THE CONSULTANT'S GUIDE TO PROPOSAL WRITING

THE CONSULTANT'S GUIDE TO PROPOSAL WRITING

How to Satisfy Your Clients and Double Your Income

Herman Holtz

John Wiley & Sons
New York   Chichester   Brisbane   Toronto   Singapore

Library of Congress Cataloging in Publication Data:

Holtz, Herman.
  The consultant's guide to proposal writing.

  Includes index.
  1. Proposal writing in business.   2. Business
consultants.   I. Title.
HF5718.5.H63   1986   808'.066658   85-32292
ISBN 0-471-83044-5

Printed in the United States of America
10 9 8 7 6 5

PREFACE

If there is one skill I have found to be utmost in importance to the success of the typical independent consultant, it is skill in marketing: the ability to win clients and contracts. And if there is one ability I have found to be utmost in importance to achieving that skill in marketing, it is the ability to develop winning proposals—that task we so often refer to erroneously as "proposal writing."

But even this, developing (writing) effective proposals, is only one element. There is another proposal-related ability that is probably of equal importance and perhaps of even greater importance: the ability to *use* proposals effectively. Many consultants who do write adequate proposals fail to use this other ability well, and so do not draw full benefits from their proposal writing skills. Helping you become fully aware of how to maximize your success and fully dedicated to doing so through wise and faithful practice in both areas is therefore a major objective of this book.

Unfortunately, many consultants groan at the mere thought of writing a proposal, and some even believe that it is an imposition for a client to request one. For the really wise consultant, however, the word *proposal* should conjure up an immediate and most welcome image of sales opportunity, as it does for others who provide professional services under contract. It has become almost a cliché that contract awards go to the best proposal writers, whether or not they are the best consultants. For anyone familiar with the evolution of consulting as a business or profession over the past several decades, it should be no surprise that the proposal has become by far the most important marketing tool for most consultants. In fact, quite often it is the final and decisive marketing tool, regardless of what has preceded it in the marketing effort. Proposal-writing skill has been and continues to be the chief instrument by which many small and independent consultants have competed successfully with well-established and much larger consulting organizations and carved out a place for themselves.

The federal government, which buys many billions of dollars' worth of consulting services every year, furnishes excellent evidence of the importance of proposals: Approximately 85 percent of the federal procurement budget (well in excess of $182 billion for fiscal 1984) is spent for goods and services purchased from contractors selected through proposal competitions. The procurement process that relies on proposals is essentially a competitive process. In fact, the U.S. Government has recently abandoned the term *negotiated* and replaced it with *competitive proposals,* to stress that the procurement is still competitive despite the fact that it is not always cost competitive (i.e., that the low bid does not necessarily have a great deal of influence over the outcome).

Note, however, that the proposal process is a true competition only when the client has formally requested competitive proposals, that is, when the client intends to compare the proposals to select the one that appears to be most satisfactory in all technical, managerial, cost, professional qualifications, and/or other respects. But when the client has asked for quotations but not for proposals, and the consultant has been sagacious enough to submit a proposal nevertheless, there is often far less competition and often no competition at all: That perceptive consultant has a clear field.

It is therefore no exaggeration to say that probably no other skill is as important to success for the independent consultant as the ability to develop proposals of outstanding quality, the quality that wins contract awards, that is.

The term "proposal *writing,*" which is often used, gives the false impression that the "quality" of a proposal is a factor of how fluently it is written, that success in creating the winning proposal is primarily a matter of writing skills. However, skill in writing, while a great help and a necessary contribution to success, is not a decisive factor by any means, because the proposal is a marketing tool. Therefore the successful proposal is necessarily based on marketing knowledge. Even the most skilled writer is not likely to produce winning proposals without a good understanding of marketing and sales techniques.

Reduced to its barest essence, the basis for any marketing success, and for proposal success in particular, is the ability to develop the right strategies and then implement those strategies effectively. Although proposal-development skills are undoubtedly essential to success, it is also true that the consultants who make proposals a sine qua non or automatic and indispensable element of their marketing are almost certain to win more contracts than are those who use proposals only now and then. There simply is no more effective way, in normal circumstances, to implement and exploit marketing strategies than through the free and frequent use of written proposals.

In one small survey of consultants that I recently conducted, 60 percent responded that they use proposals frequently, 20 percent replied that they used them invariably, and 13 percent reported that they used them only rarely. The remaining 7 percent reported that they used proposals only when the prospect requested one. The last is the most significant figure because it reveals that only a small minority wait for a proposal request, while some 80 percent recognize the wisdom of using proposals whether the prospect requests one or not (despite the fact that only 20 percent believed that they should make the proposal a major marketing tool in all cases).

Unfortunately for consultants who do not prepare proposals unless requested to do, but fortunately for those who don't wait to be asked, the wait is often in vain. Despite the growing popularity of competitive proposals as a guide to selecting the best consultant for given needs, many clients still do not make full use of this modern and most effective method for selecting the best consultant for their needs. There are several reasons for this:

Many are not fully conscious of all the advantages to be gained from this method of selecting a consultant.

Some believe that the proposal request is suitable only for large projects. (Sadly, many consultants share this illusion.) Some may not even be aware that proposals need not be massive documents, but may be quite simple and informal for small projects and yet provide all the benefits of the large, formal proposal.

A few are reluctant to undertake the chore of writing a request for proposals because it means extra paperwork. Moreover, they sometimes cringe at the thought of reviewing a large number of proposals, for that is work, too. They are evidently unaware that they can not only issue a proposal request without all that extra work but actually reduce the effort they must exert to find and select a suitable consultant.

Finally, many clients are unaware that the use of proposals reduces the risk of making costly mistakes or errors in judgment when retaining a consultant. This consideration alone can be a major influence in favor of the consultant, if used effectively, especially for the consultant who doesn't wait to be asked.

I have, then, more than one purpose here: (1) I intend to impart to you what I know of the art of writing effective proposals, (2) I intend to help you understand the several general and many specific types of proposals, and the need to select the right type for each occasion, and (3) perhaps even more important than (1) and (2) in some ways, I wish also to convince you of the need to use proposals as one of your major marketing tools, if not your principal one, and induce you to do so from this time forward.

HERMAN HOLTZ

Silver Spring, Maryland
February 1986

CONTENTS

THE CONSULTANT'S GUIDE
TO PROPOSAL WRITING

CHAPTER 1

AN ORIENTATION
IN PROPOSALS

A proposal request is an invitation to make a sales presentation, and that is a marketing opportunity.

WHY SHOULD CLIENTS WANT PROPOSALS?

Some clients always request proposals when seeking to retain a consultant. Some request proposals only when they anticipate a sizable project. And some never request proposals at all. Nevertheless, all are in quest of the same thing: information on which to base a decision as to where, how, and from whom to purchase professional services. That much is fundamental: The proposal is one way, and an increasingly popular way, for clients to establish a base of information on which to make an evaluation and reach a decision. Most clients embrace the proposal approach to their quest for consulting services once they become familiar with it and understand fully its usefulness.

The chief difference between the client who makes a practice of asking for proposals and the one who does not is usually simply a matter of the latter not having had experience with proposals and thus lacking familiarity with this method of purchasing services. Being unfamiliar with proposals, for whatever reason, such clients are usually not fully aware of the benefits—or even, perhaps, of the necessity— of the proposal request as a key to finding the right consultant, even for small projects and transient needs.

Properly implemented, the RFP—Request for Proposals—is by far the most efficient and effective tool the client can use for finding the right consultant. The response to the RFP provides all the information necessary for the client's final decision, if the client has provided an adequate "bid package" (solicitation information) and the consultant has responded effectively. (If the consultant fails to respond effectively that fact is itself useful to the client in reaching a decision.).

There are a number of obvious reasons for the proposal request, and there are some less obvious ones. Let's look at the obvious ones first.

Technical/Professional Capabilities

The client seeking a consultant has two important concerns. One is of what the client wishes to accomplish. Quite often this is a matter of great importance to the welfare, perhaps even the survival, of the client organization. For example, an ailing organization urgently in need of added vigor in its marketing may be gambling its future existence on the effectiveness of the help provided by the consultant.

On the other hand, even a healthy organization must steer clear of undue risks. In many if not most cases, the client gambles more than money in retaining a consultant. Quite frequently the client's direct welfare—its business welfare, that is—is very much at stake. On the results of the consultant's work and on the basis of the consultant's recommendations, the client may very well undertake major projects and spend large sums of money in marketing campaigns, reorganization, purchase of capital items, or any of many possible costly and perhaps risky undertakings. If the advice is the result of gross misjudgment, or is based on capabilities the consultant claims but does not truly have, the client may meet with disaster. (This has indeed happened, especially in the days of the so-called "efficiency experts" of a number of years ago.)

The other concern in the client's search for a consultant is the personal welfare of the individual who retains the consultant. This individual may or may not be the proprietor or chief executive of the client organization, but his or her personal position with the organization, or even careeer, is also at stake. An unfortunate decision can destroy a position or career.

So quite often there are, on the part of the client, both general business and personal concerns involved in requesting proposals and evaluating them to reach a decision. Ergo, the importance to the client of identifying and assessing each proposer's (consultant's) capabilities.

What Are "Capabilities"?

In light of these concerns, it should cause no wonder that the alert client seeking a consultant is looking for hard evidence of a consultant's capabilities. If a client in the cosmetics field perceives a need for a marketing consultant, he or she is going to want some clear and convincing evidence that the consultant offers not only general marketing capabilities but capabilities in marketing cosmetics. Further, the client will certainly want evidence that those cosmetic-marketing capabilities are genuine and not merely claimed. (The client who is new to the use of proposals in choosing consultants soon learns to seek evidence and not mere claims of the capabilities required.)

This does not mean the client is necessarily correct in assuming that the marketing consultant must have specific background in marketing cosmetics to handle the assignment effectively. The fact that a market-ing consultant has not marketed cosmetics before does not preclude that consultant's producing a highly successful marketing plan for the client. But that is not the point. The point is that this particular client perceives cosmetics-marketing experience as a need, and will there-fore scan proposals for evidence of that experience as a capability. Whether the client's premise is valid is another matter, one that we'll return to and discuss later, when we focus on proposals from the pro-poser's viewpoint.

Experience, both in general fields (e.g., marketing) and in specific fields (e.g., cosmetics), represents certain capabilities. But these are rather general capabilities, and there are others that must be listed. There are, for example, the applications in the field. In marketing, some of the applications—what the consultant can do for the client—might be these:

Develop general marketing strategies
Write advertising copy
Devise packaging alternatives and recommendations
Conceive special promotional campaigns and plans
Conduct market surveys
Scout and analyze competition
Make presentations to the top officials of the client organization
Train staff people in the client organization
Design and recommend distribution systems
Segment the market and plan strategies and promotions for each segment
Devise and conduct research

The Question of Competence.   The kinds of capabilities enumerated are one thing. But another distinct aspect to the entire question of capabilities is the matter of technical/professional competence. That is, given that the consultant can point to specific experience in the many tasks and disciplines in the field of interest, the client wants to know how competent the consultant is in these things. For the client will soon enough learn that evidence of experience per se is not enough, because even inept practitioners often can point to a great deal of experience in the field. The client will want to see evidence that the consultant has an acceptably high degree of competence and is good enough at the tasks required by the client. And here are some items of information that help the client judge the competence of the consultant:

Formal education and academic record
Understanding of client's problem/need, as evidenced in proposal
Proposed solution/approach to solution
Track record: verifiable history of success at the tasks
Outstanding accomplishments: remarkable successes, innovations
Other noteworthy and relevant achievements
Career history: former employers, positions, clients
Honors and awards
Testimonials from former employers and/or clients

Other Benefits to the Client

Not all clients realize it at first, but there is another and quite substantial benefit they can derive from requesting and reviewing proposals. This benefit makes it worthwhile for the client to encourage the greatest number of responses, despite the time and energy required to review a large number of proposals. The benefit is this: The client gains multiple analyses of his or her problem (in a sense all client needs are problems and may be so characterized) from a variety of specialists, reflecting a wide variety of views and approaches.

Obviously, the consultants who submit proposals are not going to carry out a complete and detailed analysis of the problem in the proposal, but they must do at least some preliminary analysis and devise at least a general approach to solving the problem. If the client has done a good job in writing the statement that explains the problem, the proposals submitted usually provide the thoughtful client a wealth of insight and expert preliminary advice. Even if many of the proposals are of little or no benefit in this regard, many will contain valuable information.

In fact, it is rarely that the proposals submitted, individually and collectively, do not reflect a greater knowledge of and insight into the client's problem than the client has. That is a bonus for the client, which alone is worth the cost of preparing the solicitation and reading the proposals, aside from the enormously improved vantage point (the much expanded base of knowledge, that is) it gives the client for selecting a consultant.

This is not to say that the client is actively seeking free consulting services, although this is what he or she gets, in effect. But that is inevitable; many business people find it necessary to furnish free samples to prospective buyers. You cannot prove your abilities satisfactorily without demonstrating them somehow in your proposals and other presentations. On the other hand, the cynical use of this means to get free analyses is not entirely unknown, unfortunately, and you must use judgment in deciding how much to reveal in your proposals and presentations. (Mercifully, the practice of deliberately "picking your brains" to euchre you into giving away your services is fairly rare, and most prospects are sincere in requesting proposals.)

HOW MUCH DO YOU HAVE TO GIVE AWAY?

Aside from the possible hazard of giving prospects—people who are not yet clients—so much information in your proposals that you are "giving away the store," there is also the matter of cost to you. Proposal writing is a time-consuming and therefore a costly marketing process. Time is not only the most costly resource you have, but it is in a large sense also the chief commodity you sell. So from that viewpoint alone you must make a judgment as to how much you should reveal in a proposal—how much, that is, is necessary to win the contract.

There is no precise formula for measuring that. Your objective is obviously to provide the prospect with enough information to prove your case and win the contract, but no more. That's a circular argument, of course, and not very helpful. But deciding how much is enough is purely judgmental, and you must base it on your own estimate. But there is something available to help you make that estimate: Perhaps the best guideline to help you judge this is a list and brief description of at least five elements that the effective proposal must always include:

1. Evidence that you have a clear understanding of the client's problem.

2. An approach and program plan or design that appears to the client to be well-suited to solving the problem and likely to produce the results desired.

3. Convincing evidence of your own qualifications and capability for carrying out the plan properly.

4. Convincing evidence of your dependability as a consultant or contractor.

5. A compelling reason for the client to select you as the winner—a win strategy.

Each of these will be discussed in much greater detail, as we proceed through the pages to come. In fact, to a large degree, the remainder of this book will be devoted primarily to discussing these items and how they are implemented, as well as how, where, and when to utilize proposals as a prime marketing tool. However, some preliminary discussion here, before we address these several items in painstaking detail, is likely to prove helpful.

Understanding of the Problem

An amazingly large number of proposals convey to the client the notion that the writer of the proposal did not understand the problem. In some cases the writer truly did not understand the problem, for one reason or another. Sometimes the consultant, eager for business, is stretching things a bit too far, trying to win a contract and project that is really not in his or her field. Sometimes the consultant has simply written the proposal in too great a hurry and has not given enough thought to the expressed need—has not studied the need at length and planned thoroughly enough to offer a convincing presentation. Most often, however, the prime weakness is neither of these, but is the result of careless writing. That is, the consultant understands the problem all right but has failed to demonstrate that understanding in the proposal.

You may argue that the client should be able to perceive your understanding of the need in the proposed project plan or design, but that is expecting the client to make extra effort—study and analysis—to make up for a deficiency in your proposal. It simply won't happen. In fact, unless your proposal demonstrates your understanding of the need quite clearly in its introductory portion the client may may decide after the first few pages that time is better spent on the next proposal. Often as many as two out of three proposals are disqualified and discarded as a result of the first reading or even partial reading.

Program Plan or Design

The portion of the proposal that establishes clearly your understanding of the client's problem should bridge logically—make a transition— into a discussion of your program plan or design. This discussion must convince the client that yours is the best approach and best design or plan for satisfying the need.

This is a place to sell your ideas, and it is a critical area, for unless you manage to convince the client here that what you offer is probably the best plan (and we will discuss later what that word "best" means, in this context), you will have already lost. Here you are going to need both sales ability and rationale, as you will see later.

Your Qualifications and Capability

Proposing, explaining, and selling a plan or design as the best one is one thing. Proving that you have all the necessary qualifications for carrying out the plan or implementing the design is another thing. And establishing those qualifications beyond reasonable doubt is only partially dependent on establishing your own technical and professional credentials. Part of those qualifications are specific experience that relates directly to the need, and general experience that does not relate directly may not be acceptable to some clients. Some projects require certain physical resources, such as access to computers and other capital items, clerical labor, people to do field surveys, and other such necessities. And, finally, there is the matter of other professionals whom you may require to support you for larger projects. Vague or general assurances that you have access to necessary resources and/or associates or others you can turn to are often not acceptable as proof of necessary resources. The typical client is likely to want some rather solid and specific evidence of adequate and assured availability of any necessary resources, including supporting professionals when the project obviously requires such support.

Your Dependability

Dependability of a contractor is always a concern, and with any client who has ever contracted with someone who proved to be less than totally dependable, it is a major concern. Given a superb project plan or design and given a superbly qualified consultant to carry out the plan successfully, the project can still founder quite easily if the consultant is not highly conscientious and properly dedicated to the project. It is not a less important consideration than that of technical/professional capability, for neither is of use without the other.

All clients want some kind of assurance that they may depend upon you, if they award you the contract, but promises and pledges alone are not enough to provide that assurance. Something more substantial than soothing syrup is needed. This is explored and studied in later pages.

A Win Strategy

There are numerous strategies possible in proposal writing, all of which we will discuss. However, there is always the question of the major strategy, the win strategy (also referred to as capture strategy and main strategy, to distinguish it from other, subordinate strategies) upon which you base your entire argument and hope of capturing the contract.

To put this another way and possibly to clarify the meaning immediately, the win strategy is your explanation to the client of why the client should favor you with the award.

In simple terms, sales techniques are based largely on giving the prospect a reason for doing business with you. The proposal you write is not a solicitation or entreaty, and it certainly should not be written as though it were. It is an offer, a business offer to *do something* for the client. But don't expect the client to think out reasons for accepting your offer. You must always furnish the reasons, make the client see why it is in his or her own best interests to accept your offer. That is what strategy is all about—the right reasons and the right way to present them.

THE EVOLUTION OF STRATEGY

Strategy was mentioned last in the series of five items, but in fact all the other four items are closely linked to this last-named item and even stem from it. Strategy should drive the entire proposal. In fact, the strategy, for even the simplest and most informal proposal, should evolve as shown in Figure 1.

This is a greatly simplified explanation, which will be expanded and presented in growing detail, as we proceed. But for the moment it captures the main steps in the evolution of basic program or design strategy, beginning with analysis of the client's need, on the basis of the client's own description of the need as filtered and interpreted through your own knowledge and experience, plus any independent observations you have been able to make. Finally you must define the client's need in your own terms, which may or may not coincide and agree with the client's identification.

As a result of this beginning analysis you must form some kind of hypothesis of the primary concerns that drive the client and inspired the opportunity to offer a proposal. (Do regard this as an opportunity, for it is just that.) Your success in evolving an effective main (capture) strategy is usually tied closely to the accuracy with which you are able to hypothesize the client's major "worry items."

The major beginning steps are, then, to identify the problem, decide what the key points of the problem and the basic reason for seeking consulting help are, and hypothesize the client's chief worries, at least tentatively. You can now begin to devise some sort of main strategy, one that addresses the client's principal worries, of course, while furnishing the client some assurance that the need will be entirely satisfied.

You should understand, at this point, that strategy does not include or embrace the first four items enumerated earlier in this discussion. Those are obligatory items that must be present in each and every proposal, whereas the strategy is something unique, devised and developed especially for the individual proposal and based on the circumstances surrounding that proposal.

Understand also that the entire process is not truly such a linear or entirely sequential one as charts and other presentations describe, but is almost always an iterative process characterized by many iterations. It is necessary to idealize the process—project it as though it were the

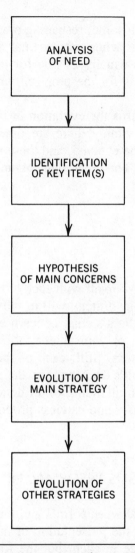

Figure 1. First steps in devising a strategy for a proposal.

orderly and sequential process described—because it would be impractical to attempt to show all the feedback loops that reflect the reality of most proposal development, even those of rather modest size. In the actual case of developing and writing a proposal there are, with only rare exception, many feedback loops, trial fits, and modifications. There is the assembling of tentative theories or hypotheses, testing them, discarding some, reshaping others, and otherwise molding the plans and approaches until a final approach and design are settled on. And this is usually as true for the proposal written by a single individual as it is for the proposal written by a large team of consultants.

The foregoing concerns the evolution of the main or capture strategy primarily. But inevitably there are other proposal elements for which strategies must be evolved, and these may or may not coincide with the main strategy. The other elements include at least these:

Program
Cost
Presentation
Competitors

You should concern yourself with each of these in any proposal you write, although the main strategy will usually coincide with only one of these. That is, the client's chief concern will usually be about one of the first three areas, or your chief problem in winning will be to outshine your competitors. Still, each of these areas makes its own contribution to the client's decision, and the surest way to be successful is to be thorough in attending to all details and so maximize the odds in your favor. Hasty and careless proposals rarely win anything except quick discard.

FORMAL VERSUS INFORMAL PROPOSALS

The chief differences between formal and informal proposals are size and format. Logically, the presentation of information and ideas follows the same sequence in each, but the formal proposal is usually one submitted for a sizable project as a discrete document, with headlines, cover and title page, and other such publication formalities. The informal proposal, however, is usually in the form of a letter of several pages. (It is often referred to, therefore, as a "letter proposal.") The fact of its being a letter does not change the philosophy of the proposal. Whatever has been or is said later about the formal proposal applies to letter proposals equally.

The fact of its being a letter proposal reflects only that the project is a small one and does not merit the cost of developing a formal proposal.

A RECOMMENDED PROPOSAL FORMAT

Occasionally a client will mandate a proposal format, specifying the order in which information is to be presented, as well as precisely what information is required. This is fairly rare however; usually, the client explains what information is required, but leaves the format up to you.

I offer here a recommended proposal format (Figure 2), with brief explanations following of those items where I believe some brief explanation is required. (Later discussions will be based on the presumption of this format and will elaborate extensively on these brief introductory explanations.) The reasons for the recommendation of this particular format are several:

1. It was developed over some years of practical experience in writing proposals.
2. It reflects many useful practices of others observed over the years.
3. It is quite similar to many mandated formats.
4. It is a logical development of ideas and information.
5. It is quite flexible, adaptable to most needs and readily modified or expanded.
6. It works. I and many of my own clients have used it successfully many times.

This is a four-part format, which can be easily expanded to five or even six parts, as the occasion requires. In some cases, such expansion is desirable and beneficial, even required. It is even readily adaptable to the multi-volume approach required for some large proposals. We will discuss these matters later, as each subject and the need for each discussion arises, when we explore the various needs and situations under which you must or should offer a proposal.

SECTION I: INTRODUCTION

ABOUT THE OFFEROR

UNDERSTANDING OF THE REQUIREMENT

SECTION II: DISCUSSION

THE REQUIREMENT

ANALYSIS

APPROACH

SECTION III: PROPOSED PROJECT

PROJECT ORGANIZATION

MANAGEMENT

PLANS AND PROCEDURES

STAFF

DELIVERABLE ITEMS

SCHEDULES

RESUME(S)

SECTION IV: QUALIFICATIONS AND EXPERIENCE

RELEVANT CURRENT AND RECENT PROJECTS

RESOURCES

MISCELLANEOUS

FRONT MATTER

APPENDICES

Figure 2. General proposal format.

I call each part a "section," use generic or descriptive titles and sideheads (I offer only a few such sideheads; most proposals of any size will use many more), and number the sections with Roman numerals, in the example here. Of course in the actual case you can call them chapters, name and number them any way you please, and make whatever changes you wish. Those are superficial matters that do not affect the final outcome. Moreover, I will have more to say about these matters later, when I will also furnish some specific examples of proposal contents for each of these sections or chapters. However, some brief explanations are in order here:

Section I

The first section should be brief, since it is only introductory, and I recommend only two subsections, although you may of course use additional subject headings, as you will see later when we discuss specifics and furnish concrete examples.

The first subsection has three aims: (1) to introduce yourself briefly (who and what you are—name and field of specialization), (2) to give some very brief idea of your credentials and experience to establish your qualifications quickly (perhaps the name of a well-known client or two), and (3) to offer something that captures attention and arouses early interest, motivating the reader to keep turning pages.

The second subsection aims to demonstrate your true understanding of the client's requirement. Since it is to be brief, it should summarize that requirement and focus on the essence of the requirement, making it clear that you are discriminating between the essential need and the extraneous or less important details.

Section II

There should be a direct transition from that second subsection of Section I to the first sentences of Section II, which starts by expanding on that discussion of the requirement to explore and probe all aspects of it, bringing the reader "aboard," with regard to your analyses and rationales, leading to the clearly defined and logic-based approach with which this section should end. This is a section for proving your approach and selling it to the client.

Section III

This is the section in which you present your plans for implementation of that approach and those plans described in the previous section. The section is a natural transition from Section II, and the major headings listed are essentially self-explanatory. (Again, you may wish to add many subheadings.) Moreover, this is not necessarily the order in which these subjects will be presented, but all should be included in this section. It is usually this section, however, that is split into two or even three sections (or even separate volumes) for major proposals essentially, offering the subject of management separately and sometimes listing deliverables and schedules separately.

Note, too, that this is the section that is, in effect, the contract or what you are offering to contract for.

Section IV

Like Section III, the major headings of this section are generally self-explanatory, may be added to and/or supported with subheadings, and may be presented in an alternate order, if your sense of order is somewhat different from that suggested here. These are, however, the typical subjects for this section.

Miscellaneous

There are several other elements referred to in Figure 2 under the general heading of front matter; they will be discussed in more detail at the appropriate time. The typical front matter for a formal proposal includes a title page, a table of contents, and some but not all of such items as an abstract, an executive summary, a foreword or preface, a frontispiece, a response matrix, and possibly even other items.

Many proposals have an appendix or even several appendices. These will be discussed in later pages also.

Application to Letter Proposals

Philosophically, the chief difference between the formal and informal (letter) proposal is that the latter will not have a title page, table of contents, and other such features of the formal proposal. (Large, formal proposals may even be multivolume; many major proposals have been prepared in four or more large volumes.) The letter proposal will, however, have an introduction, discussion, proposed program (or procedures), and qualifications of offeror. It may have some front matter, principally a summary, and may have an appendix, as well. Bear that in mind, as we proceed through these pages.

Bear one other, equally important, fact in mind at all times: Don't wait to be asked for a proposal, formal or otherwise. Whenever you believe that you have a serious prospect or a prospect with a serious need, and you think that you know enough of the need to offer a proposal, do so. Do so even if you have not advised the prospect in advance or asked for permission to submit a proposal. A letter proposal is always an excellent way to follow up an earlier contact with a prospect, and often it is by far the best way to do so.

Chapter 2

WHAT IT TAKES TO WRITE A GOOD PROPOSAL

A "good proposal" is, by definition, one that wins the proposal competition. But there are other measures, and it is certainly necessary to examine and understand these other measures, if you are to become an expert in the writing and use of proposals.

IS IT REALLY PROPOSAL *WRITING*?

There is no doubt that the proposals we are discussing here are written presentations, so it is natural enough that we all refer to "proposal writing." Yet, what is the significance of that word "writing" in this use? How important, that is, is the skill of writing in the process of producing a successful—contract-winning—proposal? To develop a sensible and reasonable answer to that question it is necessary to first analyze just what a proposal is, why we write it, and what we expect it to do for us.

We looked at this briefly in the first chapter from the client's viewpoint, from what the client expects or should expect, and why the client wants or should want proposals as part of the process of selecting a consultant. And that, understanding the client's purposes and intent, is, of course, the key to understanding why we write proposals, how we should write them, what should be in them, how we should use them, and what we should expect them to do for us.

The client's basic purpose in requesting proposals is to establish some basis for selecting the best possible consultant to satisfy his or her need. Perhaps the client knows or thinks he or she knows precisely what the problem is and how it must be solved. But that is not necessarily so. The client may be familiar only with symptoms and may or may not even be aware that these are only symptoms, which do not of themselves define the problem. In that case, the client is dependent on the consultant who wins the contract to determine precisely what the problem or need really is. That is quite often the case.

Whichever the case, however, unless you are quite sure that the client has correctly identified the problem or need, you must recognize that you must assume a need to educate the client. (Unless you accept this, you risk disaster.) But you must also manage to somehow persuade the client not only that you are right in your analysis and evaluation, but do it diplomatically enough so that you do not give offense in telling the client he or she is wrong.

In short, you must manage somehow to be several things in writing proposals, and the writer hat is only one of the several you wear. You must also be a marketer, sales expert, diplomat, analyst, subject-matter expert, designer, and perhaps even one or two other things, with all the other things those terms imply. A deficiency in even one of these areas or functions can easily cost you the contract. As Dave

Hamilton, Operations Manager for the Quadrex Corporation's Tulsa Division wisely observed, proposals must be reviewed and revised continuously to ensure that they include "selling statements" and are not confined to being straight technical dissertations. The technical explanations and arguments are necessary, of course, but they do not and cannot alone sell the project.

SKILLS NEEDED TO WRITE WINNING PROPOSALS

Were I were to rank-order the major skills required to turn out effective proposals, proposals that win contracts, that is, I would say that they are these, in descending order of importance:

Marketing and sales skills
Analytical and creative skills
Subject-matter expertise
Writing skills

This is not to say that any of these not at the head of the list is unimportant. All contribute heavily to final success, and strength in all is the most important factor for success in proposal competitions, while weakness in any single area may easily prove to be fatal. And writing should not be underrated, despite what is said here: It is quite important as the vehicle for implementing these other skills effectively by skillful integration of all in the form of a written presentation. It is therefore with some trepidation that I list writing at the bottom of the scale, for fear that you may gain the wrong impression. However, it is true enough that despite some exceptions, even the most skillful writing alone rarely, if ever, wins proposal competitions, while marketing and sales skills alone have often carried the day, even with weaknesses in the other areas. Hence, the significance of the estimated rank ordering, the chief purpose of which is to establish an appreciation of all the several skills and capabilities that make up successful proposal "writing." I shall therefore continue to use the term "proposal writing," when I really mean to refer to the entire process of proposal development, of which writing is essentially only the final act.

Marketing and Sales Skills

A later chapter is devoted entirely to the subject of sales and marketing, but it is virtually impossible to discuss even the basics of proposal writing without casting that discussion in the reference framework of sales and marketing. Therefore, I must preview that later chapter here to establish the ground rules for the discussions in this chapter, although I will really discuss the principles of sales more than those of marketing here, and will not go much beyond basic principles.

Some Typical Kinds of Fumbles

Bear in mind at all times that whatever else it may be, a proposal is first and foremost a sales presentation. (Other objectives of the proposal, if any, are in addition to and subordinate to that main goal.) One of the most common underlying causes of proposal failure is the failure to recognize this simple fact. The following are a few examples of proposals written to other objectives and thus failing to become winners.

1. *The aggressive/defensive proposal.* Some consultants write proposals with a main focus on the terms they expect the client to agree to. They tend often to achieve a tone of aggressiveness, coupled with a definitely defensive stance. In so doing these writers often tend also to hedge all promises and commitments with numerous escape clauses, thereby suggesting doubt as to the client's integrity and intentions to deal honorably with the consultant.

2. *The loud-claims proposal.* Some consultants labor under an inability to distinguish claims and laudatory self-appraisals from sales arguments. Their proposals contain few facts, but are characterized principally by a generous measure of hyperbole, being heavily sprinkled with adjectives and adverbs, superlatives alleging the writer's great accomplishments, highly respected place in the profession, and marvelous abilities. The strategy evidently is to overwhelm the client by outshouting all the other proposers. Almost needless to say, this is a not very successful tactic.

3. *The "me too" proposal.* Some proposals appear to say only that the writer can do the job as well as anyone can, so why not make the award to that proposer. Such proposals usually succumb to the competition of other proposals which are based on legitimate sales arguments and strive to be originals and not carbon copies.

4. *"I'm-not-really-sure-I-know-what-you-want" proposal.* There is one type of proposal writer who appears to believe that the client knows exactly what he or she wants and wants to see proposed, and who will award the contract to the fortunate writer who succeeds in guessing exactly what the client wants. This consultant is very much afraid that whatever he or she proposes will not be exactly what the client wants, and therefore this type of proposal is evasive and general, never says anything very concrete, and especially never proposes a detailed plan of action or even a clear-cut analysis of the problem, as the consultant views it. (In fact, this is the underlying reason for many "me too" proposals.)

5. *The canned solution.* Some consultants evidently have one or two canned solutions, old reliable standards they offer every potential client, no matter what the client stipulates as the need. And some of this genre even have preprinted proposals, with a few blanks to fill in with the client's name and address and a few other minor variables. They manage to win an assignment once in a while, when the need happens by chance to coincide with the canned solution, but it doesn't happen very often.

The Problem Is Important to the Client

All of these approaches—and a few other typical and characteristic duds—ignore the client's interest. They reflect indifference to the client's need, intended or not, and suggest that the consultant who writes them doesn't really care what the client's problem is, or at least does not consider the problem serious enough to merit much study and thought. Whether the cause for all these almost certain-to-lose approaches is fear, laziness, indifference, arrogance, or plain lack of understanding of what is wanted and needed, all radiate the same philosophy: Just give me the money and I'll do whatever it is you want done, but your problem does not merit much of my time now, before

I have a contract. Whatever it is, I'll take care of it when the time comes.

Of course the problem is important to the client, who would not be seeking or even considering consulting help if it were not. It is therefore a fatal error to convey to the client, directly or indirectly, any suggestion that you low-rate the importance of the problem. And if you happen to hold that opinion, it will almost surely manage to show, to shine through your writing.

The only way to avoid this is to be deeply conscious of the client's feelings and make it clear that you respect the seriousness of the problem. To write anything effectively, but especially to write a successful sales presentation, you must be able to perceive the problem from the client's perspective, to understand and even actually feel the client's concerns and most earnest desires. That, in a nutshell, is the essence of selling. Your own perceptions are of no importance in selling; only the client's perspectives matter—for everyone acts in his or her own self-interest at all times. The client does not care what you want, except as your wants are necessary or an avenue to achieving his or her own wants. His or her own wants are first and foremost, and the way to sell anything is to identify what the client wants and then show the client how to satisfy that want.

Needs and Wants

Marketing people sometimes refer to needs and wants as though they were different things. They are not. "Want" meant lack of, in an earlier time (e.g., "for want of a nail . . .") but is used today to mean desire, whereas "need" is generally used to refer to a necessity. Practically, however, when a client decides to want something, that want becomes a need, as far as you are concerned, and the sales/marketing problem is now one of how to persuade the client that the best or most desirable way to satisfy the need is to accept your offer.

A common failure in marketing is failing to accurately identify the client's need. You cannot sell the client something the client truly does not want—does not identify as his or her need, that is, or as the best way to satisfy the need, which is essentially the same thing. And that is something that merits a brief discussion to ensure understanding of what may be a hair-splitting point, but often makes the difference between success and failure in the marketplace.

Let us suppose that the client has announced a perceived need for a better inventory-control and -management system to replace the one currently in use. The client's objection to the existing system is that it is wasteful of both warehouse space and capital, with too many slow-moving items kept in stock. Several consultants have offered proposals. All the proposals offer more or less standard or classical solutions to the problem through computer control which bases ordering of each item of inventory on complex calculations involving required lead time for ordering, history of traffic in the item, current orders, antici-pated orders, and estimates based on trend lines and what those trends project. All of those approaches or solutions appear suitable for satis-fying the client's perceived need, as the client's request for proposals defines or identifies that need. You, however, do not accept the client's definition of need without question, but you study it carefully and in greater depth to either validate the definition, as described in the RFP, or to amend and correct it before writing your own proposal. You decide that the client's definition of need is a bit shallow and needs more careful thought. You redefine it accordingly, and then offer a somewhat different approach, one that is considerably more sophisti-cated than the one just described and better suits the need as you per-ceive it.

Sensible though others' approaches are, yours now necessarily goes a step or two beyond them and recommends the addition of equipment and software which will enable the client to keep close track of the supply situation in real time and order items accordingly, via computer-to-computer connections, thereby reducing the lead time by days and thus reducing total costs for the client. And you might even propose a study of suppliers to identify those with whom such computer-to-computer monitoring and ordering automation is pos-sible, thus maximizing the use of the method and paving the way for a turnkey project.

The client now decides that this—ordering all inventory via com-puter to reduce the lead time and minimize the time items reside and age in storage—is really the need. You are now the only consultant offering the right solution, the one that satisfies the real need, as you have now persuaded the client to perceive the need.

In one sense, you have created a new need by showing the client a better way. (Many marketing and sales successes are the result of skill-ful "education" of the client, helping the client discover the "truth" about his or her need.) But in another sense, there is no such thing as a new need, for basic needs never change. Only the ways of satisfying those basic needs change.

Many new products and new services struggle for success in the marketplace. Some succeed in becoming large successes after a long time. Some become only modest successes, no matter how long they struggle for preeminence in the marketplace. And some never find success. On the other hand, some become instant successes. Television is one such example, and the videocassette recorder is another. Microcomputers and pocket calculators also were accepted by the buying public instantly and enthusiastically, as was the xerographic copying machine.

On the other hand, all those other xerographic copying machines that had to use specially treated paper cast hardly a shadow in the wake of Xerox® copiers because only Xerox machines could make copies on plain paper, at least until Xerox machine protective patents finally expired years later.

The "need," then, was defined by the public in all cases. And while you may argue that the invention of TV created a need for TV, the fact is that the need for home entertainment always existed, and TV was one of a long series of steadily improving means of home entertainment, the latest of which is the videocassette recorder and the predecessor of which was the radio.

Copiers that required specially treated paper were modest successes because plain-paper copying was a clearly and dramatically better way to satisfy the need for copies: It was swift, convenient, and produced copies of steadily improving fidelity, until the most modern copier models produced copies that sometimes were even better than the originals. So Xerox Corporation was immensely successful, in contrast with its rivals. (There had been several earlier types of office copiers, none of them very convenient or very efficient, and hardly an improvement over carbon paper, in fact. They succeeded in finding acceptance, for a time, because there was nothing else available to satisfy the need for copying, and for that reason only, but they all disappeared from view almost literally overnight when xerographic copying on a practical basis made its appearance.)

Examine the apparent need, then, in terms of (1) what the basic and classic need it represents really is (which is not always readily apparent), and (2) of how you can perhaps satisfy that need in some better way than it has ever been satisfied before or, at least, probably a better way than your competitors are likely to offer. And "better" can mean faster, cheaper, more conveniently, with better reliability, or with any other benefit.

Creativity

Finding or devising a new and better way to satisfy a need is a creative process, and should be recognized as such. Here again, we will explore the nature of creativity in some depth in a later chapter, but I must mention a basic principle or two about the subject here because one of the characteristics required to write a really good proposal is creative imagination.

First of all, creativity is rarely, if ever, the result of a truly new or revolutionary idea. Instead, it is generally a new combination of ideas, an extrapolation of what is already known. TV owes its basic circuits and technology to the earlier radio sciences, for example, but it did not become a practical reality until the picture tube was added as the means for displaying the output of the system. (Early models used unsatisfactory devices called "flying spot scanners.") But the picture tube was not really a new invention, either. It was an adaptation of an established device, the cathode ray tube used in a laboratory instrument, the oscilloscope. Nor was the transistor a brand new idea, since its predecessor devices and basic technology go back to 1870 at least. And the modern personal computer is a new combination of radio, TV, early computer, telephone, and other communications technology. Creativity is, thus, largely a matter of reassembling known ideas into new patterns or adapting established ideas, devices, and methods to new uses.

One of the obstacles to creativity—an inhibiting factor, that is—is the all-too-human resistance to change. Giving up established ways that are familiar and comfortable, and accepting the hazard of the unknown, gives rise to a sense of insecurity for many, especially for those who are considered experts in the known. Thus Thomas Edison, Louis Pasteur, Charles Kettering, and many others were assailed for their "ignorance" and "stupidity" in attempting to achieve what the experts knew were impossible goals—the incandescent electric light, proof that microorganisms do not evolve spontaneously out of inert matter, and the automobile self-starter, respectively. And these are only three of literally hundreds of such possible citations, not the least of which was Admiral William Leahy's confident assertion that the atomic bomb would never detonate, with the notation that he spoke as an expert on explosives.

It requires a sturdy and dedicated individual to proceed in the face of such sneering, condescending condemnation by those regarded as notable experts. Courage was not the least of the characteristics that enabled such creative individuals as Edison, Pasteur, and Kettering to press on with their efforts. Almost an absolute prerequisite for creativity is courage, courage to ignore conventional wisdom and courage to be unmoved by criticism, no matter the source.

On the intellectual side, however, creativity also requires knowledge, deep and broad knowledge of one's field and related areas.

Subject-Matter Expertise

A great many breakthroughs are based on original ideas by individuals who are not regarded as experts in the fields of the breakthrough and are, in fact, sniffed at somewhat disdainfully as amateurs. If Thomas Edison were starting out today he probably could not get a job as a scientist or engineer in any organization, and probably would have trouble being hired as even a lab swipe. When I was employed at Philco-Ford's government communications and weapons division some years ago, the engineer there with the greatest number of patents to his name (some 65, if memory serves me) had never seen the inside of a college. Moreover, the engineer who was designing some of the most sophisticated digital-data secure-communications devices was likewise from the "old" (non-college) school and, moreover, did not know how to draw up a functional logic diagram or utilize Boolean algebra for his designs (both considered by others to be a sine qua non for such work), but drafted everything laboriously in complicated electronic circuit diagrams. (He was most grateful to me for simplifying his diagrams by translating them to the much simpler digital logic drawings.)

This is not to decry the need for conventional formal education and experience. It is to point out that it is the knowledge and ability per se, no matter how and where acquired, that makes the difference. You can hardly be creative without knowing what you are doing—without, that is, knowing your field thoroughly and examining the problem or need *objectively*, no matter what others say or think. Kettering was himself widely quoted as saying that education was all right if one did not permit it to interfere with thinking. (Nor does this denigrate or make light of the instinctual urges, which are probably the logic of the subconscious mind, that characterize many acts of creativity.)

Marketing/Salesmanship Considerations

One of those ingenious home-workshop inventors, Fred Grise, had a great idea, early in his career. (He has created a great many successful inventions since.) He invented a solution to a problem that vexes a great many of us: He devised a way to make the ketchup flow easily out of that traditional narrow-necked bottle. And so off he went to sell his invention to the leading manufacturer of ketchup, convinced that his fortune was ensured.

To his horror the officials of that firm all but threw him down the stairs when they heard his proposition. They could not get him off their premises fast enough. Later, Grise philosophized that he had learned his lesson: he would sell clients what they wanted, in the future, not what they needed.

Brilliant and imaginative inventor that he is, he was slightly off target in his ruminations about a lesson learned. The ketchup manufacturer's whole advertising and marketing campaign is based on that "slowest ketchup in the west" theme. Grise's invention would have totally destroyed that carefully crafted and slowly built-up image of quality, which was based on a message strongly implying that the thicker the ketchup, the higher was its quality. From a marketing and sales viewpoint, the ketchup manufacturer not only did not need that new invention, but they needed to bury it as quickly as possible, as a direct threat to their existence or at least to their commanding position in the ketchup market.

To write a good proposal, you must have a good understanding of marketing, and often, as in the case cited here, you must understand the principles of sales and marketing from the client's viewpoint also.

Writing Skills

Finally we come to that subject of writing per se, which has been relegated to last place, despite the use of the term "proposal writing."

And to summarize briefly the main significance of writing skill it is this: Writing is the means by which we implement and exploit all that other work that has gone into devising a program and a set of sales/ marketing strategies. Unless those are well done, the net result—the persuasiveness of the proposal—is less effective than it could have been.

Consider, for example, that situation postulated earlier where you did not settle for the client's description of the need but decided to study the need in some depth—to validate the need or, if you could not validate it, correct the definition. Having decided that the client had not probed deeply enough in defining the need, you redefined it in your proposal and offered what you thought was the best possible solution.

Handled properly in your written presentation, this can be the basis for a powerful strategy: (1) it demonstrates your own sincerity and perceptiveness, and possibly even a superior approach and greater ability than other proposers have demonstrated, and (2) it virtually compels the client to reconsider all other proposals in light of your own to see how others measure up by comparison. (Inevitably, no matter what a client says, much of the proposal evaluation must be a comparative one, as well as a competitive one.)

If you have done a proper selling job, convincing the client that yours is the best way to go, you have knocked out most—and maybe all—of your competitors without making any reference to them in any manner. Later, in a chapter dealing with writing persuasively, I will suggest wordings and arguments to maximize these effects without "knocking" competitors.

The effectiveness of all the strategies you devise will be heavily dependent on the quality of your writing. And that does not refer to literary elegance or grammatical perfection, but to the persuasiveness of your prose. We will discuss the factors that achieve persuasiveness, too, in that later chapter.

DEVELOPING THE NECESSARY SKILLS

The first step in developing and/or honing existing skills in these several areas is to recognize and accept the need to do so. Nothing is so destructive of these skills as the stubborn refusal to accept the need for improvement, the stubborn insistence of many individuals, in fact, that they know all they need to know about these matters. (The true experts are those who accept imperfection and continue to learn every day of their lives.) A major purpose of this book is, in fact, to help you in developing or further developing your skills in the several areas necessary for proposal success, even in that of the subject-matter knowledge. And perhaps it is in that very area where you perhaps believe—quite possibly with a good deal of justification—that you do not need my help, that I propose to begin. But before we get involved in these discussions, let me point out to you that you will find that some of these areas are actually closely intertwined, and that separating them into separate discussions in earlier paragraphs was a purely mechanical device to make certain points. In the following discussions, I will not make any great effort to so separate the topics, so that you can see their close interrelationships.

First of all I freely acknowledge that you almost certainly are already far more expert in your field or fields than I am, intend to become, or ever could become—that field or fields, that is, in which you specialize as a consultant. I am therefore not qualified to impart to you any subject-matter knowledge per se, nor shall I try do do so.

On the other hand, do you really know as much as you should about your own field and—think carefully about this—other, closely related fields? Are you keeping up with your field? Reading at least some of the literature? Active in a relevant association or two? In touch with others in your field? Attending conferences and conventions? Making at least occasional contributions to the literature, even if that is only a trade journal or two? Do you think that you know all you need to know, now or ever, about your field and related subjects?

If you are not answering "yes" to at least a few of these queries, and "no" to that last one, you are in danger of becoming a dinosaur in your field. The world won't wait for you to catch up; you have to keep up, even if that means running a good bit of the time. If you are not more expert, more imaginative, more enterprising, and more dedicated to your profession than are the nine-to-five masses in your field, you are probably not truly suited to the consulting profession, and certainly you are probably not going to become a really good proposal writer.

My obvious point is that you should be able to answer "yes" to most of those questions I postulated a paragraph or two ago. Your creative output is most definitely related quite closely and in some proportion to your information input. But information input is only one ingredient necessary to create new ideas. The next required ingredient is introspection.

Creative people are people constantly in quest of more and/or new information about a great many things, but quite aware that the information they seek may not exist anywhere. That is, they may have to generate that information themselves. Consequently, creative people are people who think about things, about what they mean, about how they can best be understood. Professor Charles H. Townes, for example, was reportedly ruminating on a park bench when he conceived the maser (microwave amplification by stimulated emission of radiation) and, soon after and more significantly, the laser (light amplification by stimulated emission of radiation), both major scientific breakthroughs. However, he had been working on the problem with other scientists for a long time, and had been gathering relevant information and pondering the problems during all that time, as had the others, before his introspection finally produced the seminal inspiration that represented the breakthrough.

The point of some earlier discussions was that new and better ways themselves create new needs. That is, you can address a client's stated need in either or both of two ways:

1. Study the need itself, as defined by the client, and decide whether that is the true definition of the need or whether you must redefine it.
2. Study the various ways in which the need can be satisfied, identify the best way, and redefine the need in terms of that best way.

In many cases, it is that second approach that works best and which we really use. Here is an example of how that might work:

The client wants a rapid-delivery service. In fact, he wants to be able to deliver documents—special reports—to the opposite coast on the same day. The obvious method is express air service, which can do the job within 12 hours. But there is another way, one that can do the job in a fraction of that time: "electronic mail," a method in which the report is recorded on some magnetic or other machine-readable medium and sent via computer-to-computer telephone-line communication. The availability of the second method makes the first method obsolescent and thus becomes a need by the simple virtue of its availability. If the client did not know that it was possible, the proposer who explains and proposes it creates a new need by simply making the client aware of the possibility.

Note that what changed the "need" here was not even the creation of a method not heretofore available, but simply making the client aware of that method. Educating the client changed the client's definition of need. It is not truth but the client's *perception* of truth that makes the difference.

A MASTER STRATEGY

The foregoing is, in fact, a general master strategy that may be used in many, if not most, proposal situations. If you are able to devise a different and better way to satisfy the requestor's basic need, you often succeed in changing the rules—writing your own rules, in essence. This is because you have actually succeeded in changing the specification of the need when you do this, invalidating all proposals that limit themselves to responding to the need as defined in the RFP. And if no one else has made the effort to develop a new and better way, you often wind up with a clear field.

There is a qualifier in all this, however: For practical purposes (as a winning strategy, that is), your new and different innovation is better only if the client agrees that it is better. Your allegation that it is better does not automatically make it so in the client's perception. To change the definition or specification of need you must succeed in persuading the client to agree with your definition. That is, you must *sell* that idea to the client. Moreover, you must never assume that the client can or will easily see for himself or herself that your solution is by far the best one; you must explain your rationale carefully, making sure that the reader is able to follow your reasoning completely. For even if the client is knowledgeable enough to make the analysis without your help—and that may or may not be so in any given case—there is no earthly reason for the client to go to that much trouble. (To expect that is to expect the client to do your selling job for you; it won't happen.) And finally, aside from all this, there is at least one other consideration: The probability is that the client, like most other people, almost instinctively resists new and different ideas, and is not likely to hasten to embrace your new and different idea unless you succeed in your persuasive arguments for it.

Most people are not visionary at all, and they tend to reject new ideas, especially those which are revolutionary and call for casting out old ideas and old prejudices. Alexander Graham Bell was unable to sell his telephone to Western Union, whose officials thought the idea of people talking to each other over a wire was ridiculous. (Of course, they also thought the telephone contrary to their interests.) Kodak and IBM, among many others, reportedly were offered and rejected the new xerographic copying invention which tiny Haloid Corporation embraced and which sparked its growth into today's giant Xerox Corporation. Those who rejected Chester Carlson's invention could not foresee much of practical value in this idea of xerographic copying, to their subsequent loss. Thomas Watson, head of IBM, which was to later become by far the leading computer firm in the world, was originally highly unenthusiastic about computers. In 1943 he estimated a world market for computers of about five buyers. And there are legions of similar stories. The platitude about the better mousetrap is a myth. The world will not beat a path to your door, no matter how good your mousetrap is, unless you manage to sell it to the world. Do not be misled by the occasional exceptions. Exceptions to all rules are inevitable, but they do not invalidate the principle.

Evidently almost no one is immune to the human tendency to wear blinders. Ironically, even those who ought to know better out of their own experience have the same frailty. As late as 1922 Edison expressed the opinion that radio was a passing fad. Lee DeForest, inventor of one of the most basic breakthroughs in radio (the "audion" tube) and considered to be at least one of the parents of radio, assured any who would listen that TV was probably a technical possibility but could never be a practical success because it was not feasible commercially or financially. And H. G. Wells, acclaimed writer of visionary science fiction novels, predicted that submarines would succeed in nothing but suffocating their crews to death.

The tendency of most of us to resist new ideas is in some proportion to how different or revolutionary those new ideas are. Those ideas with which we are most uncomfortable are those that require us to discard the familiar notions and opinions we already hold, so we are far more resistant to revolutionary change than we are to evolutionary change. The latter are new ideas we can accommodate side-by-side with those we already hold or by minor modification of the latter, instead of requiring us to cast them out totally. We are also uncomfortable with new ideas that we do not really understand, and so tend to reject ideas for that reason as well.

The means for presenting and selling new and different ideas to clients must take these principles into consideration also, to avoid traumatizing the client with new ideas that the client will find extremely difficult to accept. There are several means for so doing, and in a later chapter we will explore some means for coping with these problems successfully, but the principles should be borne in mind as we proceed next to discuss the various kinds of strategies that can be and should be embodied in most proposals.

CHAPTER 3

THE DEVELOPMENT OF EFFECTIVE STRATEGIES

In marketing, as in waging war, strategy is a prime factor of success and failure. And as in military matters, discriminating among the many possible strategies and tactics to identify that one most likely to effect success is much more art than science.

THE MAJOR STRATEGIES

The concept of a marketing or sales strategy can be most confusing when applied to proposals because we must discuss more than one kind of strategy. It is possible and necessary to have a master strategy (known variously as capture strategy, main strategy, win strategy, etc.), but there are at least four other major strategic concepts to consider, as well as some others which we will discuss here. First, however, a few introductory thoughts about these major strategies:

Technical or program strategy
Cost strategy
Competitive strategy
Presentation strategy

Usually the win strategy, that strategy upon which the proposal and the hopes of winning are based, is one of these, although it may even be something of a lesser strategy which is a subset or component of one of these. Or it may be some combination of two or more of these. In fact, most effective win strategies have cause-and-effect links to more than one of these, but one clearly defined strategy must dominate the proposal. It is the process of deciding what that strategy is to be that should be a major objective of the preliminary requirements analysis, which ought to be the first step in the proposal process.

Whatever the specific situation, it is always essential that you identify your elected win strategy as early in the proposal process as possible, since it has such a great effect upon all elements of the proposal. (At the same time, you need the flexibility to modify or even change your win strategy if later developments suggest that as the sensible course of action.)

IDENTIFYING A WIN STRATEGY

The main (win) strategy many employ is to try to utilize and maximize all of these, in a kind of "buckshot" approach, based on the hope that the more buckshot—strategic ammunition—scattered by the proposal, the more likely it is that some will strike the target in a vital spot and thus produce some kind of salutary effect—a contract, that is.

Alas, it rarely happens. This approach is very much like that of trying to please everyone: The result is almost invariably to please no one. And compromise among many strategic factors vitiates the effect overall so that none of the strategies strikes a telling blow.

Trying to be all things results in a dissipation of your effort. You scatter not only your strategic ammunition but you scatter also your energies. To be maximally effective and to become a decisive factor, strategy must have a clear focus. It can hardly help your cause to argue the technical merits of your proposed method or the virtues of your specialized experience when the client has shown concern for costs only and appears to be unconcerned about those other matters. You must have decided which is the most critical matter (critical in the client's eyes, that is), crystallize your strategy around that specific idea, and suspend your entire presentation from that superstructure. To try to strike everywhere at once suggests uncertainty, weakness, almost desperation, a tacit admission of the lack of a grand strategy. (Of course, the client is not thinking in terms of strategy per se, but in terms of what your main point is.) When you turn to this you risk leaving your reader—the client—with quite a distinct impression that you are not really sure what is the most important aspect of the requirement. The reader should never have the slightest doubt as to exactly what your principal argument is. Nor should you.

That lack of clear focus, that vague meandering around the subject without ever coming to grips directly with it, is characteristic of too many unsuccessful proposals unfortunately. And that weakness usually reflects the lack of commitment to a main strategy as a base for the proposal. It is probably the reason for failure of about two thirds of all proposals.

There is, of course, a hazard in the decision that commits you to a specific strategy, the hazard that you will make the wrong decision and waste all your efforts in pressing home the wrong strategy. It is undoubtedly that danger that impels so many proposers to try "polypharmacal" proposals, offering so many kinds of "medicine" to cure the client's ills.

The danger of making the fatal error is real. But the proper approach to avoiding that error is to do that which is necessary to identify the *proper* win strategy. It is far more a matter of doing the right thing than one of avoiding the wrong thing.

This is not to say that the many other strategies are not to be utilized. They can and should make their own contributions. But they should be most definitely in supporting roles, linked to the main strategy, and clearly subordinated to it. But let us have a brief look at each of these major strategies listed.

Technical/Program Strategy

Technical or program strategy includes such matters as your approach to the solution of the client's problem or satisfaction of need, the characteristics of the design, the procedures prescribed, materials to be used, special features, innovative ideas, use of specialists/special resources, and/or other such features. These may have direct effects and be closely linked, even in cause-and-effect relationships, with such other matters as costs and schedules.

Cost Strategy

While cost is rarely the sole consideration and often not even the chief consideration in the client's choice, it is never unimportant. And cost strategy is possible because, contrary to popular views, cost is rarely an absolute term or an absolute quantity. In most cases cost is a relative term and has numerous qualifiers that point this out for various situations, such as for acquisition costs, maintenance costs, installation costs, support costs, cost of ownership, and life-cycle costs. And even then there are related cost considerations that should be taken into account, such as the possible effects of the consulting work on other costs the client normally experiences.·

In a great many cases it is simply not possible to determine precisely what the final true costs will be or, perhaps more significantly, who the low bidder is among all the proposers or bidders. In this basic anomaly there are the conditions for the evolution of cost strategies, a few of which we will explore shortly.

Competitive Strategy

It is a competitive world, and you are only rarely fortunate enough to be the only consultant invited to propose. In most cases you are only one of at least several—sometimes many—able consultants vying for the contract.

No matter how capable you are or how well you write, it is likely that at least some of your competitors are as able as you and write as well as you. To operate on the premise that none of your competitors approaches you in competence or capability for presenting credentials to a client is an almost certain road to disaster. Remember at all times that with only occasional exception the client judges the capabilities and competence of the proposers primarily by what they say in their proposals and how credible the client finds those statements. As far as the client is concerned in most cases, proposal quality equals consultant quality. (True or not true, this is the client's perception, and it is the client's truth.)

That means that you must have some kind of competitive strategy so that you help the client find reasons to rate your proposal higher than those of competitors. In fact, competitive strategy should be based ideally on one prime factor that somehow dramatizes the issue in your favor.

Presentation Strategy

Your proposal is a presentation, a sales presentation. There are many presentation strategies possible, strategies that can make your presentation (proposal) more effective by increasing its impact, by capturing the client's attention in some special way, or by otherwise maximizing the benefits by various artful methods of presentation.

Don't underestimate the contribution to success that a good presentation strategy can make. It is often only in the presentation strategy that the other strategies are implemented successfully so that you can gain the benefits of those other strategies.

STRATEGIES IN A MINOR KEY

There are many problems that require the development of minor strategies to cope with them successfully. Some would call these measures tactics, rather than strategies. But whichever you call them, strategies or tactics, they are necessary to overcome special problems. In fact, we might and perhaps ought to grant them a special category of "assets and liabilities strategies."

It is not often that you are so precisely "right" for a client's requirement that your qualifications represent 100 percent assets and zero liabilities with regard to the requirement. More often you must weigh your assets and liabilities vis-a-vis the requirement, in evolving some kind of strategy. However, there is, aside from the question of a win strategy and those other major strategic factors, the question of exploiting your assets and overcoming your liabilities. For example, suppose you must write a proposal to offer your services in an area where you have little or no specific experience to present as your technical/professional qualifications. How can you cope with this? Some requirements may clearly call for the services of a sizable team, one considerably larger than your own staff. How do you satisfy the client that you can meet this need successfully and without risking failure? A requirement may be for services primarily in your field, but still require special capabilities for some aspect of the project, special qualifications you do not possess. How can you overcome this liability in your capabilities?

On the other hand, you also need to evolve strategies for maximizing the benefits of your assets. If you have extraordinary experience or other resources that are directly relevant to the client's need, you can benefit from exploiting these as an advantage over competitors. But you will gain the benefits of exploiting them properly only by utilizing specific strategies to do so. It won't come about spontaneously.

HOW IMPORTANT ARE THE MINOR STRATEGIES?

These latter strategies are referred to as "minor" strategies only because they generally affect only relatively minor matters. But that is not always the case. Often the strategy that began life in connection with some apparently minor asset or liability begins to assume more and more importance, as the proposal evolves, and sometimes becomes the pivot upon which success turns. One small firm (total staff of four), for example, was among those invited to submit proposals to create and present a training program for a large firm managing a federal (Energy Department) facility in Idaho. The problem was that the schedule was exceedingly difficult to meet because it was so short. However, this small firm happened by pure chance to have an unusual asset: they had a proprietary program on the shelf that was so close to what was needed that it could be adapted to the need with only a few days' work. This asset translated into both a probably unique ability to meet the impossible schedule and a cost advantage. However, the schedule advantage was all that was required to win the job easily: no one else could offer a firm guarantee to meet the schedule. Thus the proposal focused the entire sales argument on this, and this became the win strategy.

THE ANATOMY OF STRATEGY

A successful strategy may be and often is the result of a flash of inspiration. At other times it may be and often is the more or less subconscious process of a talented individual. But most of us cannot afford to be at the mercy of uncertain and unpredictable inspiration and subconscious mental processes, nor can we accept any premise that requires these for the development of effective strategies. We must have something much more dependable, something that can be employed methodically and produce results—effective strategies—on demand and as required. We must therefore analyze strategies logically to find those basic elements that are the ingredients of all successful strategies.

One thing we may be reasonably sure of immediately is that every successful strategy is based on a clear and unambiguous objective. That appears to be transparently obvious, so obvious as to be hardly worth observing. But let us see if it is truly so obvious as to be unworthy of saying:

> If we consider that which we call a win strategy, is not the objective—winning—implicitly clear and unambiguous in the very fact of its name?

The fact is that winning is a general goal, rather than a direct objective. One thing that makes this assertion true is that not every proposal competition results in a contract award directly and immediately as the result of evaluation of the proposals and selection of a winner. In fact, in quite a large number of proposal contests, and especially in the case of the large contracts, proposal evaluations are followed by such activities as calls for presentations, best and final offers, discussions, and other kinds of negotiations or preliminaries to negotiations.

In short, many clients use proposals as the mechanism for narrowing the field to acceptable candidates, from whose number the client will eventually choose a contractor.

In this situation a go-for-broke win strategy may be a mistake, at least in that it distracts you from what ought to be your true objective: surmounting that first hurdle and getting into the finalists' circle.

It is not possible to know always whether the client will choose a winner without postproposal activity. However, should the client do so, having based your main strategy on the objective of getting into that second-stage phase will not hurt you in any way. But the reverse is not necessarily true. Shooting for a direct win when there are to be follow-up activities can hurt you because you had your eye on the wrong ball. It's a matter of knowing or not knowing where you wish to go. If you do not know exactly what you are aiming at, don't be surprised if you don't hit the target.

But even that is not the entire essence of the matter. The fact is that it is so much in your interest, normally, to be invited to make a presentation or best and final offer that many wise marketers of consulting services do not even try to guess whether the client will issue that invitation. Instead they do everything in their power to persuade the client to do so. That is, they set themselves a clear and unambiguous objective of inducing the client to call on them for proposal follow-up marketing, and they structure and design their win strategies to include achieving this objective as the first step.

The objective is nothing by itself, however. It's a statement of what you wish to bring about, but it contains no hint of how you can make it happen. It becomes useful only when some method of implementation is designed and employed. It's well and good to decide that your first objective is to persuade the client to invite you to make a presentation and discuss your proposal, but what can you do to bring that about? You need some kind of plan to put your strategy to work and produce that result, as the following consultants did.

Case History No. 1

A consultant we'll call X was invited by a large organization to propose to them services to develop their Annual Report. The consultant was to interview the staffs of and report on some 22 engineering projects being conducted for the organization and to compose and print the report in 500 copies. The report was estimated at 150 pages, to include approximately 75 color photographs. And that was the full extent of the specification, at least as far as quantified data was concerned, although there were several pages of text in the request for proposals.

Consultant X had a problem in pricing the work, of course, since there are so many alternatives in typesetting and printing. Moreover, the client had not specified where the color photographs would come from—that is, whether they would be supplied or had to be made by the consultant. But that handicap was very much to X's taste. He saw a way to make lemonade out of that lemon, and his basic strategy was based on a plan for persuading the client to call on him for a presentation and discussion. That was his "clear and unambiguous objective."

His method was simple: He explained the pricing difficulty—the lack of sufficient quantified data—but offered his own suggested specifications and explanations of what they meant and why he thought them suitable. He thus tactfully made the client well aware of the client's own shortcomings in knowledge necessary to specify the project properly and demonstrated his own expertise, along with his ability and willingness to educate the client suitably in the relevant subjects. However, he went on to suggest several alternatives as distinct possibilities, listing the pros and cons of each, as he saw them, and leaving the door open for modification of his basic proposal with diplomatic implications of the need for face-to-face discussion. And in his letter of transmittal he was highly specific in offering to provide any additional information desired, to answer questions, and/or to make a formal or informal presentation on the client's premises.

The client saw immediately the need to discuss the matter face to face with this expert, and Consultant X had no difficulty converting that meeting into a successful contract negotiation session.

Case History No. 2

Consultant Y had a client who requested proposals to develop a public-information program. The request listed several possible elements, such as press releases, brochures, and posters, but asked proposers to suggest some ideas of their own, and made it clear that the client was looking for fresh and innovative ideas. In fact, it appeared rather obvious that the contract was likely to be awarded on the basis of the most attractive innovative ideas offered.

Consultant Y also perceived a face-to-face presentation and discussion as the most desirable outcome of the proposal competition, and set about to persuade the client to ask for exactly that. She did offer a few innovative ideas, but stated clearly that they were entirely preliminary and intended to serve only as examples. The final set of ideas would come out of a contract first-phase brainstorming session, to which she now invited the client staff as active participants, and she hoped earnestly that they would attend and help plan their own project with their own contributions.

The strategy worked admirably, and Y was entirely successful in winning the contract after making her presentation.

Other Objectives

Here are a few—a very few—other kinds of objectives you might find it useful to consider in various proposal circumstances:

☐ Persuade the client to modify the statement of work.
☐ Make the client perceive unusually splendid qualifications in you.
☐ Persuade the client to see extraordinary assets in your proposed design.
☐ Sell the client a different approach than the request suggests.
☐ Sell the absolute need for some unique resource you offer.
☐ Alert the client to the hazards of the project.
☐ Convince the client that any cost in excess of that which you estimate is sheer waste and totally unnecessary.

Of course there are thousands of other possible objectives, each clearly defining or at least implying a strategy, which may be a win strategy or only a subordinate strategy. However, in either case it is necessary to do more than merely state the allegation of the objective. Strategy is the means of persuading the client to agree with the statement, to perceive the situation as you perceive it. Flat statements are not enough to do the job, for they represent opinion or claims, not demonstrated facts or what the client will accept as facts. (Note that last observation carefully, for we will discuss this again.)

If you wanted to alert the client to possible hazards of the project called for, for example, you might validate your allegation (and so implement your strategic objective) by citing case histories, published papers, public statements of prominent authorities, or simple logical analysis. And to add weight to your arguments you might even reproduce some of the relevant published material, drawings, photographs, or other supporting materials.

THE OPPOSITE POLES OF STRATEGY

There are two angles of attack open to you as a proposal strategist, which we might call the positive and negative approaches. In the classic tradition, that stance referred to as the positive one, you try to better your position by boosting yourself and what you have to offer. In the negative approach you try to better your position by trying to knock your competitors out. In some cases you might use one or the other of these two general approaches, but more commonly you will employ both. Both are entirely legitimate in this competitive world, even that one of attacking competitors and doing your level best to discredit them in the eyes of the client.

Positive Strategy: Gain

Most of what we have been discussing has been geared to boosting your own image and ideas. Philosophically, this approach is based on the promise to the client of gain. It strives to persuade the buyer that this proposal offers the client the greatest gain of all the courses open for whatever reason the basic strategy dictates, such as better schedule, lower cost, greater dependability, or other such boon.

Obviously, this approach clearly implies, if it does not boldly state, that you offer more gain—that is, better results—than do your competitors in general, although it never ventures to knock competitors directly. In fact, the implication that competitive offers and competitive capabilities are inferior to your own is so subtle or low-key in this typical presentation strategy that rarely does the client even sense that implication in reading your proposal. Of course, all of us have come to expect that every advertisement and sales presentation will necessarily make the claim of superiority of product or service. We would be dumbfounded at any presentation that neglected to make such a claim.

For practical purposes, then, the strategies underlying these kinds of presentations do not qualify as competitive or competitor strategies. They are not aimed directly or indirectly, except in that most general sense, at invalidating competitive claims, and therefore represent only one of the two basic strategic orientations. But it is possible to draw a bead on competitors without appearing unethical or in violation of good taste.

Negative Strategy: Fear

Boosting your own position at the direct expense of competitors, while yet avoiding the stigma of directly knocking competitors, calls for a great deal of delicacy. And probably the most effective way of doing this is to use fear motivation, generally a most effective motivator. One way to do this is to combine the gain motivation with the provision of a worry item, and present this with a twist: You alert the client to the problems and even disasters that are possible (perhaps even probable) unless certain measures are taken, certain capabilities at hand, certain resources available, certain foresight present, etc. And, of course, you are the only proposer who has that foresight and can offer whatever it is you say is necessary to avoid disaster.

Now in that latter sentence lies the root of the strategy. For it to be effective it must meet certain conditions:

1. The problems or disasters predicated must be legitimate (believable) eventualities. (That is, you must identify real possibilities and make them believable.)
2. They must be things your competitors are not likely to think of or point out to the client in their own proposals.
3. You must provide some credible evidence of your own unique capabilities to cope successfully with the projected problems.

That last-named condition is the hardest to satisfy, inasmuch as probably all or nearly all the proposers in any given proposal competition are competent providers of whatever consulting services are required. And to succeed with the first two items but fail totally with the last one is to probably make yourself appear somewhat foolish, but worse still, give your competitors more of a boost than a kick. Therefore, give careful thought to that aspect of this strategy. But here is a bit of guidance in that matter.

If you have some special and unique or probably unique asset, such as some kind of helpful proprietary resource or some highly specialized experience, you can probably make that the basis of your claim. If you do not have that kind of advantage, there is always one other way to address this, a way that has proved successful many times. Base your claim on the need for foresight and advance planning, pointing out that you are now demonstrating that foresight and advance preparation. But be sure that you have identified real problem potentials that probably no one else will think of, or even if they do think of them, will mention in their own proposals.

In short, the essence of this technique is to find or create the worry item that, properly employed, gives you some special advantage over competitors in terms of the image you present in your proposal.

IMAGE STRATEGY AND THE CAPABILITY BROCHURE

The image you strive to create for yourself is itself a strategy, one on which you normally base all your marketing effort. And one place you try to create that image is in your brochures, especially that type of brochure that is known in some circles as a "capability brochure" or "capability statement."

For many consultants the capability brochure is itself virtually a standard proposal and is often used as a major element of the consultant's proposals. In fact, 69 percent of those surveyed in gathering material for this book reported that they employed brochures and/or other boilerplated material as major portions of their proposals, and only 31 percent reported that each of their proposals was a completely custom-written original.

A well-designed capability brochure is itself based on a major strategic concept, usually one that strives toward creating a specific image for the consultant. Computer Programming Services, Inc. (CPS), a computer consultant in Prairie Village, Kansas, supplied a sample of the CPS capability brochure, which they use as an integral part of their proposals. The basic strategy underlying the firm's posture is quite evident in that brochure. It is a clear message that the firm sells absolutely no proprietary products, neither hardware nor software, but offers only custom services to clients. The firm has therefore no commitments to any proprietary products, and for that reason has no difficulty being completely impartial and objective in recommendations to clients. The stated firm policy of the firm with regard to proprietaries, the brochure explains, makes possible an objectivity that enables the firm to truly represent clients and the clients' best interests.

The capability brochure is an excellent idea for anyone offering custom services of any kind. It is itself a basis for many, if not all, of your proposals (depending on several factors to be discussed later). It is a guide to and aid in preparing individual proposals, also: A well-designed capability brochure greatly facilitates and speeds up proposal writing. And, not the least of its virtues, it is an excellent means of establishing and promoting your professional image, as CPS does with its own brochure.

An image strategy should send a message. CPS's image is one of deliberately engineered objectivity to enable unflinching loyalty to the client. But here, as examples, are images other brochures present:

- "Quick reaction" services, available to support clients on short notice, with impossible schedules, and in emergencies of all kinds.
- "One stop" services, a resource to handle virtually every related requirement within the general field.
- Unparalleled experience in the field, possibly even unique in quality of experience or capability.
- Top-drawer; the *ne plus ultra* of such services; expensive, but the very best.

Unfortunately, many of the brochures offered by consultants reflect no strategy at all, image or otherwise, but pursue the futile allegations of the consultant's superiority in all respects by self-appraisal, with generous use of superlatives. Obviously, the strategy here is to overwhelm the reader with claims and hyperbole, which is, of course, no strategy at all.

As a consultant, you probably should have a capability brochure of some kind (format and content will be suggested later), and it should most definitely be based on some strategy that is designed to create a suitable image for you. That image should be the one that you wish customers to see in you generally, but it should also be the underpinning for not only your proposals specifically but for all your marketing presentations.

The strategy underlying brochures and proposals has still another aspect, a related subject to consider. The subject is theme.

THEME

Theme is a word that has several meanings and yet is a difficult concept to define in terms of what it means in proposals and other sales presentations. It is closely related to strategy and should reflect the strategy. Properly used it is also a reinforcement and continuous reminder to the client of your image and of your strategy. And if we have trouble defining theme briefly, we can at least study some examples.

A company proposing to design for the Department of Defense an airplane that could be used by both the Air Force and the Navy decided that their theme was to be "an aerodynamic solution to an aerodynamic problem." A competing company offered their own proposal, presenting their own technical arguments for their proposed design, and used the theme "commonality."

The first company used a theme that appealed to logic, assuming that the client accepted their technical arguments for their design and agreed with their claims of superior technical/scientific aeronautical engineering expertise. The second company used a theme that appealed to emotions, assuming that the Department of Defense had a truly great desire to achieve commonality. If we were to infer from the statements of theme what image and strategy each proposer wished to project, we would have to draw the following conclusions:

The first proposer, using the "aerodynamic solution to an aerodynamic problem" as their chief argument, was striving to project the image of an organization of superlative technical expertise and unflagging devotion to related scientific integrity, employing the related strategy of offering what it insisted was the only design that made good engineering and scientific sense.

The second proposer focused their efforts on an image of total devotion to the client's goal, taking the position that their technical/scientific competence was a given, with no need to argue it, since the company was well known in its field. The strategy, on the other hand, was to portray a project and staff so committed to the client's desired end goal—commonality—that it never took its eye off that target, not for a single page.

It is probably not necessary to identify the winner here; by now you should be able to project that from the information supplied. And certainly you should be able to make that projection later, if not now, after we have further probed the nature of sales persuasion.

In another case the client had asked for a computer/data-processing service that was difficult enough to supply at best. Briefly, the request called for a contractor to supply on demand the services of any of quite a vast number of computer specialists, each with different qualifications of expertise in computer languages, machines, kinds of programs, and job functions.

The proposal request suggested that the successful proposer would need to be an organization with all such experts on staff, readily at hand. This would, not surprisingly, have slanted the requirement toward only the largest of the computer service companies.

One proposer decided that they could not make their strongest possible presentation if it were based on that suggested modus operandi, since that approach denied them the opportunity to take advantage of their strengths as an organization. They were sure that they could do the job very well and make a strong argument for themselves if the approach were such as to exploit their strengths as an organization. They therefore took the sensible course of exploring ways of meeting the requirement through employing those methods which did take advantage of their own strengths. And, accordingly, they pursued the proposal presentation along the following lines:

1. They first isolated the desired result from the suggested method, and pointed out that the suggested method was, first of all, only one of several possible approaches to satisfying the requirement.

2. They argued against the suggested approach, pointing out its weaknesses, that even if there were a company or two large enough to have all the cited kinds of experts on staff (which

was itself a doubtful supposition), there was no guarantee that the one expert required for any given task would always be available immediately, when needed. Quite the contrary, chance being the perverse factor that it so often is (per Murphy's Law, of course), that expert would probably be the only one of that kind in the company and would be already engaged several thousand miles away on another assignment.

3. They suggested a different approach, one that they could employ successfully, using their own large rosters of consultants (a large part of their business was precisely the provision of technical/professional temporaries) and argued for it.

4. They expressed their firm conviction that this was an even more responsive proposal than would be one offering the suggested solution because this would guarantee the same result, which they said was the true test of responsiveness, and would be a more efficient, more dependable, and less costly approach.

The strategy was to take advantage of their strength by changing the rules of the game—invalidating the suggested approach—thus also denying competitors the advantages of *their* strengths. The theme was then one that reflected the proposer's basic strength as a leading provider of technical/professional temporaries, with an already-in-place staff accustomed to filling such requirements every day.

It is almost unnecessary to say that this approach was a successful one.

DESIGNING STRATEGIES FROM STRENGTHS

In a later chapter we will get into specific tools, methods, and procedures, even offering forms, for developing strategies, and you will then find that we have barely penetrated the outer skin of the subject here. But in the meanwhile remember, if you have not already perceived this for yourself, one of the basic approaches to developing a win strategy is to first identify clearly the *end result* the client seeks. Then take an inventory of all your strengths and weaknesses—assets and liabilities—vis-a-vis the requirement. Next study all the possible ways to achieve the desired end-result. Finally select a way that enables you to utilize your own greatest strengths as a consultant, while still an effective way to achieve the desired result. And then devise the arguments to sell that approach to the client.

In the next chapter we are going to probe that subject of selling your approach to the client, and we will probe much more deeply into the nature of persuasion generally as the essence of sales and marketing and into the specific do's and don'ts of sales activities.

CHAPTER 4

SOME BASICS OF SALES
AND MARKETING

Despite the mystique with which some have surrounded sales and marketing, the fundamental principles are quite easy to understand and are, in fact, in themselves a basic explanation of human behavior in sales situations.

NEEDS, WANTS, AND PERSUASION

There are a number of immutable truths in selling, truths that apply to all kinds of selling under all kinds of circumstances. They are, in fact, truths that apply to all kinds of persuasion, for that is what selling is, of course, an act of persuasion. Sometimes the buyer is persuaded by an effective sales presentation, sometimes simply by the appearance of the item, sometimes by a description of it, sometimes even by curiosity. But selling is always an act of persuasion, even if the buyer is motivated by self-persuasion. And if someone buys something without being persuaded, that isn't selling, marketing, or advertising; it's simply order-taking. Thus, to understand selling at its most fundamental level, it is necessary to understand the art of persuasion.

We all want most earnestly to believe that we are totally rationale animals, logical thinkers, easily able to behave according to that which reason dictates. And that is a truth, but a qualified one. We are, indeed, reasoning creatures, seeking to reach logical conclusions upon which to base all our decisions and actions. However, with perhaps a rare exception here and there, we do more often than not subordinate our reasoned conclusions to our emotional reactions and impulses, consciously or unconsciously. Who has never overcome restraining efforts of reason and yielded to an impulse to inflict verbal or even physical violence on someone else? And even when we regret so yielding or "losing control," as we often put it, have we not often rationalized our action and justified it by assuring ourselves that we had been "pushed too far"? And who has not bought something on impulse and regretted it later in that phenomenon that salespeople refer to as "buyer's remorse"?

In most cases we try to rationalize decisions arrived at tentatively on an emotional basis, and discard or reverse those tentative decisions only if and when we are unable to rationalize them satisfactorily. This is perhaps especially true in sales situations, as witness an example to two: When television receivers first appeared, shortly after World War II, they were quite expensive, as new luxuries tend to be. A few people bought receivers, but most of us felt unable to afford this new delight, much as we wanted it. The cost stayed our hands, preventing us from acting on that emotional desire to have this new adult toy. Some even rationalized that it was smart to wait until TV was "perfected" before buying a set. (Some individuals are reluctant to admit even to themselves that they cannot afford something they want and so rationalize even that situation.)

On the other hand, many who perhaps strained their financial resources badly wanted TV enough, even at those high original prices, so that they managed to persuade themselves that they could afford it or that they really needed it. There is plenty of evidence for unrestrained and unwise buying behavior today with the appearance of what some have called "credit card junkies."

Bear this emotional influence in mind, as we proceed to study the subject of sales and marketing in this chapter, and you will see evidence of this again and again, even as it was suggested in an earlier chapter. Understanding of this is essential to understanding all selling and to the development of successful proposals, for it applies to the business world as much as to the non-business world.

Only a few pages ago we discussed the subject of needs and wants briefly, in general terms, pointing out that a need is usually perceived as an absolute requirement which we recognize through pure objective reason, whereas a want is something we desire, although it may not be an absolute requirement. For example, my own word processing system was a perceived need for me and was the only reason I bought a personal computer, but the word-counting program, the spooler software, and a few other items, such as the A-B switch and modem, were expensive wants because I could have managed quite well without them, as I had for many previous years.

On the other hand, although I did very well without those items for all those many years, once I decided to want them I had no difficulty convincing myself that they were needs, and that I must have them. (I did write many books, proposals, articles, and other things on a typewriter before I owned a computer and word processor.) So while I regard all of these as needs, before I bought them they were wants, and as long as I felt unable to afford them I persuaded myself that they would not really be of much use to me. My reasoning changed abruptly, however, when circumstances enabled me to afford a system of my own: I had no difficulty then in reframing that want as an absolute need, a need that had to be satisfied without further delay.

In fact there is no practical difference between a want and a need, at least not for marketing purposes. They are the same. The want becomes a need instantly when the individual succeeds in rationalizing the want—or when the effective sales presenter helps the client make the rationalization successfully.

That is the essence of all selling: Identify and/or stimulate the want and provide or support the rationalization. The means for doing so, however, are somewhat varied, and are what sales and marketing are all about.

WHAT IS A NEED?

Sales experts sometimes identify two different kinds of needs, naming one a "felt" need and the other a need that has been "created." In general, this concept attempts to distinguish between the buyer who sets out deliberately to buy something he or she has already perceived as a need and the buyer who is persuaded to recognize or "feel" a need. Thus the idea of creating a need assumes that an effective sales presentation can persuade a prospect to develop a want for an item. There are two things wrong with this idea:

1. There is ample evidence around that efforts to create needs by persuading uninterested prospects to become interested are almost always wasted. In fact, it is a truism that you cannot really sell a prospect anything the prospect has not persuaded himself or herself to become interested in.

2. Needs are really never new, and have never changed throughout the course of human history. We have the same needs our ancestors had, even when they were living in caves.

The Felt Need

Some products and services are instant successes. Commercial radio and TV caught on with the public very quickly, as did movies, the personal computer, air travel, xerographic office copiers, express mail and package services, fast food establishments, and a great many other things. That means that the public quickly decided that they had a need for these things.

It might be said that these new developments created new needs by the simple fact of their availability. Obviously, one could not have a need (as marketers use the term) for something that did not exist and was not even dreamed of. (Or could they?) So it is valid to think of the rapid acceptance of new items as reflecting a need that had been heretofore unfilled and even perhaps unperceived.

On the other hand, perhaps there is another way to explain the swift success of these and many other new creations: Is it possible that these items succeeded almost instantly because they satisfied *felt* needs that had either never been satisfied before or they satisfied those felt needs in a far better way than they had ever been satisfied before? Let's consider this in terms of some of these items by identifying what needs some of these items serve.

Radio and TV are among the latest (the VCR—videocassette recorder—is *the* latest) home-entertainment devices. They were new and better ways of satisfying a long-standing need for entertainment, especially in the home. Witness what they have done to theatre attendance, public band concerts, public lectures, and many other older forms of pastime for adults. And if there is any doubt as to whether there has been a long-standing need for better means of calculation, consider the Chinese abacus and how long it has been in existence.

The message here is plain enough, even as it was suggested in another context earlier: First determine what the client really wants— the truly basic want, that is, for that is the need—and then show the client a better way to satisfy that need. If you can persuade the client to accept your argument that yours is truly a better way, success is almost inevitable.

Clients Do Not Always "Feel" a Felt Need

Oddly enough, in the face of all that I have said here, the client's felt need is one that is often not felt consciously, but only unconsciously. As many people have observed, they "know it when [they] see it," but not until then. Consciously, they feel only a vague discontent, an unrest, an awareness that something is needed, and yet are unable to actually "put your finger on it," as many express that vague discomfort. It is a sensation somewhat akin to that of trying to recognize a face you know you ought to recognize or recall a name you know that you should know, some knowledge that probably lies deeply in your subconscious, but won't come forth on command.

This comes through often in proposal requests and statements of work written by clients, as they describe what they are not able to identify clearly enough to specify. It is readily apparent in such cases that the client is troubled and feels a need for help (that is indeed the universal reason for using the services of a consultant) but often the help needed includes help in deciding what the problem is.

DIRECT BENEFITS COME FROM GOOD PROPOSALS

The proposal itself is a direct benefit to the client, if the proposal is truly a good one. So often is the client unable to actually identify and define the problem accurately (and sometimes not able to even describe the symptoms with any great accuracy of detail), that a most important element of proposal writing is the proposer's analysis of the client's statement to determine what the problem is. This alone is often the critical difference between successful and unsuccessful proposals. And the proposer who does an effective job of making that identification and defining the problem does the client a great service—provides valuable client education—as well as bettering his or her own position as a contender for the contract.

MANY CLIENTS NEED EDUCATION

In a great many cases there is a distinct need for client education. Educating the client—selectively, that is, in terms of the immediate problem and its solution—is often the key to a successful main strategy. However, this must be done judiciously. Often enough the client would not care to admit such a need as this, and may even feel defensive about it. It's important to be aware of this, for obvious reasons, and exercise a great deal of diplomacy in administering the necessary education. But that aside, never underestimate the importance of the education, and quite often it is most needed by clients who appear to have the least need for it! Witness my own case, vis-a-vis buying a computer and word processor:

With a fairly extensive technological background in modern electronics, including much experience with mainframe computers in a variety of major applications, I was sure that I fully understood the significance of personal computers and word processing. I thought myself to be in an especially privileged position in this respect. Moreover, as the successful professional writer of a large number of books and other publications, I was sure that I had a realistic grasp on what word processing would and would not mean to me as a writer. I thought it would be pleasant and convenient to work with this new technological miracle, and I planned to do so eventually, but I didn't think that the use of word processing would contribute much to my efficiency or effectiveness. In fact, I was convinced that it would not greatly increase my productivity, since I was already making free and effective use of all the time- and labor-saving cut-and-paste techniques I had learned in my years in the technical-publications industry, and had even developed a few special techniques and tactics of my own, in this respect. I thus kept my retyping of revised manuscript copy to a minimum. And I did not see how this system could do very much to increase the quality of my writing, since I already did what I believed to be an at least adequate amount of self-editing, rewriting, and revision.

I was wrong on all counts. I didn't find out how wrong I was until I began to use a word processor. And the chief reason I bought a word processor when I did was that I was beginning to write books about computers and their use, and I found it embarrassing, as well as ludicrous, to do so without owning a system of my own.

I believe that I would have bought one much earlier had I been educated by someone in what a word processor would really do for me—had I somehow gained a more accurate and insightful grasp of what word processing really is. (In retrospect, however, that is not too surprising, considering how little of the outpouring of printed words on the subject have shown a true appreciation of word processing. Relatively few users seem to understand it yet, and many tend to use it as an automatic typewriter, rather than learning how to gain the advantages of using it as the revolutionary new, different, and better way of writing that it is.) In fact, when I did buy a system, after fairly extensive research, I bought one featured in full-page advertising in the *Writer's Digest*, that enduring journal of freelance writing that I have read for a great many years. (I think it was at that point, when I read that advertising copy, that I began to suspect that perhaps word processing offered more for the professional writer than I had previously believed.)

Incidentally, inasmuch as word processing is reported as by far the most popular use of and outstanding reason for buying personal computers, it has always struck me as odd that so few manufacturers and distributors of personal computers have focused any significant portion of their advertising efforts on media and means for reaching writers. And what has been and is published on the subject tends heavily to stress the technical advantages of the system being touted, rather than its functional advantages, with virtually no advertising devoted to explaining the true advantages of word processing over the more conventional means of writing. (We will be returning to the subject later, when we discuss ways to use computers and word processing to add leverage in proposal writing.)

This reveals quite clearly a shortcoming of many marketers in failing to understand what business they are in.

WHAT BUSINESS ARE YOU IN?

In conducting seminars in proposal writing I sometimes ask my attendees, "What business are you in?" I get such answers as these:

"We provide accounting services."
"We are marketing consultants."
"I am an interior designer."
"I teach people how to use their computers."
"We help clients design their office systems."

All these answers suffer from the same deficiency: each definition of the business is focused on "we" or "I" and describes what the consultant sells or wishes to sell. None of these statements reflects what the client really wishes to buy or even shows concern for (or is it awareness of?) the probable client want.

As everyone knows today, the railroads represent the classic case cited so often to illustrate the point. Becoming "fat, dumb, and happy," as modern vernacular puts it, the prosperous railroad magnates sneered at change and stubbornly insisted that they were in the railroad business, even as they watched their dwindling freight business transfusing to the huge tractor-trailers multiplying on the rapidly growing network of superhighways, while their vanishing passenger business was flowing to the growing number of airports, large and small. Only when they had begun to founder did they begin to reshape their thinking, but it was too late then to salvage more than a shadow of their former industry.

The problem is that each of us tends to think in selfish terms, in terms of what we want rather than in terms of what the client wants. We even rationalize that what we want is what the client ought to want. And even when the subject of educating the client arises, most of us—at least until we come to know better through getting a proper education in the subject ourselves—we believe that educating the client means making the client understand why what we want is what he or she ought to want.

Of course, this is getting it all backwards. It is we who should want what the client wants. It is we who should—*must*—sell what the client wants, and must identify and define our business in those terms. Even today, many do not understand what the railroads were or should have been selling. Some people who ought to know better believe that the railroads were actually in the "transportation business," but that is wrong too because even that is a bit too abstract to come to real grips with what customers want and so to properly orient and focus marketing. It is not "transportation" per se that customers want to buy, as they perceive their wants, but it is getting their goods delivered to customers and getting themselves to wherever they are going. And customers want efficiency, speed, comfort, convenience, and economy in doing these, although not necessarily in that order.

Airlines offer much greater speed in actual in-transit time than do railroads, although they do not offer as much convenience in many respects, due primarily to the remote locations of airports and the hassle of transportation to and from those airports. Nor do airlines always offer greater speed in total travel time, especially in short hauls of a few hundred miles where passengers spend much more time traveling to and from airports than they do in the air. Rail travel, in portal-to-portal terms, is often as rapid as air travel, as well as much more convenient, more comfortable, and less expensive. Had the railroads focused on those advantages and concentrated on increasing them, they would almost surely have retained much of their passenger business. And had they thought out and maximized the advantages they could offer in freight forwarding—delivering the goods to customers—they would have kept much more of their freight business than they did. But the railroads failed to even think out marketing strategies, much less do anything to put them to work. At least they did not do so until the damage was done, when it was too late to salvage very much, even with the help of the federal government.

Nothing has changed very much. Not everyone has learned from that classic case of the railroads, and many of us are making those same kinds of mistakes today, albeit on a smaller scale and in less dramatic industries.

The business you are in has nothing to do with what you want. It has everything to do with what the client wants. And in a very large sense we are all in the same business: helping the client. The differences among us are in how we help clients, or perhaps more accurately, in what help the client needs.

To help you to gain a firm grasp on this and apply it to your own case, try your hand at the exercise presented in Figure 3. The idea here is to first study the typical consulting services numbered as 1 to 10, and then match up those services with the kinds of benefits suggested in the second part of the figure by writing in the number(s) of each kind of service you believe can be fairly represented as offering that/those benefit(s). Of course, some of the services offer more than one kind of benefit or the benefit can be represented in more than one set of terms, so you should wind up with many more than 10 numbers written on the lines following the list of possible benefits.

You should also, at whatever point you wish to do so, write in a description of your own services, and also add your own ideas as to benefits offered by any of these services, including your own. (That is the purpose of the blank lines provided.) That, conceiving of additional benefits and words with which to express them, is an important part of this exercise, designed to compel you to think seriously about this. This is an opportunity to orient and sharpen your thought processes vis-a-vis this aspect of marketing, and the time you spend in this will be well-spent time.

Finally, go to the third part of the figure and write out a statement of the business you are in, as you now see it. Be sure that this is a statement that stresses what you do to help the client directly, and do not overlook the emotional element in articulating that main benefit. Don't worry about how many words you need to make your statement, and don't do it mentally only. Actually write it out, and return to it later, and see whether you are still satisfied with that definition or

CONSULTING SPECIALTIES

1. Marketing services
2. Interior design
3. Office systems design
4. Computer systems specialist
5. Hypnotist

6. Speech coach
7. Publications specialist
8. Conference management
9. Investment advisor
10. Real estate appraiser

11. Your own specialty(ies) _____

_____

_____

PRIMARY BENEFITS

Maximize profits _____   Reduce risk _____

Stop smoking _____   Raise efficiency _____

Save money _____   Increase sales _____

Be in style _____   Gain personal prestige _____

Avoid making a mistake _____   Improve business image _____

_____

_____

_____

THE BUSINESS YOU ARE IN

_____

_____

_____

_____

_____

Figure 3.   Exercise sheet.

wish to revise it, as you gain more insights into successful proposal-writing strategies and tactics.

Note also the point made earlier that the most basic appeals and motivators are emotional ones, not rational ones. Study those benefit items and note that most have an emotional appeal—to be in style, to gain in personal prestige, to make more money, to improve one's business image.

This is not by chance. All experienced marketers and sales experts are well aware that the prime motivator is emotional, and that logic and reason play supporting roles in marketing and sales.

MOTIVATORS

Earlier you read that fear and greed are prime motivators. People act out of the desire to avoid something they fear and the desire to gain something they want. And there is a great deal of evidence around that fear is probably by far the more persuasive motivator. And that is itself not too surprising, when you consider the ever greater pressures of modern life and what that inevitably does to increase the sense of insecurity that most of us have to some degree. (In fact, is there anyone who is not insecure to at least some degree in this uncertain world?)

Motivators are Emotional

Note carefully that these are emotional motivators. Study all successful advertising and especially those appearing on TV as commercials. You can easily tell which are the most successful ones: They are the ones that are repeated again and again, over a great period of time, those, that is, that have proved their effectiveness. Study these for their emotional content, for that is the common factor.

Invariably, successful advertising is addressed to the emotions, to what people are most likely to want to gain or avoid. Insurance, smoke detectors, burglar alarms, locks, security systems, safes, and a great many other items are sold principally through fear motivation, often with a generous measure of appeal to guilt thrown in, as insurance advertisements urge prospects to remember their obligations to provide for their families, even after they are gone from this sphere.

Many other items are sold through promises of gain—money, love, fun, prestige, and other such endowments. And sometimes advertisers manage to incorporate both kinds of motivators, as in the case of some securities advisors who promise to reduce the risks—safeguard your capital—while helping you make profitable investments and even offer discounted stockbrokerage fees.

Selling Benefits—What the Item *Does*

Note how many of these successful advertisements do not even attempt to sell the product or service directly, but instead focus the major persuasive effort on the claimed benefit directly, and then describe and sell the product or service only as the means to the benefit. Rare indeed are the advertisers who make even an effort to prove their product better than anyone else's product, except to support their claims of what the product does for the buyer. Kitchen or dishwasher detergents are not of better quality per se, in the TV commercials, for example; they simply produce better results, such as literally spotless glassware and dishes that shine so that you can see your face reflected in them. And once the advertiser has established that claim of beneficial result, the time comes to support that claim with some evidence to help the prospect believe the promise of pleasing results.

"Proving" the Claim

Wherever possible, that "evidence" (which may or may not be legitimate evidence, but which the advertiser hopes the prospect will accept as evidence) is linked logically and directly to the qualities or characteristics of the product or service. For example, claims of better riding qualities in an advertiser's automobile might be supported by technical or semi-technical descriptions of the suspension system. This is the best kind of evidence, usually, and should be used when possible.

In some cases, it is not possible to link the promised blessing with the qualities of the product or with any direct claim to superiority of product. Beer is one such case. Beer advertisers rarely base their advertising on any claim of product superiority in quality. (Not only would that be almost impossible to prove, but beer drinkers couldn't care less about the technology of making beer or the logic of one method over another.) Rather, beer advertisers only suggest broadly that it's more fun to drink their beer by showing their beer being consumed in a good-times atmosphere. And, as another (and less powerful) theme, they try to portray their product as the "in" product by commercials that attempt to prove that "everyone" (or at least everyone with good taste) orders their product.

In another case, where there is no logical basis (and probably no valid basis) on which to lay a claim of superiority, the advertiser might simply claim superiority and "substantiate" that with testimonials by some public figure from the sports or entertainment world. Or, as an alternative, an actor dressed appropriately as an authority with relevance to the advertised product or service, such as in a white laboratory coat, might offer the "expert opinion."

Humans have a herd instinct, too, and tend to join the flock, rather than go it alone. Probably this is another manifestation of our common sense of insecurity, but it can be used effectively in marketing. The influence of testimonials and other data that demonstrates widespread acceptance of your product or service is not entirely logical or evidence that yours is a good product or service, but is also an emotional appeal to the human instinct to join the crowd and agree with the popular view. Possibly this can be explained as fear motivation, reflecting the fear many of us have to go it alone.

WHAT DO YOU REALLY SELL?

I once had the opportunity to observe an outstandingly successful Fuller Brush salesman at work. His technique was really quite simple. He went through his entire case of samples—he carried perhaps 30 to 40 items—showing each to the customer with a few words of introduction, watching the customer's eyes intently. If the eyes remained vacant, he went on. If he detected a spark of interest, he stopped and began to sell that item, usually with great success.

There were many other aspects to his technique, but this was the basic one and it was the one that most clearly explained this man's basic success. He understood that it was impracticable and wasteful of time to try to sell something the prospect was not really interested in, when the time could be invested much more profitably in selling something in which the prospect showed some immediate interest. His tactic was simply to find out which items captured the prospect's interest, and to do so as quickly as possible so he could get on to the more important business of getting the maximum-sized orders for those items. (He also had effective techniques for maximizing those orders, but that is not relevant here.)

That's a universal truth. You can't sell the client what the client really does not want. The most effective tactic is to first find out what the client really wants, but remember that clients often do not know what they want. At least, this is often true in the sense that they do not know precisely how to identify or specify what they want and need your help in doing so.

We All Sell the Same Thing

Buyers are motivated by the desire to gain or avoid things. If we look at this from the sellers' viewpoint, we all sell the same thing. We all sell help. And while that is true for everyone who sells anything, it is especially true for consultants because the desire for help is usually the conscious and direct objective of clients who go in quest of consulting services. We sell help in avoiding things, help in gaining things, help in achieving things. But even more fundamentally than that, it is not help that we sell; we sell the *promise* of help.

A BASIC MARKETING PROBLEM

Why is it important to recognize that fact—that what we sell is the *promise* of help? It is important because it illustrates both the basic difficulty in selling consulting services and the importance of the proposal in marketing. It is important to have a realistic appreciation of the marketing problem, with all its difficulties. Of course selling a prospect a tangible object, even such a costly one as an automobile or house, is far less difficult than selling any intangible, such as a service. And on that latter level there are sublevels of marketing difficulty too, for it is obviously far easier to sell mundane, workaday services such as automobile repair and accounting services than it is to sell the relatively sophisticated and mysterious services known as "consulting." And when those latter services are such that they mandate entrusting a stranger, no matter how well recommended, with confidential information and perhaps even with the welfare of a business enterprise, clients need a great deal of reassurance before they agree to undertake the risk.

In the face of this almost overwhelming need for gaining the client's complete confidence if you are to win the contract, it is not surprising that conventional advertising does not work well for consultants generally. And it explains why the proposal must be considerably more than a brochure and a quotation of price and terms. It must satisfy a number of requirements, *at the minimum*, including the following:

☐ A persuasive demonstration that you fully understand and appreciate the client's need.

☐ A believable promise of help that is appropriate to the client's perception of need.

☐ Evidence that you can and will deliver that promised help. Evidence that you are a dependable and trustworthy consultant.

CHAPTER 5

GATHERING MARKET INTELLIGENCE

The effectiveness with which the consultant gathers information and the quality of the information so gathered often make the difference between winning and losing the proposal competition.

THE BASIC SOURCES OF INFORMATION

Very much as in the case of making a decision, the quality of your proposal is heavily dependent on the quality of the information upon which it is based. That is a truth about proposals generally, but it is especially true as it applies to approaches and strategies. It's hard to imagine how anyone can devise effective approaches and strategies without basing them on an adequate store of accurate information, properly organized and properly utilized.

Of course, much of your proposal content stems entirely from your own judgment, but there must be other sources also. And this applies equally to formal and informal proposals submitted in response to specific requests from clients and to unsolicited proposals you submit as a followup to earlier marketing approaches.

Gathering suitable intelligence necessary to the development of a successful proposal is often not at all easy. More often than not it requires both a great deal of effort and a great deal of imagination and ingenuity. But that effort and resourcefulness are what make the difference in most cases.

There are many potential sources of information—market intelligence—to support your proposal-writing effort. Following are some of the typical sources:

- [ ] The client's request for proposals.
- [ ] Conversations with the client.
- [ ] Other client materials, such as brochures and reports.
- [ ] Other readily available public information about the client.
- [ ] Your own experience, knowledge, and judgment.
- [ ] Your proposal library and files.
- [ ] Study/analysis of the requirement and related research.
- [ ] Special methods and sources.

Although at least some of these items are self-explanatory or have been covered in earlier discussions, others merit some special consideration and discussion here.

The Client's Request for Proposals

How to Read a Proposal Request

Surprisingly often the answers to questions that arise in a consultant's mind and the information the consultant seeks in developing a proposal, are readily at hand, although quite often they are overlooked. Ironically, that may be simply because they are so nearby. The sardonic observation that enjoins us, "When all else fails, read the instructions," has true application here; we often neglect to take advantage of the prime and most important source.

It is easy to understand why this is so. The client's statement of the requirement and other portions of a formal RFP (request for proposals) are often neither well organized nor fluently expressed, and that can easily lead the consultant astray. Impatient to get on with important work, the consultant is unwilling to indulge in what appears to be a waste of time because the quality of the writing suggests that there is little of value to be gained from study of the request.

That is not the only problem. The consultant must guard against an unconscious tendency to leap to conclusions in reading the request and reading what is not there. (It's quite easy to see what you expect to see, rather than what is actually written there, and in reading proposal requests this tendency must be specifically guarded against.) This often leads to offering the client a ready-made solution that may be a reasonable approach but not the best one.

Acres of Diamonds

Despite the apparent uselessness of much of the written material that forms the request for proposals, the contrary often proves to be true. Again and again I have found the information I needed in the request, after all, after lengthy investigation into other sources. Quite often the search through the formal request is a painstaking one and not at all easy, but it is almost always more efficient than most other ways you can pursue and uncover the information. Moreover, it is almost always more reliable information than any you can gather in any other manner. The time spent in studying the client's representation of requirements and what is wanted in the proposal is usually a worthwhile investment. One of the reasons many consultants miss so much information of importance in reading the client's request is that they, the consultants, often content themselves with a single reading of the request and an occasional brief review. That is rarely sufficient, for several reasons. For one, the first reading of a request normally produces only a superficial understanding of the client's needs and desires. One of the benefits of preparing the checklists recommended in Chapter 6 (to follow) is the enforcement of a discipline in the reading, compelling you to read with great care, as you deliberately and consciously search out specific items for your lists. (Even if the preparation of the lists did nothing more than that the time would be well spent.) However, additional readings, as you study the problem and begin to conceptualize an approach and design, have greater significance than the earlier readings because you now have specific questions and are in quest of specific information. Ergo, it is quite important to continue to reread the client's request continually, while you are developing the proposal, regarding it as the prime source of information.

Serendipity

Finding answers to specific questions or finding specific information you believe you need is one reason for that careful and continual study of the request. But another is that without it you might simply miss some important piece of information, perhaps even something that will spell the difference between success and the lack of success in winning. Sometimes information that seemed trivial on the first reading assumes great importance after you have worked on the proposal for a while and developed a much more in-depth appreciation of what you need to know to write the winning proposal. You must therefore satisfy yourself that you have indeed extracted everything of worth to be extracted from the request.

Reading Between the Lines

Another common mistake some consultants make in reading a client's request is to assume that anything not stated plainly is simply not present in the request. That is, they fail to even make the effort to read between the lines, much less do so effectively. Often the most valuable information lies there, between the lines, information that is implicit and not explicit.

Perhaps you have to be something of a detective to do this reading between the lines well, but it may be the key to winning. If you do not naturally tend to think deductively, train yourself to do so. You will be rewarded with a great increase in what you can infer from your reading.

There are several reasons for information being or appearing to be implied, rather than stated plainly. Quite often it is nothing more nor less than simple weakness in writing or a peculiarity in the writer's style. Some clients will simply be unable to express themselves as clearly as we would prefer them to or will have a difficult writing style, a not unusual circumstance. In other cases, the subtlety is deliberate, for one reason or another. There may be "political" considerations in the client's organization that prevents the client from writing as plainly as he or she would wish, and compels the client to do little more than hint at certain facts. And sometimes there is a specific effort to hold back certain information, for such reasons, but the information gap is often quite apparent, and the resourceful consultant will at least know that such a gap exists, and may even be able to gauge what it is that is being withheld.

There may be a personal bias in the client's view of a situation, also a not unusual condition. Or there may be other reasons. But whatever the reasons, it is important for you to gain as clear and objective a view as possible, if you are to benefit from everything that is or should be available to you.

Conversations with the Client

Information received verbally from the client is second in usefulness and value only to that contained in a formal written request for proposals, and in some cases may even exceed that latter source in its importance. In fact, in the case of submitting an unsolicited proposal on your own initiative, there will be no formal written request, and perhaps not even a verbal one, from the client. It is especially important to have made notes of your conversations, preferably during the conversations, if possible, certainly immediately afterward, while your recall is fresh. If possible, it is advisable to tape-record the conversation, but be sure that the client does not object to this by asking specifically for permission to do so.

In the case of responding to formal requests, especially with any government organization, it is usually a mistake to ask questions that you do not truly need the answers to (and you can almost always find a way to write your proposal without asking those questions). In the case of an unsolicited proposal or one that you are asked informally to submit and are the only consultant invited to propose, the situation is quite different. It is usually "safe" to ask questions in these situations, as long as you are sure that it does not annoy the client nor lend any impression of uncertainty or lack of know-how on your own part. One word of caution: Be sure to first explore all other readily accessible avenues of information, but especially that of available client materials. It is embarrassing and quite often harmful to your image to have the client point out that he or she has already supplied the information you seek.

Other Client Materials

Quite often, regardless of other circumstances surrounding the proposal situation, you have or can gain access to many kinds of client materials, such as annual reports, brochures, newsletters, article reprints, and other such items, many of them freely available to everyone. Whatever other sources you have, you ought to utilize these also, and should keep such materials in your proposal library and resource files. All such materials should be studied to learn as much as you can about the client before deciding on your proposal strategy and approach.

Other Readily Available Public Information About the Client

There are often other sources of information about the client, especially if the client is a well-established organization. There are, for example, D&B (Dun & Bradstreet) reports, listings and descriptions in various kinds of directories (e.g., the Thomas Register and Standard & Poor, two of several such directories), and various other public sources of information, much of it available in any well-stocked public library. These sources can tell you a great deal about the client, and provide valuable input and idea starters for your proposal effort. And if your clients or potential clients are business firms, make it your business to read the appropriate business periodicals, including the daily newspaper financial sections and perhaps the two most important financial newspapers, the *Wall Street Journal* and the *New York Times*.

Your Own Experience, Knowledge, and Judgment

Of course a great deal of the content of your proposal comes from the depths of your own knowledge and judgment, developed over the years of your formal education, supplementary studies, and career experience. And that applies to both your general knowledge of your field and to the special research, analyses, and studies, which will be normally be central to the beginning phase of your proposal development.

Your Own Proposal Library and Files

One of the basic marketing resources you should have been building up from the first day you entered practice is your own proposal library and files. If you work at maintaining this resource, it expands and improves steadily, and your success rate with your proposals should likewise continue to expand and improve.

There are several basic elements to a proposal library:

Copies of Your Own Proposals. Those proposals you have written in the past that were successful in winning contracts are valuable as models, since they are, presumably, models of and for success. However, that does not mean that the remaining proposals you wrote have no value. There is much in them that has potential value, items that are salvageable for other use, and they should never be discarded, but should be filed away as permanent items in your proposal library.

For one thing, many of those contain valuable analyses and studies that will save you a great deal of time and money, and often even make it possible to write a new proposal that would not be viable if you had to write it all from scratch. But they also often contain many illustrations, tables, discussions, and arguments that you can use again and again, sometimes with minor modifications, but often without even these.

Competitor's Proposals.   Opportunities arise to get copies of competitors' proposals. Take advantage of all such opportunities and study those competitive proposals. And if you are conscious of a need to get copies of competitors' proposals, opportunities to do so will arise. (Perhaps you will unconsciously work at creating such opportunities.) Then add them to your library in that special section reserved for competitors' materials.

Reference Books.   If you maintain an adequate library, you can carry out a great deal of your research, even special research, without stirring from your desk. *Everything* goes into your library against its potential usefulness to support a proposal effort.

Client Information.   Here is where you deposit those clippings you make from stories you read in periodicals about your clients and potential clients, as well as brochures, annual reports, and all other information relevant to clients and prospective clients.

Miscellaneous papers, drawings, price lists, catalogs, reports, and other such items all belong in your proposal reference files, as part of your proposal library. Give serendipity a maximum chance to happen and favor you.

Study/Analysis of the Requirement and Special Research

Naturally you will be making routine studies and analyses of the client's requirement. On some occasions special studies and research are required to carry out a proper analysis of the requirement. It may not be viable to do this yourself, if the effort required is so extensive as to require an excessive investment in the proposal. As an alternative to dropping the proposal entirely, in such cases, you may wish to consider some kind of an arrangement with another consultant, one whose field enables him or her to handle the special study as a routine analysis. You can, for example, be co-proposers and partners in any resulting contract, the other consultant may be a subcontractor to you, or you may be able to find some other mutually agreeable business arrangement.

Special Methods and Sources

There are many special situations where special and sometimes even unorthodox methods of intelligence-gathering are necessary, if you are to maximize your probabilities of winning. These are problems which call often for imagination and resourcefulness, and the contracts tend to go to those who find ways to gather the information they need.

Advertising for Information

In one case, the project called for operating a client-owned installation that employed a number of people. The grapevine reported that the client was unhappy with the incumbent contracting firm and would like to make a change, if they could find someone who appeared suitable to take over the project.

The request for proposal, while not exactly cryptic, was not as enlightening as it could be. It did not specify, for example, just how many people were employed by the incumbent contractor, and did not furnish much information about their professional specialties, the total payroll the contractor would have to handle, or any of a number of other details one would usually want to have to support proposal development.

The successful proposer ran a number of carefully worded help-wanted advertisements, designed specifically to draw responses from those currently employed in the project, and specifying that respondents must submit up-to-date resumes.

Resumes resulted in abundance, with a satisfying number coming from those working on the project in question. The resumes received were in themselves a mother lode of priceless information, but the proposer also invited some of the respondents—those who appeared to be key people and therefore knowledgeable of important details— to visit and be interviewed. These interviews produced even more useful information. In fact, the proposer reported that she had never had better information and she had had little difficulty developing a powerful proposal that won the contract.

In a somewhat analogous, but yet different, case, a consultant found herself invited to propose an on-premises project several states away. The project required the hiring of several local people to do certain specialized work on the client's premises. Uncertain as to local

rates for the kinds of specialists required in the client's area, the consultant placed advertisements in a local newspaper and arranged to
travel there to conduct interviews. As a result of those interviews she
acquainted herself with the local supply of qualified labor for the project, learned what rates she would have to pay, made tentative arrangements to hire several people, and got permission to incorporate their
resumes in her successful proposal.

This is not uncommon. Many small consulting firms, and even
some not-so-small firms, use this method for gathering resumes of
qualified individuals to be included in their proposals (with the individuals' consent, of course). In the course of doing this the truly alert
proposal writer manages to gather a great deal of useful information,
even if that is not the the specific reason for requesting the resumes.

Clipping Services

If you do not wish to take the time to do all the reading and clipping
you ought to do to build files on clients and prospective clients, you
can buy the service from any of several firms that operate clipping
services. For a per-clipping fee, such agencies scan newspapers and
magazines for you and clip out items you specify as those you want.
(PR firms, for example, order items about their own clients, to both
check on their own effectiveness and to provide their clients proof of
results.)

Computer Online Database Services

One way to get a great deal of research done without leaving your
desk is to order information from any of a growing number of online
public databases. This can be done with almost any personal computer
equipped with a modem, a device that permits your computer to "talk"
to another via telephone, so that you can request and receive information in this manner. In one case, to illustrate, I was able, for only
about $100, to carry out in less than an hour a research effort that
would have cost me several days otherwise, and would even then have
produced less precise and less reliable data as a result. With the right
equipment (which is quite simple) and only a little practice this becomes as convenient and easy to do as making an ordinary telephone
call.

There are many online databases available to anyone equipped to reach them via modem-equipped computer and dial-up telephone connections. There are several popular and well-known online services aimed at serving the general public, such as The Source and Compuserve. But aside from these, there are many specialized ones, designed primarily to serve the needs of specific interests, such as lawyers, engineers, retailers, government contractors, bankers, investment brokers, and the medical profession, as well as business and the professions generally. The fees charged for subscriptions and access to most of these are relatively modest, as my own case, cited in the preceding paragraph, illustrates.

There are many ways in which your personal computer can support and aid the gathering of intelligence for your proposal-writing project, adding to and aiding the implementation of many of the ideas expressed earlier in this chapter. Here are just a few suggestions for using your personal computer in this effort.

Gathering Information Generally.   Proposal writing is almost always done under the duress of difficult and often virtually impossibly tight schedules. This means that there is often not enough time to wait for such services as D&B (Dun & Bradstreet) reports to arrive via the mails. However, it is often possible to get information of this type immediately, via access to some of the online databases. Dun & Bradstreet, for example, operates its own online database service. But there are many others, and the number has been growing. Following are just a few of the kinds of databases made available by the services referred to, along with the names of some of the services. (These were selected from a list of GTE Telenet users, which alone includes some 300 different databases offered by well over 100 information services and yet is by no means a complete or exhaustive listing of all such resources.)

APTIC—air pollution control	Dialog Information Services
AVLINE—av programs on health sciences	National Library of Medicine
BOOKS INFO—Data on books in print	Brodart Co.
CITIDATA—financial indicators	Citishare Corporation

DRUG INFORMATION—data on 1,100 drugs	GTE Telenet
GRANTS—federal, state, local grants	SDC Search Information Services
HAZARDLINE—2,000 hazardous substances	Occupational Health Services
MANAGEMENT—business/ management literature	SDC Search Information Services
MERLIN—technical database on securities	Remote Computing
MNT—literature on mining technology	TEXT Information Services
MORT—mortgage amortization program	QL Systems Limited
PATSEARCH—patent information	Pergamon InfoLine

Online Programming Services.   One other service offered by a number of online systems is that of assistance in running computer programs, especially in those cases where the consultant's personal computer is not suitable for the task, for personal computers are relatively small and limited in their capabilities, compared with the mainframe and minicomputers, which are considerably larger. Using the usual computer-to-computer link, the service can run a program for and download the results to the consultant's personal computer. Too, such services can often make special programs available to the consultant to handle such functions as the following few examples:

Computer conferencing	Electronic mail
Financial analysis	Job costing
Inventory control	Pension management
Econometric modeling	Communications network design
Energy auditing	Simulation and modeling
Flowcharting	Market research
Mapping	Media research

"Machinable" Library Files

Your proposal library does not necessarily consist solely of ink and paper. Quite the contrary, in many ways it is more useful to have as much of your library as possible in machinable form. That means in some form which your computer can scan, usually magnetic recordings on tape or disks. The advantages of putting as much of your library as possible in machinable form are several:

The files are more readily accessible—much more easily found because the computer itself helps find the right files quickly.

The information in individual files can be found more quickly because, again, the computer can help with this through its search functions.

Its easy to copy and/or print out files or portions of files for use in your research studies.

It is not suggested that you "computerize" (convert to machinable form) those library materials which you acquire as ink-and-paper materials. The labor involved in doing so is usually too great to be a practical option. However, much of the information you accumulate for your library, such as your own prior proposals and data files acquired earlier in prior information searches via computer and online databases, should be saved and filed in their original magnetic form, rather than in hard copy (printout) versions. And that points out another advantage machinable files offer: Paper files become so voluminous that finding or making space for them often becomes a problem in itself and compels you to consider whether it is worthwhile to keep them at all, much less whether to devote valuable live-storage space to them. (And, of course, the minute you place old files in dead storage you have need for them and must go in search of them.)

That is not a problem with computer storage media, for a desk drawer and even a desktop can hold many thousands of pages worth of information when it is in magnetic form. (The equivalent of approximately 8,000 pages of typed material resides within arm's reach on my own desk, as floppy diskettes stored in two convenient disk "trees," with several times that amount of recorded data within a step or two of my desk.) That alone makes it possible for most of us to maintain a much larger resource library than we would be able to do without the aid of the computer.

Collaborative Efforts

When you undertake a joint effort with another specialist to help you write your proposal, as suggested in an earlier paragraph, the problems of proximity and schedule coordination sometimes arise. Working together on a proposal requires frequent discussions and exchanges in a close coordination. It is rarely that each of you can work independently on portions of the proposal, in relative isolation from each other, and find that it all fits together properly in the end.

The personal computer can solve problems of schedule conflicts and long distances between you and your collaborator if you have compatible systems. Fortunately, the influence of IBM in the marketplace and a growing number of software programs designed for the purpose are making personal computers more and more compatible with each other, at least for simple communication and exchanges of data, so that you can work closely together without either of you leaving your office. Through intercomputer linkage you can exchange copy, comments, ideas, and virtually anything else you might otherwise do in a face-to-face meeting.

GETTING INFORMATION FOR DEVELOPMENT OF GOVERNMENT PROPOSALS

The government issues a great many contracts for consulting services, although most of the contracts are not characterized as consulting for a variety of reasons. The problems of writing proposals to government agencies are similar to, and yet in some respects somewhat different from, those of writing proposals in the commercial markets.

This applies to the gathering of intelligence, as it does to all other aspects of proposal development. There is, of course, a great deal of information readily available about government agencies and their programs, and you can gather up a large library of materials, much of it free of cost. But there is also one significant difference between intelligence-gathering for the development of proposals to government agencies and that for developing commercial proposals. That is the law which makes it mandatory for government agencies to release, on demand or of their own volition and initiative, all information that is not classified—covered by the needs of national security—and/or does not infringe on individual privacy or the right to hold certain information proprietary and confidential. That law is, of course, the Freedom of Information Act.

Under that act you have the right to demand certain information. The following are typical items of information you can and should normally request:

- ☐ What the government is now paying for a given service (in the case of a competitive procurement to continue a service now being provided).
- ☐ The name of the incumbent contractor.
- ☐ A copy of the successful proposal. (Confidential and proprietary data will be excised from the copy you get.)
- ☐ Copies of reports and/or other documents generated earlier in the performance of the contract or related contracts.
- ☐ Records of work required and performed under the existing or earlier contracts.

In connection with these items, you can often get these even without invoking the Freedom of Information Act by visiting the agency's library and reading some of the reports and other documents on the shelves. And in some cases a visit to a Government Printing Office bookstore will produce a great deal of useful information available in publications of the Government Printing Office.

To some degree, owing to this, it is often easier to gather information necessary to writing proposals to government agencies.

CHAPTER 6

MAKING A BEGINNING

Success in marketing is rarely a chance occurrence. It comes to those who think ahead, plan ahead, and act accordingly.

THE RIGHT TIME TO MARKET

There is no doubt in my mind, based on my own observations, that the single most common cause of failure in consulting enterprises is the failure to market effectively. And one reason for this is a failure by many new to consulting to understand that consulting is not a "one call" business.

What that means, in practical terms, is that for most consultants there is never a time when he or she can afford to neglect marketing. Typically, the newcomer to the field has begun practice with a single client and gives no thought to the day when he or she must find new clients. Instead, those new to the field tend to wait until they have no current assignment to begin the quest for clients. And since marketing consulting services normally produces clients and assignments only months, sometimes many months, after the marketing contacts, many newcomers to consulting find themselves unable to survive while waiting to land that second client.

The time for marketing is always, preferably starting immediately with the decision to launch an independent practice, and never ending. The independent consultant cannot afford to ever be too busy to maintain marketing activities. It's part of the price for being an independent consultant.

Proposal writing is a most important part of marketing, but a great deal of work must precede the proposal writing. And the successful marketer will review a great many opportunities to write proposals, more than he or she can or should respond to. But that raises the question of the need to make the inevitable bid/no-bid decision, itself a most important element of marketing.

BID/NO-BID DECISION MAKING

Every proposal represents a serious commitment by the consultant. In fact, it really represents two commitments: One is the pledge that what is proposed is a firm offer to the client. The other is the time and money spent in writing the proposal. And in many cases this latter is by far the greater commitment, for while many proposals are relatively minor efforts, the simple and informal ones known popularly as "letter" proposals, many others are major undertakings, requiring rather extensive expenditures of effort and money.

For this reason those large organizations who write a great many major proposals, who get all or most of their business in this manner, in fact, often have rather formal systems for analyzing each bid opportunity and reaching decision on whether or not to submit a bid in each case. And many of these firms have standard forms with which to document and report the results of each such analysis. Figure 4 typifies such designs and is the basis for the following discussion of bid/no-bid analytical procedures.

Analytical Procedure

The head data on the form are self-explanatory, serving merely to identify the bid opportunity and list its basic characteristics. The significance of some of the other entry blanks provided may not be as apparent, but should become so as the discussion progresses.

First of all, such an analysis is rarely cut and dried but is almost always linked to conditions of the moment. That is, the bid opportunity that is eagerly seized on one occasion might well be turned down on another occasion, depending on such variables as the current in-house workload, how urgently new work is needed, and spin-off benefits (e.g., getting a foot in the door with a new client or diversifying experience and market possibilities). Ergo, on one occasion you might make the investment in a proposal for which you rate your chances at only 25 percent, whereas in another case you would not undertake one in which you rated your prospects for winning at less than 75 percent.

It is largely for these reasons that a relatively large section is provided at the bottom of Figure 4 for remarks, immediately following the space provided to record your conclusions and recommendations. In that remarks section the evaluator, or evaluators (in larger organizations, there may be several people making independent evaluations and then meeting to discuss them), makes pertinent observations and recommendations. On some occasions an organization undertakes a project at cost or on a most narrow margin because they need the work to keep the organization going or they believe that there is some spin-off benefit that makes the risk a good one.

The uncertainties and the transient conditions that have such pro-

RFP HEAD DATA

Title: _____ Due: _____

Client: _____

Requirement summary: _____

Formal proposal [ ] Ltr. proposal [ ] With pricing [ ] Separate pricing [ ]

EVALUATIVE ESTIMATES

Est. value ($): _____ Est. bid/proposal effort (hrs): _____

Probable competition: _____

*Rank order (vis-a-vis other bid opportunities available now): No. _____

Our major strength: _____

Our major weakness: _____

RATIONALE

*Arguments pro: _____

*Arguments con: _____

CONCLUSION AND RECOMMENDATION

Est. win probability (%): _____ *Recommendation: Bid [ ] No bid [ ]

*REMARKS

*Consider all related factors.

Figure 4. Bid/no-bid analysis and reporting form.

found effects on decisions are realities over which you do not always have any control. However, you can pursue a few marketing measures that will help you to increase the odds in your favor and vastly improve your proposal "batting average" over what it might otherwise be:

1. Do everything possible to become the recipient of a maximum number of opportunities to prepare and submit bids and proposals. The more such opportunities you have, the more selective you can be in choosing only those which appear to offer you the greatest possibilities for success. However, do not confine these efforts to getting yourself on as many bidders lists as possible, but also take advantage of every opportunity to submit unsolicited proposals where you believe you have a fair chance of winning a contract or where, at least, the cost in time and money is relatively insignificant.

2. Maintain constant intelligence-gathering awareness so as to maximize your knowledge of competitor activities and other relevant facts. Gather as many of your competitors' brochures as possible, and be alert also to opportunities to acquire copies of their proposals. (Such opportunities do arise, but you must be alert for them.) Remember that the quality of the proposal is linked directly to and is dependent on the quality of the information upon which the proposal is based.

3. Build the most extensive proposal library you can manage. It should include as much competitor literature as you can acquire, copies of your own past proposals, useful "boilerplate" materials and "swipe files," reference books, rosters and resumes of specialists you might have need of for some projects, and whatever else might be helpful to your proposal efforts. And if you are using a computer and word processor, you should have a disk library, with as much material in disk files as possible.

4. Try to evaluate the possibilities of follow-on work with current clients so that you can consider this too in assessing your probable need for new contracts and project assignments. You often get surprising benefits by being simply honest and direct. Try telling your clients frankly that you are planning your schedules for the near future and need help in anticipating your probable workload.

PREPARATIONS FOR PROPOSAL WRITING

One of the most common mistakes in proposal writing is that of beginning to write too soon, writing before doing the necessary advance planning and preparation. The consequence of that haste is often a rough draft proposal that requires more work to revise than it is possible to do in the time allowed for proposal submittal, compelling you to submit a proposal that is not your best possible presentation. And in some cases the cost of the revision is far too great with respect to the size of the contract.

The only way to minimize rewriting and revision is to plan ahead before you begin to write so that you know your precise objectives in advance and you have planned the route to reach them.

Planning Essentials

The main elements of planning a proposal are simply these:

1. The major objective.
2. The approach.
3. The grand strategy.
4. The itinerary (outline).

Of course, all of these are closely related to each other, and rarely does anyone have these fully detailed in advance when writing a proposal because the time element and the cost of writing proposals bars that excessive degree of advance planning. However, if the proposal writing is to be accomplished with any degree of efficiency and economy, some planning along these lines ought to be done before investing any large amount of time in serious writing efforts.

Obviously, the data required to establish these elements must come from somewhere before the serious proposal writing begins.

The First Input

If you have carried out a bid/no-bid analysis and recorded your estimates, you already have some data that ought to be the first inputs for your proposal planning. Most of the items you will have recorded are of direct interest in writing a proposal, and you should be conscious of this probability as you develop the estimates and judgments that you record in that initial analysis. Following are some notes on each of those items that are not completely self-explanatory:

RFP Head Data.   Aside from identifying the request for proposals, the client from whom the request comes, and the due date for the proposal, there are some items here of direct interest in reaching a final decision. One is the kind of requirement, of course, and an accurate summary of the requirement is an important item here. Another important item is the type of proposal required, especially as compared with the estimated size (dollar value) of the contract and the estimate of cost in labor hours required to write the proposal, and recorded in the next item. (You might, for example, decide to write an informal or letter proposal, even when you do not rate your chances for success very highly, because the proposal is easy and inexpensive to write.)

Estimated Value.   This is a measure of the size and importance of the proposal and should thus be something of an indicator to the amount of effort and size of proposal justified and necessary. This is a rough indicator, of course, because it is only one of several ballpark estimates you will have made in analyzing the RFP but it is nevertheless a guideline for you.

Probable Competition.   This is quite important. Your ability to judge this depends on several factors. One is your familiarity with your special field. If you have been in your practice or have been working in the field for someone else for some time, you probably have a very good idea of who all the general competitors in your field are. That gives you some beginning idea of probable competitors for any given contract. And if you have a great many acquaintances in your field, you may very well be in touch with a kind of grapevine that exists in all fields and is often a source of information. There is also the possibility that a pre-proposal conference was held by the client, and in attending that you had the opportunity to observe and note the other attendees. And sometimes the client will tell you frankly, if you ask, who the others were who were invited to propose.

Whatever the case, the information is usually useful and may affect your strategy decisions. Certainly it will affect your decisions as to what competitor strategy to use.

Rank Order. This calls for you to consider the other bid opportunities that are available to you and make your best estimate of how you would rank this one in comparison with the others. This automatically also enters into the estimate the factor of the total number of bid opportunities available at the time. If this were your lowest-rated choice, for example, it would be number 35 in a field of 35 opportunities, but number 1 if there were no others available at the moment.

Major Strengths. This is a critically important item, and may even be the basis for your grand strategy in some cases. Caution: This item refers only to your major strengths vis-a-vis this contract. It has nothing to do with any major strengths you may have that have no relevance to the requirement. For example, you may be a computer expert, but unless the project you are pursuing entails computer work as a major element, this is not a strength in this case.

In all cases it is important to take as objective a look as you can at this item. If you find it difficult to be objective about this estimate, get someone else to play devil's advocate for you to help you make an objective estimate.

Major Weaknesses. Everything said about the major-strengths item applies equally to this item. But in some respects this is an even more important item and requires careful consideration. You must be sure that any weaknesses you perceive will not be fatal ones, and you must have some reason for believing that you can offset or overcome any weaknesses, if you decide to develop a proposal.

Arguments Pro. Here you should summarize the logical arguments for going ahead with the proposal and trying to win the contract even if you have decided not to propose. That is, this is a polemic exercise, recording the logical arguments for proposing, without regard to the arguments against proposing or to your decision to propose or not to propose.

Arguments Con. This is the other side of the coin, and should be recorded in the same philosophy as arguments pro.

Estimated Win Probability. This, like the arguments pro and con, should be as objective an estimate as possible. It has nothing to do with your final decision or recommendation regarding the development and submittal of a proposal. On the other hand, your estimate of win probability may or may not affect your final decision or recommendation.

Recommendation. Here you simply summarize what you believe to be the logical conclusion of all the data you have analyzed and recorded and make your recommendation to bid (propose) or not to bid (propose.)

Remarks. This area is used to supplement or explain any of the previous items or to add comments that are germane but not covered by any preceding item. Obviously, this may be supplemented by additional sheets, when necessary. The footnote is a reminder to do this, also, suggesting that while some of the items can be estimated without regard to other factors, many cannot be estimated on an absolute scale, but are necessarily estimated only after taking into account other items and/or to specific conditions which are peculiar to the specific situation. Obviously, the final recommendation is the total of many factors considered together, for example.

There is a rough logic in the order in which the items are listed, but this is not absolute and is not necessarily the precise order in which you might enter your estimates and appraisals. Too, there is nothing sacred about your initial estimates, and you may find it a wise procedure to make rough preliminary guesses first, making up an initial, rough-draft form. There is absolutely no reason for not revising that form several times, until you are satisfied that you have reached as accurate a set of estimates as possible. In fact, the probability is that you are far more likely to make a realistic and dependable appraisal by doing this than by trying to create a do-or-die first effort. (This is an excellent application for your personal computer, since the revisions and updates are virtually painless when done on-screen and on-disk.)

This discussion has been predicated on the assumption of a more or less formal request for proposals having been made by a client, whether at the client's own initiative or as a result of your suggestion to a prospective client to write out a description of the requirement. However, as you will see, it is not only when you have received a written request for a proposal that you are faced with the task of writing one. (Actually, it should be regarded as a marketing opportunity, not as a task, when you have a prospective client willing to accept and consider a proposal from you.) If you are a perceptive and aggressive marketer of your services, you will always be alert for opportunities to offer a proposal to a client or prospective client. Therefore, your input information may be only verbal information gathered informally in conversation with the client. That does not make the bid/no-bid analysis any less a valid and sensible procedure to follow, although the information may have to come from your verbal exchanges with the client and perhaps from other sources, such as the client's brochures and annual reports, from your own library and files, and/or from calls to other people who can supply useful information.

In such case, that form of Figure 4 is a useful one to guide you in gathering information upon which to base a proposal. However, there is one question that does not appear on the form suggested, and which may be quite pertinent in the circumstances described here: In the case of your volunteering a proposal to client with whom you have had informal conversation the missing item is this: "Probability of award," which refers to the question of whether there will be an award to anyone. That is, has the prospective client merely humored you in agreeing to consider your proposal, or is it likely that the client is serious and will, indeed, make an award to someone?

(On the other hand, this probability of award is usually a consideration only when the proposal is a fairly costly effort because it is possible in some circumstances to submit an informal or letter proposal at hardly more cost than that of sending the prospective client a printed brochure, so the question of how serious the client is about making an award is of no real importance in this latter case.)

The Second Input

With the basic data of the bid/no-bid analysis at hand and a decision to proceed with the proposal, specific data gathering and organization are logical next steps. And the place to gather these are from the client's request and specification of work to be done, where there are such documents, and from whatever other sources you can find, in other circumstances.

Some requests and their work statements are quite well organized and in logical order. Unfortunately, many others are not. Quite the contrary, many are vague, rambling, sometimes almost incoherent. The same consideration applies to gathering information from other sources, when it is necessary to do so. Sometimes you can get a wealth of reliable and helpful information from other sources, whereas at other times the information is scanty and of doubtful accuracy or usefulness. Nevertheless, it is necessary to manage somehow to cope successfully under all these conditions and circumstances, and a method that has proved to be quite effective at doing so is the checklist, which you should be developing as you study the requirement.

Figure 5 suggests one format for such a checklist. Actually, there are two or three lists: a list of items specified as requirements in the proposal itself, a list of items that must appear as elements of the project or program called for, and, in some cases, a list of evaluative criteria specified by the client. (This latter is a requirement of federal agencies requesting proposals, and may be found in proposal requests from other clients as well.) The same format may be used for all three lists, merely changing the heading in each case. Or you may prefer the design of Figure 6, which lists all the items on the same page, in parallel columns, with notes at the bottom or on a separate sheet. The advantage of this arrangement is that having the items side-by-side helps you to perceive correlations among the various items, and that can be a useful contribution. However, the format is not the important matter; the completeness of the listings is.

PROPOSAL REQUIREMENTS CHECKLIST

Item	Page Par Nos.	Notes
State major project objectives	pp 2, 11, 33–37	Milestone chart?
Describe relevant experience	p 7, par 2.3, pp 8, 9	List specific contracts, clients
List, describe entire staff proposed	p 12	Needs 6 or more professionals; offer resumes of associates

Figure 5. One possible format for a proposal checklist.

REQUIREMENTS CHECKLIST

Proposal	Project	Evaluation
1) State major project objectives, pp 2, 11, 33–37	1a) Must be in place in 30 DAA	1b) Understanding: 10 pts
2) Describe relevant experience, p 7, par 2.3, pp 8, 9	2a) Must be validated at 90/90	2b) Resumes: 20 pts
3) List, describe entire staff proposed, p 12	3a) Final report & manual due 120 DAA	3b) Viability of design: 30 pts

NOTES:
1) Milestone chart? 2) specific contract clients 3) Needs 6 or more professionals; offer resumes of associates

Figure 6. An alternative checklist format.

WHY USE A CHECKLIST?

There are several reasons for making and using a checklist, such as that suggested here, for even the small or informal proposal. Here are a few such reasons, which, in fact, furnish the rationale:

1. For the vague or haphazard request, the checklist helps to bring order by revealing the focal points—what the client really requires—which are otherwise often buried in and obscured by the verbiage. In short, it helps you to identify and define the true need of the client, even when the client is not entirely clear on just what that need is.

2. The checklist often brings anomalies to the surface, especially when various items are compared and correlated, which otherwise often go undetected. These are important to you from more than one viewpoint: They are the basis for the creation of "worry items," thus strategies; it is necessary to identify and recognize these to design a sensible and efficient project; they are potent ammunition for the development of competitor strategies, as you point out problems that competitors often miss.

3. The lists are a valuable aid in identifying the most critical and most important points in both the project requirement and the proposal requirement, at least partly because they offer you an opportunity to see all items arrayed.

4. Every requirement entails a deliverable item of some sort, but precisely what that is is not always clear. In fact, it is sometimes in question whether the client knows exactly what is to be delivered. The checklist is a help in identifying this clearly and, for that matter, even in helping the client understand precisely what it should be.

5. The list has another use, to be described later when discussing front matter of formal proposals, in creating a "response matrix," a device that is instrumental in maximizing the technical rating given your proposal.

A GRAPHIC EQUIVALENT

The use of graphics in proposals is a highly desirable measure in general, for a variety of reasons, not the least of which are these:

1. It makes study and understanding of your proposal much easier for the client, and the desirability of making things as easy as possible for the buyer is a basic objective of all enlightened sales and marketing activity.
2. Used judiciously, graphic devices displace more than their "weight" of text, thus reducing the labor of writing and the sheer bulk of the product.
3. The "right" graphics can help you, the writer, gain a better understanding of the requirement and the best approach to satisfying it.

That last-named consideration is a useful next step in preparing to write the proposal (although in some circumstances, to be described, it is better employed to precede the development of the checklists). And the specific graphic device referred to here is something usually referred to as a "functional flowchart."

The concept underlying such a chart is that the work of the project is a flow process, a series of steps arranged in some logical sequence wherein each step, proceeding from left to right, is a necessary prerequisite to the next step, and each "next step" is a step closer to the goal or objective of the entire flow. There is thus a "why" logic in such charts as you examine the flow from start to finish, and a "how" logic as you study it in the opposite direction.

While not exactly an equivalent of the checklist, a well-conceived functional flowchart summarizes the project in the most efficient presentation possible—a single drawing or, in some cases, a set of several drawings—revealing all the significant steps of the project together with the logic of the design and delineation of the extremes, from the starting first step to the final step and the final deliverable items.

In fact, the functional flowchart of the project often comes to the client as something of a shock, showing the client a much deeper insight into the requirement than he or she had had before, and often

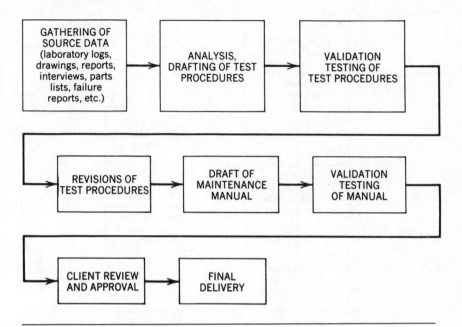

Figure 7. Simple functional flowchart of a proposed project.

revealing that the consultant has a better view than the client has. The development and presentation of a really good functional flowchart is thus usually an impressive performance, and the client is often somewhat awed by the consultant's demonstrated x-ray vision, which can pierce to the heart of the requirement.

Figure 7 is a simplified example of such a functional flowchart. (For many projects such charts extend six feet or more in length, and include more than one stream of flow.) This simple chart explains how the consultant proposes to develop a set of maintenance procedures and appropriate documentation. In the actual case, such a project requires many more steps than those shown here.

There are two ways to graph this. One is to develop a fully detailed single chart that reveals all the steps in a single flow representation. The other is to offer a set of several functional flowcharts, one "top level" chart showing only the main phases or functions, and the others each showing one of those main phases or functions in greater detail.

Figure 7 shows the flow as we normally read, from left to right, descending a step as we run out of space on the right. However, some

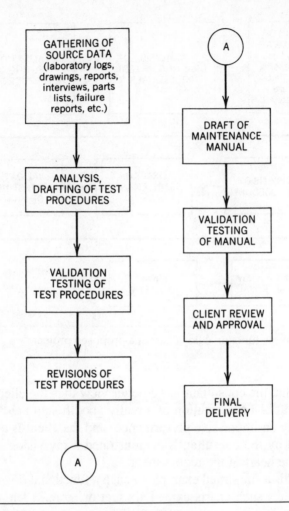

Figure 8. Alternative flowchart presentation.

individuals, especially those who work with computers, prefer to show the flow from top to bottom, as shown in the next figure, Figure 8. This has a some advantages, as well as disadvantages: It's easier to create, especially if you do not have a professional illustrator available and must create your own charts, and perhaps it is more efficient in its use of space. Too, since this format invokes fewer lines connecting the boxes with each other, it is somewhat "cleaner"—less cluttered

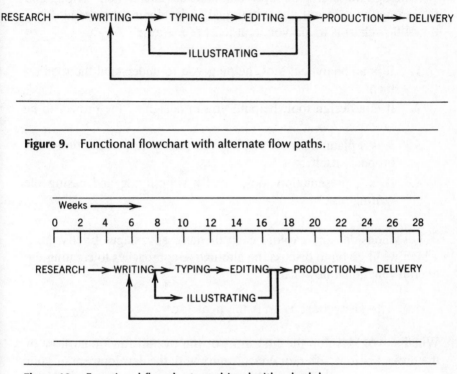

Figure 9. Functional flowchart with alternate flow paths.

Figure 10. Functional flowchart combined with schedule.

and perhaps less confusing—than is the left-to-right presentation. On the other hand, since we all learn to read from left to right, it takes a little more adjustment to learn to read charts using this alternate orientation.

The chart shown as Figures 7 and 8 is a functional flow in its simplest arrangement, as a purely linear and unambiguous process. In fact, few projects are that simple. Most processes entail iterations, options, and/or feedback loops, as in Figure 9, which is still relatively simple, but demonstrates that illustrating is a parallel or concurrent function, and editing creates a feedback loop for corrections and revisions.

As a further refinement that makes the proposal easier to write and easier to read and understand, it is usually possible to add a milestone or schedule chart to the functional flow, as in Figure 10.

Although these graphic representations are aids in both writing and in reading the proposal, the initial goal of developing the overall functional flowchart is to aid you in at least four ways:

1. It is an analytical tool, helping you to understand the requirement.
2. It is a design tool, helping you in designing the project to be proposed.
3. It is a planning tool, helping you plan your presentation—the proposal itself.
4. It is a presentation tool, greatly simplifying and easing the writing task.

Let's consider and explore each of these advantages briefly, after which we'll go on to discuss the alternative approaches to creating the overall functional flowchart.

The Flowchart as an Analytical Tool

Whether you develop the first draft of the overall functional flow of the project before, after, or concurrently with the development of your checklist, the fact of compelling yourself to depict the project process flow graphically enforces a discipline of thought—analytical thought—upon you. It is relatively easy to generalize in verbiage and even easier to deceive yourself about your understanding, but it is much more difficult to do so when you attempt to portray the process graphically, depicting the logical order in *how* and *why* sequences. (That will become much more apparent shortly, when we discuss the several options of approaches to development of the chart.) The result of that enforced study is to achieve a far deeper and clearer understanding of the requirement and what is necessary to satisfy it properly.

The Flowchart as a Design Tool

The analysis of any problem, when well done, leads inevitably to the synthesis of the solution: the design. The anomalies, the inconsistencies, and the non sequiturs which can be found so often in proposal requests and their work statements are not always readily apparent in verbal form, especially in lengthy and complex statements. This is because perceiving these kinds of problems in text requires that you picture mentally the processes, as you read, and attempt to visualize all the phases and functions in relation to each other. This is obviously a most difficult task for any but the simplest situations and requirements, so it is not surprising that so many such logical absurdities elude us in reading proposal requests.

Once committed to paper (or computer screen) as a functional flowchart, however, those things show up quickly, simply because the flowchart is inherently a logic-based presentation. Redundancies, dead-end flows, and "you can't get there from here" anomalies fairly leap from the graphic presentation, all but guiding your hand in making the changes necessary to a successful and efficient design.

The Flowchart as a Planning Tool

In a sense we have already discussed the flowchart as a planning tool in considering its utility in planning the project design. But it is also a tool for planning the proposal itself, for it is the representation of the proposed project, and virtually everything in your proposal that pertains directly to the project is geared to that flowchart. The flowchart should be the unifying theme, and everything your words say should be entirely consistent with what the chart says graphically. You should therefore plan and outline your proposal with an eye on that chart so that your proposal "proves" your design and *sells* it to the client as the most dependable, most efficient, lowest cost, or most whatever your chosen strategy dictates as sales arguments.

The Flowchart as a Presentation Tool

The benefits of using a well-designed flowchart as a presentation tool have been touched on already and are fairly obvious in any case. Properly designed, the flowchart (or any other graphic representation, for that matter) should require little explanatory text, or it fails in its basic purpose. On the other hand, it should also serve as a reference for much of the related text, also easing the burden of textual explanations. In fact, the really well-designed functional flowchart does far more than explain and support the basic design and schedule presentations. It also explains and supports arguments for the proposed design, for the features, the costs, and for many other factors that must be explained and sold to the client, if the proposal is to be the persuasive presentation it must be to be successful.

CREATING THE FUNCTIONAL FLOWCHART

The flowchart, like the text, must go through at least one rough draft stage before being finalized, but there are alternatives to the creation of the first rough draft, depending usually on the quality and abundance of the beginning information available to you. In some cases the client has furnished such detailed information and ideas about what is needed that a rough-draft flowchart can be constructed by the simple expedient of translating the words into their graphic equivalent. However, in a great many other cases this is not a practical option because the available information is imprecise and/or inadequate in other ways. In these cases the rough-draft flowchart must be constructed by other methods, methods which are considerably more difficult and more time-consuming, but probably even more necessary, if the ultimate proposal is to be at all effective.

First Steps

There are at least three alternatives available for creating a functional flowchart in the second case described. The easiest case is that in which the requirement is totally conventional and uncomplicated, involving well-established routine procedures and processes. For example, if the requirement is to develop a manual, conduct a survey, or write a computer program, the expert consultant who specializes in the appropriate field knows in advance what all the major steps and procedures must be. If you are faced with a requirement of this nature, you begin your flowchart by first depicting the typical functions and phases of the work and then seeking out any special conditions, problems, or requirements and modifying your draft chart accordingly.

In another case you may have little useful information beyond a definition of the required end-result—a manual, report, computer program, installed system, training program, or other end-product. In such case you usually find the most practical approach to be one that

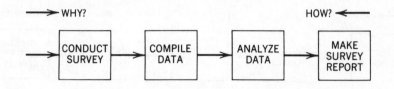

Figure 11. Beginning a functional flowchart: developing the chart from the end.

starts at the terminus of the chart with a symbol or box depicting that end product. You then must work backward, using the *how* question to determine what must be the preceding step, and the *why* question to check and verify your chart. Figure 11 illustrates this. The requirement is for a survey to support a marketing campaign. The product required is a report of survey, the details of which will be resolved later. But now a draft chart must be constructed.

The preceding steps are obvious ones, at least in general terms, although they will have to be detailed to fit the specific application and circumstances. But that will come later, in revising the chart. For now the need is to make a beginning, to create something as a beginning.

The steps leading to the development of the deliverable item are logical necessities. The survey report is created by analyzing the data, the data are analyzed by compiling them, the data are gathered and compiled by conducting the survey. And in the other direction, the survey is conducted to gather and compile the data, the data are compiled to be analyzed, etc.

Asking these questions helps you construct the chart, and the answers help you examine the chart to be sure that all necessary steps are in there.

Working From Both Ends

In most cases you know what must be at both ends of the chart because you must know what the required end-result is to be, and you usually have knowledge of what you will have to start with. In the case hypothesized in Figure 11 the assumption was only that of a requirement to conduct a survey. Obviously, a client requesting proposals to conduct a survey must have given at least some basic infor-

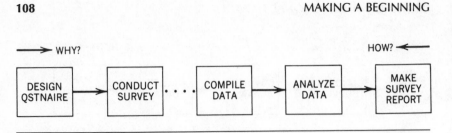

Figure 12.   Developing the flowchart from both ends.

mation about the requirement, such as where the survey is to be conducted, whether a survey instrument (e.g., questionnaire) is to be supplied or must be constructed by the consultant, and at least some other beginning information. Consequently, the actual case is likely to be more along the lines of Figure 12, where you can work from both ends to first define the requirement in at least broad functional terms, and then go on to refine the chart with all the details necessary to carry out a custom project. These charts are obviously so general that they can apply to virtually any or all such projects, and the typical consulting job is a custom project that is shaped and characterized by individual, often unique, needs and considerations.

Despite this, the situation may very well arise wherein you do not have definite information as to a desired end-product or even a specific starting point. This might well be the case, for example, where you have met a prospective client, discussed a problem the client is experiencing, and been invited to or volunteered to and gotten agreement from the client to submit a written proposal for solution of the problem. In such cases the client may simply say something to the effect, "I really don't know how to proceed, but I am willing to listen to any ideas you have."

This is a completely open-ended opportunity, and it is left almost entirely up to you to propose a project, based on your expert knowledge. You must decide where the project begins and where it ends, and you would presumably have asked the right questions to serve as guides in designing a project. This, however, does not change the basic situation: You still have the problem of making your prospective client understand what you offer, and selling it effectively through a persuasive proposal. And you should still develop a functional flowchart to explain your plan and point out its merits.

This is a double-edged sword. On the one hand you have carte blanche to propose, and it may well be that you have no direct competitors for the work. However, you are still in competition, for you are even then competing with other possible expenditures of available dollars, and possibly with other departments and their needs. You must still convince the client that the project is of great enough importance to earn a priority for funding. If you go overboard in what you propose you may thus price yourself out of the job, not necessarily losing it to a direct competitor, but causing the client to decide the postpone having the work done or foregoing it entirely.

(However, it is also possible, if the client believes your proposed project too extensive and costly that some of your direct competitors will then be invited to propose, despite the fact that the proposal opportunity resulted from your lead.)

If your work is such that you do essentially the same kind of work most of the time, albeit customized for each client individually, you may very well find it practicable to construct one or more standardized functional flowcharts which can be adapted to and customized for each individual project. Obviously there is a great advantage to you if you can do this.

WHICH COMES FIRST, CHECKLIST OR FLOWCHART?

There is an apparent anomaly here in that I have suggested both developing a checklist and developing a draft flowchart as a first step. The fact is that there is no flat rule possible for this because circumstances vary so much from one case to another, and circumstances often dictate what you must do first. If you have enough information to develop a substantial checklist of items, it is usually advisable to do that first, and then utilize that checklist as an information source and guide in drafting the functional flowchart. However, if you have in hand a request and work statement that lend themselves to direct translation into a functional flowchart, it may prove more fruitful to do that. In the actual case, I find it possible quite often to do both concurrently, developing them as I study the request, and correlating the two sets of results as they unfold. This latter course is probably the most effective, and I recommend that to you for all cases where you find it it a practical possibility. (The opportunity to correlate the two sets of results is especially helpful for finding potential problems as incipient worry items and devising stratagems therefrom.)

A COMMON DILEMMA

One question almost always arises at my seminars during discussions of making and presenting such analyses as these: How much information can the consultant afford to offer in proposals? That is, won't unscrupulous clients steal the ideas and information from the consultant who is too generous with such detailed information, and use them in ways that are contrary to the consultant's own interests, such as doing the job themselves? Or, once the consultant has revealed how to go about it, won't unscrupulous clients pass such information on to competitors whom they favor?

This is a legitimate concern; such unfortunate exploitations of consultants have happened, and this creates a serious dilemma: How much of your expert knowledge and analysis—that knowledge and skills that you normally sell—can you afford to reveal gratuitously without "giving the store away," while still offering that minimum necessary to persuade the client to opt for your proposal.

It is worth noting here, before going on, that a great many consultants worry about giving away information free of charge, and some who write and lecture on the subject of consulting even offer specific lectures on "how to avoid giving away free consulting." This concern is the result of some sense of insecurity, the notion that one's security lies in being secretive about one's special work. (Some writers and lecturers who purport to teach consulting even offer lectures on how to make clients dependent on the consultant for all time to come!) These attitudes bear the seeds of their own defeat within them. If you are going to be effective in marketing your services, you cannot avoid giving away a few samples of your knowledge and consulting skills. Those samples are the very best evidence of your abilities, and it is difficult to convince any prospective client that you are the consultant to retain simply on the basis of broad claims to excellence as a consultant. You simply must get down to present-case specifics, to be effective in selling yourself.

This is especially the case when it comes to submitting proposals. The typical client wants to compare you and what you propose with your competitors. But that comparative evaluation goes far beyond a comparison of the universities you attended, the organizations who employed you, and the positions you held in the past. It is focused largely on what you have to say about the client's expressed requirement and what you propose to do to satisfy that requirement. That is obviously the client's primary concern. If you avoid entirely a technical discussion and a projection of your approach to satisfying the requirement, and ask the client to settle for a personal bio and set of claims to excellence, you might as well forego writing the proposal entirely and save your time and money, for you will be simply wasting both. In short, you cannot completely avoid the risk of having your "brains picked" unfairly. It's an occupational hazard.

This is rarely a serious problem when dealing with clients in the public sector—government agencies—but it can be a real hazard in marketing to the private sector, even with the largest companies. (I confess to having been so victimized twice, in dealings with large corporations in both cases.) In all fairness, to such companies, however, it should be noted that when such things happen in dealings with large corporations, they are almost invariably the unscrupulous acts of individuals seeking personal advantages in their companies, and are not sanctioned by management. Management, in fact, would be outraged by such actions, and would probably make a serious internal investigation if charges of such depredations were made by any proposer.

There is no absolute safeguard against this danger, but following are several measures you can take to reduce the danger of such unethical appropriation and misuse of your proposal. They are written here with formal multipage proposals in mind, but are equally valid for application to informal, letter proposals, and can be easily adapted to use in those kinds of proposals:

Limit the Proprietary Information. Try to gauge that minimum amount of information necessary to demonstrate your competence and sell your approach/design to the client, and don't go beyond that minimum. At least, try to hold back the most specialized and most proprietary information.

Copyright Your Proposal. Place a copyright notice on your proposal, and make it a prominent notice. Here is how to establish a common-law copyright:

Near the bottom of an early page, usually the title page, type the words: "Copyright (date) by (your name)." The date used is usually the year or the month and year, although nothing prevents you from using a more specific date. You can use the abbreviation "Copr." or the symbol (C) instead of the full word "copyright," but the soundest practice is to spell out the word. One note: Many people follow this notice with other words, such as, "All rights reserved" and " Not to be duplicated without express permission." This adds no statutory protection but does advise readers what that copyright means and what your position is with regard to it.

You can register your copyright with the Copyright Office of the Library of Congress, but you are not required to do so to get common law copyright protection. (You do need to do so if you get into litigation with anyone over your copyright. However, you can register the copyright at that time, if such an eventuality ensues.)

Use a Notice of Proprietary Information. Since the Freedom of Information Act has given anyone a legal right to demand and get a copy of a proposal submitted by someone else, the federal government has urged proposers to advise readers of any proprietary information contained in their proposals so that such proprietary and confidential information will be excised from any copy of a proposal made available to requestors under the Act. It's a good idea to do this in the private sector too. Here is what to do:

On the title page of your proposal type a notice along the following general lines:

> The information contained in pages _____ and so noted is proprietary and is not to be revealed or utilized except for evaluation of this proposal and/or in performance of the services proposed herein. This, however, in no way inhibits the revelation and use of this information in behalf of the client in the event of award to this proposer.

Then you must indicate on each of those pages listed that material you claim as proprietary and so mark it "proprietary" and/or "proprietary and confidential."

Do not attempt to claim that the entire proposal is proprietary, as that would weaken and possibly invalidate totally any later claim of rights to recourse, in event your admonition was totally disregarded, since there is always some material in your proposal that is obviously neither proprietary nor confidential.

In this connection, however, it does not hurt to mark your entire proposal "confidential," and to make this marking a prominent one.

None of these are absolute guarantees against violation of what most of us believe to be an ethical code of behavior, but they do seriously lessen the danger in two ways: One, by advising those who might act innocently in revealing information they did not even suspect was confidential or proprietary; and two, they serve notice on and should give at least some pause to those who might act wrongfully with full knowledge, but in the hope that their action will go unnoticed or that they might be able to plead ignorance, if detected.

APPLICATIONS TO LETTER PROPOSALS

All of the foregoing pages of this chapter were written with formal proposals in mind. The informal proposal written as a letter of several pages is ordinarily written to propose a small project. Often it is written as a follow-up to an earlier contact, with no real assurance that the prospect will award a contract to anyone. These are necessary marketing activities and should be carried out as energetically and as often as possible, still recognizing that in such cases as these an elaborate study is not warranted, and should not be undertaken.

On the other hand, you should not go to the other extreme and simply "dash off" a quick letter carelessly, for disaster can result from such a hasty action. Rather, you must judge the real prospect of winning some business and estimate the possible benefits, both immediate, as reflected in the probable size of the contract, and long-term, as reflected in the probabilities of other, follow-on business and/or other benefits.

Therefore, do take advantage of all opportunities you encounter or can create to offer a prospect a proposal (for it is a marketing opportunity, and one you can often create by offering an unsolicited letter proposal to prospects). Do prepare these proposals according to the same principles and philosophy followed in developing formal proposals for major contracts. But do scale the effort to the size and nature of the proposal, and do not make the mistake of one nationally known electronics/defense-industries engineering company that all but bankrupted itself by continually spending more to create the proposal than the total size of the possible contract that might result.

CHAPTER 7

PROGRAM DESIGN

Program design is a must of proposal writing, and it calls for clear, independent, and original thinking if it (the design) is to be effective in creating a persuasive proposal.

EVERY PROPOSAL MUST BE DESIGN BASED

If it is to be properly focused and make its points, a proposal must be based on and built around some specific program design. Many proposals call for the original design of products of various kinds, some to be mass manufactured, others to be produced singly or in extremely limited quantity as custom products. In such case the design of the product, as well as the design of the proposed program to produce the end-item, must be considered in the discussions. But even when R&D—research and development—is itself the principal service required, acceptable preliminary design goals and approaches must uually be proposed. Success in the proposal competition depends heavily on the client's reaction to the proposed beginnings of design and their apparent appropriateness and probability of success.

Proposals Usually Describe Programs

Many proposals call for services that do not involve products per se or, at least, do not involve products directly. Nevertheless, there is still a need for clear designs or, at the minimum, clearly defined approaches to design of the service program. Even simple or apparently simple services, such as the provision of technical/professional temporary staff, generally must present a design for the carrying out of the obligation. There are such matters of concern to the client as assurance of an adequate supply of qualified individuals and the ability to replace any without delay, should replacement become necessary. And in some cases the consultant organization is required to manage the individuals assigned, although they are working on the client's premises. (In federal contracts, this is required by law.) It is also not unprecedented, where a large number of specialists are required, for the client to request details of the consultant's recruitment program for finding the specialists to be assigned to the project, whether they are themselves individual consultants or are to be new hires.

Program Designs Must Consider Possible Problems

It is essential that you think out all the possible problems, especially those which are likely to have been already perceived by the client, and provide for their solution in your design. Even when the client has not thought to ask for many of the specific details, the more pertinent details you include in your proposal, the more impressive and more foolproof your design appears to be. And that is in itself at least the beginnings of a design or program strategy.

What this means is that the design or at least the factors surrounding it—approaches, design philosophy, and design logic—must be clearly apparent to the client. Mysticism and generalizations are not convincing or persuasive, for they are not the evidence you need to sell your proposed program to the client; only the details can "prove" the merit of what you propose.

DESIGN VERSUS STRATEGY

Comparing program design and program strategy to determine which is cause and which effect is like the chicken and egg question: There is no firm answer. You may have developed a brilliant design concept and derived your strategy from that. But you may do it the other way, too, evolving a strategic concept first and basing your design on that. Actually, the two are probably inseparable and evolve together in an iterative creative process, each consideration guiding the development of the other. But the question of creativity does enter into it, for it is possible to create pedestrian designs based solely on one's technical or professional discipline, rather than on true creative inspiration. They are usually the classic designs taught in formal training courses and often to be found in various texts and reference works, from which they may be borrowed.

Such ready-made designs exist in abundance, which is not always a fortunate circumstance. Ready-made solutions tend to arouse little enthusiasm on the part of clients, most of whom have retained a consultant because they are convinced that they do need custom services, which call for original thinking and a good measure of creativity. (Is that not essentially a trait that characterizes consultants?) Such designs also bear little relationship to anything that might be fairly called a strategy.

THE OLD VERSUS THE NEW

In proposal competitions, this clinging to yesterday's solutions is likely to be effective, if at all, in only those cases where no proposer has offered anything more imaginative than the "tried and true" design bromides of yore. The client who was hoping to find something refreshingly new and different will generally sigh and select a proposal reluctantly. But there have been many cases where a client, disappointed by all the proposals, has simply rejected all and cancelled or postponed the procurement. One cannot depend even on being selected as the best of a bad lot.

This is not say that every proposal must be a display of creative genius or a bold departure. Quite the contrary, there are clients who prefer old, established approaches, regarding them as the low-risk, tried-and-true methods. Still, even they are attracted to fresh ideas, and it is possible to have it both ways—to be refreshingly original and yet not represent radical departures from convention.

CREATIVITY

In 1899, Charles H. Duell, Commissioner of the U.S. Patent Office under President McKinley, recommended closing down that office, saying that everything that could be invented had already been invented. Ludicrous although that may seem today, the thinking of many has not changed greatly: There are many who show that same peculiar mental stance. Evidently those who are lacking in creative imagination are unable to understand creativity at all, even as exhibited by so many others. But that is not the only startling aspect of the subject. It also shows an almost inexplicable tendency by many to cling stubbornly to old and long-established biases, despite mountains of contrary evidence. So many "know" so many things that are not so. There is a quite enormous reluctance to give up the familiar and secure beliefs of long practice, and this is a factor that must be considered also in developing proposals that prove persuasive.

Education Versus Creativity

Studies of creativity turn up many surprising facts. One is that virtually all of us are far more creative as children than we are as adults because our educational systems and societal standards tend strongly to stifle our creative instincts, and to actually wean us from them, as we grow up. In fact, it has been shown that in general terms creative imagination is inversely proportional to levels of formal education. Obviously we tend to rely primarily on what we were taught over all those years of inculcation in formal doctrines and beliefs. And we thus tend strongly to mistrust our instincts and independent judgments, and to resist new ideas, no matter their origin. Probably a great majority of us operate on an at least unconscious conviction that when we have completed our formal education we have all or nearly all the important learning we shall ever need. In fact, we are quite sure are we that most of the answers reside in those textbooks, reference books, professional papers, and other such formal documentation.

Ironically, most such documentation is heavy with bibliographic notations and citations of many sources, so that it begins to reach the absurdity of an endless circle of scholarly authors quoting and citing each others' work, each to prove the soundness of his or her own work. This, presumably, enables an author to escape culpability (in the event of challenges) by assigning it to those presumably authoritative sources so painfully reported in the endless footnotes and other bibliographic annotations. And this only supports the tendency to resist new ideas, which for this purpose can be characterized as any ideas for which one cannot find suitable bibliographic citations to defend its use!

Sadly, scholarliness is represented more often by knowledge of and research into other writings than by independent and original thinking.

Conventional Wisdom

All of this is conventional wisdom with a vengeance, relying unquestioningly on consensus, rather than on independent reasoning. It is certainly the antithesis of innovation and originality. New ideas cannot survive in such an atmosphere. New ideas spring from a seedbed of questioning and seeking better ways, from a basic philosophy that there is always a better way. We need merely to seek it energetically enough, with an open mind, and we shall find it, but comparatively few of us do so.

Conventional wisdom bears within it its own negation, for in this fast-changing world—and the *rate* at which changes take place is itself increasing steadily—those ideas and methods which become conventional wisdom are already obsolescent by the time they begin to assume that status. Thus anything that is recognized as conventional wisdom should be regarded with some skepticism.

Even the acknowledged thinkers of the world, our scientists, are susceptible to such human frailties. It was once a widely circulated idea that not more than six of the world's scientists understood the theories of Albert Einstein. That was something of a distortion. Most of the world's true scientists understood Einstein's equations, theories, and their subsequent implications well enough. What was probably true was that not more than a handful of the world's scientists *believed* Einstein's ideas and accepted the conclusions that had to be drawn therefrom. Those ideas were radical departures from the old scientific beliefs. To accept Einsteinian physics meant giving up many treasured notions, almost tantamount to starting over in some areas of scientific thought and speculation. For example, accepting the new physics of Einstein required the abandoning of a physical law that said that matter could neither be created nor destroyed. (The atomic bomb, for example, compelled changing that physical law to recognize that matter is a form of energy, and the two are interchangeable.)

VALUE MANAGEMENT: METHODOLOGY FOR CREATIVE THINKING

Value management is a discipline known also and perhaps more popularly by such other names as value analysis and value engineering. It sprang into existence in the engineering field as a pure result of serendipity, that mysterious art of finding things you didn't know you were looking for. (It is, in fact, a characteristic of creative minds to recognize the opportunities in sudden and chance discoveries.) The problem with that latter name (value engineering) is that it tends to mask the fact that the discipline is applicable to virtually all human activity, that value can be managed in fields other than engineering, despite its origin there.

The Origin of Value Management

During the Second World War, while utilizing substitute materials as a typical result of wartime shortages of strategic materials, a General Electric Company executive made the rather curious discovery that often the substitute material was better for the purpose than the original material for which it was a substitute, and often was less expensive in the bargain. He observed this to be a fact often enough so that he dismissed the idea of it being a freakish exception, and thought it a phenomenon worthy of serious investigation. That serious investigation, carried out by General Electric engineer Lawrence Miles after the war had ended, produced the original methodology, to which a number of enhancements and improvements have since been made.

The Essence of VM

In its barest essence, VM, as value management is often referred to for convenience, is an organized method for creative improvement. Unfortunately, it is too often used only on existing products and systems in which so much investment has been made that even beneficial improvements are often impractical to implement. For example, in many manufacturing processes the initial investment in tooling (and sometimes in parts and raw materials inventory, as well) is quite enormous. And in such cases a saving brought about by design changes is often impossible because the design changes would require retooling and the scrapping of many inventoried parts and materials. The write-off of some of these original costs, would often nullify any possible saving, unfortunately. To this extent, the benefits of value engineering have some built-in limitations, at least when practiced in this after-the-fact manner.

Obviously, the right time for value studies (by any name) is early in the design or predesign stages, long before front-end investments are committed. This makes the method nearly ideal for application in the proposal process, where penciled-in designs and design approaches are being made.

I will not attempt to make a detailed or in-depth presentation of VM here. It is neither necessary nor desirable to do so. The principles upon which the discipline is based, not the several detailed procedures and methods, are what is significant for our purposes here.

WHAT IS VALUE?

The most difficult and least precise idea with which we must come to grips in making value studies is that of value itself—of what it is. Dictionary definitions require several column-inches of fine print, and yet they do not come firmly to grips with the definition, and certainly do not produce an unambiguous definition.

Value is not an absolute nor a constant. It is an abstraction, in fact, a notion, an idea. It changes frequently, with changing circumstances. It is a noun that must be qualified by an adjective to have any substantial meaning at all. The value of the American dollar, for example, is quoted on financial exchanges, as are other countries' currencies, every day because it is changing constantly as a *market value*.

Art works have what might be called *artistic value*, and many other objects have an *esteem value*, as well as a market value. Those values may be poles apart. You may, for example, have such esteem for the house you wish to sell so that you place a far higher value on it than the market says it is worth. Or you may esteem and want something badly enough to knowingly pay "over the market" to get it.

A piece of jewelry may have an *intrinsic* value, which is the market value of the materials in it—e.g., gold, silver, and precious stones, for example—but it may also have an esteem value which is greater than its intrinsic value and equals its market value, as long as others esteem it equally.

So value is an elusive idea, and yet we do need to arrive at an agreement as to what we mean by the term if we are to agree on ways of managing value.

Fortunately, value management does not require that we agree on or even establish any absolute definition of value, intrinsic, market, esteem, or any other variety. In VM we can deal with value as a *relative* term only, without regard to its original idea, for the entire idea of VM is to increase or improve value, by whatever yardstick that value is measured. VM can be used to improve esteem value, intrinsic value, market value, or whatever other kind of value you wish to apply.

VM does this by making beneficial changes to one or more parameters of the item under study. The parameters of value are cost and utility. If we can make beneficial changes to either or both so that the result is greater utility at the same or lower cost or lower cost at the same or greater utility we have increased the value of the item.

Neither of those two terms, *cost* and *utility*, are as simple or absolute as they appear, however, as will become abundantly apparent in these discussions. There are many kinds of cost and utility, and an agreement on what these are is essential to an understanding of VM principles and methods. However, before we attempt to come to grips with these terms and ideas, we must have a look at another fundamental of VM: the idea of function.

THE IDEA OF FUNCTION

The heart of VM lies in the understanding and analysis of functions. It is on the basis of function analyses that VM studies begin, and on this basis that improvements in value are predicated. However, experience has demonstrated rather clearly that a great many people with non-technical backgrounds have some difficulty with the term and its significance. This may be due to the tendency of many technical professionals to speak in the jargon of their professions, rather than in everyday layperson's English. Whatever the cause, it seems necessary to discuss this term and its meaning.

Like the term *value*, *function* is multifaceted in meaning, and we shall have to examine these several facets. However, function is not as difficult to define as value is. It is fairly well defined by stating simply that function is what the item *does*. But that, what an item does, is itself at the heart of VM, at the heart of value itself, as we shall soon perceive.

The first question VM asks of an item to be studied is: What is it? And the answer to that question may be simply the proper or generic name of the item, in such manner that it describes the primary purpose of the item. The purpose of the question is to identify the item in terms that make its general purpose clear, in preparation for addressing the question of general function: What does it do?

How Many Functions or Kinds of Functions?

Only the simplest of items do only one thing—have only one function. Most items have several functions, even many functions. A wrist watch, for example, indicates the time of day. But many of today's watches also indicate the date, can act as stop watches or timing devices, some are miniature calculators, some are decorative—fine jewelry—and some have even other, additional functions. So, "what does it do?" is not so easy to answer unambiguously.

In the practice of value management, the question is taken to refer to the main (sometimes called *basic* or *primary*) function of the device. In the case of a watch that is not difficult to discern: There is not much question that the main function of a watch is to indicate the time of day. All those other things it does are secondary functions.

Identifying the Main Function

It is not always so easy to decide what the main function is. Consider, for example, the typical accounting system employed by businesses large and small. Ask business people what they think the main function of the system is and you will probably be advised that it is to "keep the books," "keep tax records," and sundry other such ideas. The problem with these definitions is a common one: They strike all around the main function, but never come to grips with it because the analyst has failed to first answer the more basic question of why— why does the system exist at all? What is the basic purpose of the system? What need does it satisfy?

The fact is, in this case, that "keeping books" is how, not why, and keeping records for tax purposes is a secondary issue and has nothing to do with the main purpose of accounting. One does not keep a costly accounting system for the convenience or enrichment of government tax bureaus (although it sometimes does appear to be so), but for the benefit of one's own enterprise. Accounting is a management function and exists to aid management by providing information necessary to make sensible management decisions. Relevant information is a need of management. Even the fact of record-keeping is not highly significant here, for that, too, is part of the means and not of the purpose, and the main or basic function always reflects the main or basic purpose.

Aids to Reaching Function Definitions

The VM methodology includes measures that are helpful in reaching function definitions and expressing them properly so that they will be useful in the analytical process. The most important of these are listed and explained briefly here:

The Verb-Noun Rule. The discipline demands that functions be defined or identified by two words only, a verb and a noun. The purpose of this (occasional exceptions are allowed, when a verb or noun must be a compound word to be clear and definite) is to enforce discipline and compel the analyst to make firm and unequivocal decisions. Otherwise, the definition of function is not at all useful.

Identification of the Purpose of the Item. You must ask yourself what is the true purpose of the item? Why does it exist? Why has someone gone to the expense of creating or acquiring the item? What is the need that must be satisfied by the item? This calls for some clear thinking and is at the heart of the discipline. Everything hinges on doing this properly, for everything that follows is based on this definition of main function.

Where the main function is not readily apparent, as it is in many but not all cases, the most useful first step is usually to identify that purpose by deciding what the desired end-result of the item is to be. In the case of accounting systems, that is the gaining of useful management information, information which enables managers to make wise and useful management decisions.

The second step is to find the verb and noun which expresses the definition most accurately and most usefully. (The significance of this will soon be apparent.) And that may entail choosing either word first, depending on the individual circumstances of each case.

In this case, we have already decided on information, and it may be wise, in this case, to use a compound noun, management information, since the unqualified word *information* is not likely to convey the full and proper meaning. In this case it is also important to choose the verb carefully, for accounting is perceived by most people as a recording and record-keeping process, which is misleading for our purposes. Again, the recording and record-keeping are part of the means, rather than the end, and it is important to take note of this. In fact, the most significant aspect of accounting's function vis-a-vis management information is that it is an active function and *reports* that information to the executives of the organization. Thus the definition ought to be "reports information" or perhaps "reports management information."

Secondary Functions

Secondary functions are of two kinds. Some are supporting functions, functions that are necessary to and support the accomplishment of the main function. Others are additional functions, not directly related to the main function.

In the example cited here, if the main function is to report information (to management), recording and recordkeeping are secondary functions, but they are also supporting functions. They are supporting functions because they are the means by which the information is accumulated and recorded steadily, day after day, so that it can be reported to managers periodically. (Monthly, quarterly, semiannual, and annual recapitulations and other derivative reports are made up for transmittal to the managers of most organizations.)

Other secondary functions, such as making up payroll checks, paying bills, invoicing sales, and calculating taxes, are not support functions because they make no direct contributions to the main function, although they may be considered to make some indirect contributions to it. (The figures explaining and describing these activities are included in the reports, but the physical processing of the payments and other paper is not in support of the main function.) In all cases you, as the analyst, must make a decision about which are the support functions and which are other secondary functions, not directly related the the main function.

THE SIGNIFICANCE OF DISTINGUISHING
SECONDARY FUNCTIONS

The purpose of the analysis is to prepare for the synthesis of a better way to satisfy the need. The front-end analysis is itself means and not end. Synthesis of improvement—a better system to propose to the client—is the end. It is thus critically important to identify the need which is to be satisfied, if you are to identify and define the main function accurately and accurately evaluate the contributions of secondary and support functions.

More specifically, once all of this is done, you can begin to make judgments as to how well the item performs its main function and satisfies the need. You can make judgments as to the usefulness or efficiency of supporting functions. And you can decide whether other secondary functions are necessary and make satisfactory contributions of some kind to the satisfaction of the need, for value improvement can result from a great number and wide variety of changes. There are many deficiencies that you can and will find among existing systems and for which you would be wise to keep an eye open. Here are just a few of the more common ones:

Unnecessary Frills.   American designers especially appear to have a weakness for loading all their designs with "whistles and bells"— numerous secondary functions that have nothing whatsoever to do with the main function but only do the double damage of increasing cost and reducing reliability.

Reluctance to Change.   In this jet/space/computer age many virtual Stone Age designs are still appearing everywhere, reflecting the reluctance to change and, to a large extent, the reluctance of many to learn new things and "keep up" with their special fields.

The Need to be Clever.   Unfortunately, many individuals design items as monuments to their own cleverness, rather than as the most effective and most efficient designs possible. The ego trip is understandable enough, but efficiency and effectiveness are the goals.

The Need to Appear Innovative.   Many individuals build designs that are Potemkin villages in that they have the facade of smart modernity, but are still early nineteenth century thinking. They recognize that times are changing, but try to disguise old designs and old thinking with fresh paint.

Conversely, here are just a few of the ways to improve value in the synthesis of better methods and better designs:

1. Eliminate unnecessary, trivial, unneeded, redundant, and/or non-contributing secondary functions.
2. Improve efficiency/effectiveness of main and support functions.

3. Reduce the number of steps required to carry out a function.

4. Reduce the human effort—labor—required to perform a function.

5. Automate functions and systems.

THE IDEA OF UTILITY

The foregoing suggests clearly that value is represented by the ratio of cost-to-function of the item. Varying either, while holding the other constant, increases or decreases value. But there is more to consider than the main function alone, in most cases. There are such items as convenience or ease of use, efficiency, dependability, durability, and other factors that have to do with the quality of the item. Improving efficiency at a sacrifice in one or more of the other characteristics may actually represent a decrease in value. In fact, the term *function* is not entirely satisfactory as one of the terms necessary to define value. We really need another term, one that considers these other factors that refer to quality and efficiency, which cannot be ignored when trying to assess value, absolute or relative. The term I choose to use here is *utility*, and it is to include the main function, with necessary support functions, if any, and those other characteristics of quality and performance, referred to here.

That poses another kind of problem, however: How does one manage to somehow quantify these other factors? Without quantification of some sort, value management cannot have even the semblance of a science.

COST IMPLICATIONS OF PROGRAM DESIGNS

It was with this kind of need in mind that the Department of Defense some years ago created the measure they called *cost-effectiveness* (which the popular press quickly explained to the public as a means of measuring "how much bang for a buck" a weapon or weapons system produced). And one way in which value management attempts to cope with this problem of quantification is in "life cycle" cost measurement, which takes in the estimated total cost of ownership over the entire life of the item, as distinct from the acquisition or purchase cost.

That life-cycle cost must include all the following costs:

Acquisition or cost of initial purchase.
Operating cost.
Maintenance cost.

Operating cost may include the cost of labor, which is usually the highest cost factor in today's economic environment. It is always important in evaluating and estimating cost consequences of a design to project the probable volume and level of labor required to implement the design operationally.

That does not necessarily mean that it is always possible to substitute equipment for human labor, even when it is technically possible to do so. Equipment entails its own acquisition costs, along with operating, maintenance, and depreciation or amortization costs. These need to be considered and evaluated versus labor costs.

Maintenance cost is not confined to machines and equipment. Even management systems and computer programs often require maintenance to correct "bugs," to update the systems, when conditions call for updating, and often to adapt the systems to new developments and circumstances.

Another factor to consider where it is applicable is the end-of-life salvage value of an item—what the remains of the used-up or obsolescent item are likely to bring in the marketplace—as an offset of those costs. Estimated with any accuracy, that total cost takes into account the other factors lumped earlier under the general category of "utility."

IMPACT ON PROPOSAL STRATEGIES

The possibility of designing your program for lowest life-cycle costs without sacrifice of convenience, quality, or utility is a most important point to consider in any proposal planning, for it points directly to a proposal cost strategy that is often highly effective. In short, discuss and explain the idea of life-cycle costs and then apply the explanation in a discussion of what you propose, and help the client to assess and evaluate the *true* costs of what you offer versus the costs proposed in competitive proposals. If you analyze and present your case well you can demonstrate most convincingly that the cost of acquisition—purchase price—is not the true cost—life-cycle costs—of ownership. In this manner you can often overcome a competitor's advantage in offering a lower acquisition cost. Moreover this concept of life-cycle costs is not confined to physical (hardware) items, but has validity also when applied to many computer programs, management systems, and other varieties of software.

Note, however, that to make the case effectively you must do more than demonstrate the validity of the principle (acquisition costs versus total costs). You must apply it to the specific case of what you propose. You must somehow manage to quantify the various cost elements by identifying and unitizing each, and do so in a convincing manner. Here, perhaps more than in any other place, you must present good evidence to prove your case, to show a logical and persuasive basis for your projections and claims.

PROPOSAL TACTICS

If designing for a low life-cycle cost is a possible strategy, tactics to sell the concept to the client are necessary, of course, and they would normally proceed along the normal lines of any sales presentation, first offering the overall emotion-based promise of greatly to be desired end-results, and then building the structure of evidence.

As a logical argument, a strong way to build the evidence, a first premise might easily be that of borrowing VM's basic idea that the item in question (whether it is a system, a service, a product, or anything else) is valuable only in what it *does* for the user, not in what it is. That's not a difficult premise to establish, and it helps greatly to set the scene and tune the client's awareness to the need to weigh results or utility in judging value.

The general evidence of an established idea and widely accepted truth as a second premise. In this case it might well be the well-known principle of trade-off, sacrificing one thing to gain another. It would be acquisition costs versus life-cycle cost here.

There is a close parallel between this and the economics of developing a computer program. One can develop the program for either low acquisition costs—fastest, easiest way of writing the program—or for low operating costs—tightly written, hence economical of running time. One cannot have both, and if the computer program were to be run only once or twice, it would be sounder economic sense to write it as swiftly as possible and so realize the lowest acquisition costs. But if it were to be run many times, as a more or less permanent element of the system, it would pay to spend more on its development so as to write a "tight" program and minimize the operating cost.

The mere fact of thinking it through and presenting this careful analysis and explanation is impressive to most clients, revelatory as it is of the consultant's knowledge and thought given to the client's need. But for maximum effectiveness, the presentation must to go on to apply the principles to the case at hand, as noted earlier.

Suppose, for example, the requirement is for the development and presentation of a training program to be presented a dozen times. Here you have that same familiar problem. The program can be developed as an instructor-dependent course, one that requires presentation by highly qualified (but costly) instructors. That makes the course relatively inexpensive to develop (since it requires only a lecture guide, lesson plans, and a syllabus, usually) but expensive to deliver.

The reverse is possible. You can develop a course that is dependent on auto-instructional programs, using videotape and other audiovisual materials, and bearing a light instructor load thereby. It requires relatively little "live" instruction and, in many cases, the instructor(s) need not be especially well qualified. The program so developed will be costly to develop and costly to produce, but be relatively inexpensive to deliver.

There is often a third possibility, one that is normally a compromise between these extremes: A "paper" auto-instructional course, as distinct from an audiovisual one, is thus relatively economical of both instructors and development/production costs, with a cost falling between those of the other two options.

Given such a case as this, your tactics would be to project and present the total estimated costs for each option and propose the one you think most economical, if achieving low cost is, indeed, your strategy. However, to be completely convincing, you must present your design factors and cost analyses in the greatest detail possible, even to the extent of validating your figures by citing the sources (e.g., quotations by vendors) and by offering specific physical evidence, such as catalog sheets and written quotations.

A typical cry comes up in the room when this strategy is offered to a group of seminar attendees: *What do I do when the RFP doesn't reveal how many times the course is to be presented?* (Actually, in many cases the desired information is at least plainly implicit if not explicit.)

That is a typical problem, but it does not invalidate the tactic suggested here, and it does not call for asking the client to clarify the point. (It's always risky to ask such questions, especially when proposing to a public-sector—government—organization, because the clarification is provided to everyone invited to propose, and you may be thus giving away to competitors much more than you get. Those are poor tactics, of course, and there is a better way: Explain the options and the considerations important to the choice. Then you can pursue either of two courses: (1) explain that owing to the lack of certain explicit information you cannot urge any specific choice on the client, but invite the client to choose one of the options, using the criteria you have provided to help guide the client in making the choice, and (2) if you think you can infer the information you need, explain the basic problem, make a recommendation of the option you recommend, but still offer the client the final decision or choice of options.

The opportunities to pursue this overall design and cost strategy are more numerous than you may imagine, for with a little imagination the idea can be adapted and applied to a great many custom developments.

This demonstrates a principle to bear in mind when developing a program design: Always consider the different possible approaches to the program, especially in terms of cost of each alternative, but do remember to consider *all* costs.

DESIGNING TO COST

Although, as already noted, VM has too often been used to close the barn door after the horse has gotten out, one of its spin-off developments has been the idea of designing to cost. That is, instead of permitting the design ideas to drive the cost, cost drives the design by basing the design studies on the premise of *how can the program be designed to achieve its goals for xxx dollars?*

This poses another possible proposal strategy, suitable for certain circumstances. For example, when the client has specified the available budget—and even government requests for proposals sometimes do that, to guide the consultant—design studies can be based on the question of *what is the maximum program/benefits we can deliver for this figure?*

Designing to cost utilizes VM in a special way, probably in the way it is used most effectively: VM considerations dictate the design by restricting it to the indispensable functions and the cost goals.

THE PAYOFF QUESTION IN VM

Mechanical although it may appear when rationalized, the practice of VM is most definitely a creative exercise, and it is generally carried out by a team, working together in a brainstorming session that I believe is more graphically referred to as "ideastorming." One of the several benefits of such a collective effort to evolve ideas is the synergy—a result greater than the sum of its parts—that normally results from this free exchange of ideas, generated spontaneously and often triggering one another.

Having arrived at answers to such questions as *What is it?* and *What does it do?*—that is, what is its main function?—there are other answers to be sought. But the most significant other questions, the ones that address the main objective of the exercise, are "What else would do that?" and "What would that cost?"

The answers to those questions point to the most effective and most efficient alternatives. However, it must be remembered that these questions are from the original value engineering/value management methodology, which was predicated on the assumption that the study was of an existing item, seeking to improve its value by reducing its production cost without losing any important function or characteristic—without, that is, losing utility or quality. But our case is different: We are projecting the use of VM-like methods to the hypothetical custom design of something new, rather than to the improvement of something already existing. That requires a different approach. If we are to pose the question of what else?—what to improve upon, that is—there must be some design to improve upon or to compare the proposed design with.

THE DESIGN APPROACH VIS-A-VIS THE SALES OBJECTIVE

This idea of comparative VM analysis, as you will soon see, gives you the basis for your sales arguments. The reason for this is simple: It is much easier to sell against competition than to sell against prejudice. Merely offering something new and different and trying to prove its worth in an absolute sense is most difficult. You are flying directly in the face of that well-known resistance to change, especially to change that means accepting new and perhaps revolutionary ideas. It's much more effective to compare your own proposed design with less-desirable options, to demonstrate superiority and sell your design. Obviously, you cannot demonstrate superiority without comparison! But here, where you are selling something unique—custom designs— you must create your own competitive item with which to compare your design. You must create what is sometimes called "a straw man" to be knocked down so as to validate your claim of superiority.

There are two ways you can create or hypothesize the competitive model against which you will sell your own ideas: One is to summon up some classic or conventional design or method that has long been used and use that as the basis for your argument. The other is to estimate one or more approaches you expect your competitors to take.

That second course can be a bit dicey unless you have some substantial reason to believe that you know what your competitors will offer. (That is the case in many situations.) Unless you are reasonably sure of that, you will be well advised to follow the first course, a much safer avenue and usually a quite effective one. If your competitors are following the conservative convention and offering conventional designs, you are selling against their designs. But even if they offer innovative ideas, you are asking the client to compare theirs with yours, and still selling against competition.

A FOR-INSTANCE

As an example of this strategy applied successfully, one consulting organization responded to an invitation from the U.S. Postal Service to develop on-the-job training for electronic and mechanical maintenance technicians in bulk-mail centers. (The students would have had training in basic electronic and mechanical technologies at Postal Service schools.)

The successful contender devised a training-development plan whose most attractive features were those that departed from the conventional design and from the most disadvantageous methods of developing such training. Specifically, conventional maintenance training almost invariably goes overboard and provides far deeper and far more wide-ranging technical training than required for the maintenance tasks. It overtrains the learners. The proposal referred to identified that as a typical weakness of most maintenance training, pointing out the several disadvantages of doing that, and promised to provide a design that would eliminate that problem. It offered, instead, to train the technicians only in the precise needs of the equipment to be found in bulk-mail plants. But to make that promise convincing and persuasive, the proposal had to offer some credible method for doing what it proposed, for making good on the promise. It therefore offered a highly innovative idea, the application of a methodology it called "failure probability analysis" (invented spontaneously for the proposal), explaining what that was, the rationale for it, and how it would be used to identify and define precisely what training was required and how the training program should be weighted. And to sell that latter idea the proposer developed another worry item for the client, a worry item that was itself the rationale for the proposed model of failure probability analysis. That was a necessary instrumentality to convince the client that the innovative method was needed. It was based on the fact that much of the equipment in the bulk-mail center was hardly beyond the prototype stage (this seems to be a characteristic of Postal Service equipment procurement) and so had no operating history to guide the maintenance-training design. The proposer stressed this problem and used it effectively to persuade the client to buy his solution. (And that points up another factor: You must "do your homework"—gather information on which to base your approach, as this proposer did in learning that most of the equipment in the bulk mail center was of recent design and therefore could provide no maintenance history on which to rely.)

Offering such innovation has two potential hazards: (1) The client may be one of the conservative types who is apprehensive of change that appears revolutionary, or maybe for other reasons—perhaps has a comfortably familiar existing system to be improved on or replaced but not changed seriously—is fond of conventional design and may be fearful of any but the slightest changes, and (2) there is the hazard that the client may interpret what you say as an attack on or criticism of his or her existing system or of the method he or she believes in. Hence, you must be careful in your presentation that you do not unintentionally give offense by saying things that the client interprets as attack or criticism. (In general, avoid the appearance of preaching, lecturing, pontificating, etc.) But you must also be careful to avoid appearing to be too revolutionary. That threatens the client's sense of security, and you must never underestimate the prevalance of that sense of insecurity. It lies buried not far beneath the surface in many of us, and is quite easy to arouse, usually with disastrous results. In fact, you want to strive for the opposite effect of helping the client feel quite secure in doing business with you.

There is something of an anomaly built into this. On the one hand, you want to be innovative and offer what someone else does not or cannot offer, selling your innovative design on the basis of advantages offered by the innovations. And yet you want to avoid being too innovative or appearing to be revolutionary. But there is still another consideration, and that is how to gain the advantage of presenting your innovative design in a manner that commands attention and makes your proposal outstanding in that respect.

The example just cited of a proposal to the U.S. Postal Service is an excellent example of how this typical problem of reconciling these conflicting needs was solved successfully, and we will return to it later to examine the methods used.

A CLOSER LOOK AT THE CREATIVE PROCESS

There are various theories of how the creative process works, and probably it works in more than one way. There are individuals, such as many prolific inventors, who can often come up spontaneously and consciously with useful new ideas on a regular basis. There are others who can the same thing, but only through laborious and lengthy processes. And there are those of us who develop new ideas occasionally, and usually do not know how we did so or even think about it a great deal. (And, unfortunately, some people develop great new ideas but never do anything about them, either through inertia or because of that common fear of being different to even a slight degree and risking possible criticism thereby.)

Some of those who have studied creativity and drawn conclusions from their studies advise us that creativity is much more often a new combination of known ideas or components than it is a completely original idea or creation. (Some even maintain that creativity is always a recombination of known factors or components into new patterns.) There is a great deal of evidence for this notion. Certainly, examination of existing devices bears it out in a great many cases, for there are few inventions or other new developments for which the antecedents are not quite apparent. (It was, for example, quite a long time before automobiles ceased to resemble "horseless carriages" and that epithet vanished from the language.) But there is ample other evidence for it.

There is also much evidence that a major element in the creative process is the contribution of one's subconscious mind. In studies of creativity, three main stages appear to exist in most cases of creative breakthrough, stages that can be fairly described by the following terms:

1. Concentration.
2. Incubation.
3. Inspiration.

Again and again we learn from many of those with demonstrated great creative powers that first they focus consciously on the problem until they have exhausted all possibilities that occur to them to be worth pursuing. Then they go on to other things, and incubate the problem, which means that the subconscious mind takes over and works on the problem. And, finally, usually when they are relaxing at something with no particular heavy thinking going on, comes the inspiration or the solution flashing into their minds suddenly.

We are told that our subconscious never forgets anything. That appears to account for its great ability to work on problems: it has far more referents—relevant ideas—to consider than does the conscious mind. How often have you been frustrated by an inability to remember a name, title, address, telephone number, or other item that you think you ought to be able to recall easily, and then had it pop into your mind much later, when you are not thinking about anything related to it? That is an example of the unconscious mind at work, as is hypnotism and its effects.

There is no readily accessible direct link between the conscious and unconscious minds. Hypnosis is one way to establish linkage. Concentration, intense concentration, is another way. Hypnosis is based on maximum relaxation of the conscious mind. Evidently it is that relaxation that opens the gate between the two, and permits communication both ways. Ergo, the need to concentrate on the problem, incubate it, and wait for inspiration, such as waking up in the morning with the answer to something that has been troubling you, a widely reported common experience.

OTHER ANALYTICAL TOOLS

The checklists, the functional flowcharts, and the VM methods are all useful analytical tools, but they are not the only tools available to provoke introspection in analyzing requirements and formulating strategies and approaches. Several others are in common use for the purpose. One used by many in proposal development is called informally the "why it can't be done" analysis. It can be utilized in all or virtually all cases, although it is more appropriate in some cases, where there is a complex or difficult problem to solve, for example, than in others, such as when the requirement is rather straightforward and calls more for management and dependability than for problem solving.

Why It Can't Be Done

One major objective of this unusual analytical attack is the development of worry items through surfacing problems not readily discerned. (This, you may recall, is also one of the objectives of analytical tools and methods discussed earlier.) Addressing the requirement from this perspective calls for deliberately seeking out problems, looking for potential obstacles to the successful accomplishment of the mission, as stated by the client.

Personification

Some analysts find it useful to try to project themselves into the problem to gain greater insight into it. Inventor Charles Kettering (inventor of the automobile self-starter and the electric cash register, among other things), when he was working on improving the diesel engine and making it a more practical prime mover, imagined himself in the inner chambers of the engine, and asked himself what he needed to work more efficiently as a diesel engine.

FAST Diagramming

Value Management has developed its own special kind of functional diagramming, which it calls "FAST" diagrams, for function analysis systems technique. Briefly it consists of making the leftmost block the one representing the main function, while the supporting functions are represented in the boxes proceeding to the right in the order of their priority. Other secondary functions, those not essential to the main function, are placed above or below the line of flow in locations suggesting their roles in the item. Figure 13 illustrates this. Note that the main function must correlate with the purpose of the item. To further illustrate this, a simplified FAST diagram of the Postal Service proposal idea is offered as Figure 14. Note the *How?/Why?* progression here, including the *why* of the main function, answered by the block that describes the purpose of the item. The *How/Why* questions verify the validity of the diagram, as they do in any other functional or logical diagram.

This is not all of it. There is more utility to the FAST diagram than appears here. Figure 15 illustrates this. A figure for whatever parameter is being addressed—money, time, materials, labor, or other—is measured or estimated for each function in the chain. And this is done first for the original model or the one to which the proposed model is

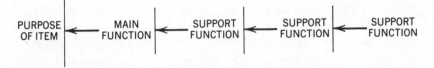

Figure 13. Principle of FAST (function analysis systems technique) diagramming.

Figure 14. FAST diagram of the Postal Service training proposal discussed in text.

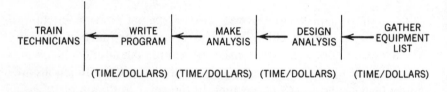

Figure 15. Further use of the FAST diagram.

to be compared, and then to each alternative model. This enables the analyst to make comparisons, of course, and decide which is the best alternative.

Note that it is not necessarily greatest efficiency of cost in dollars that is the objective of the study. This kind of study may be undertaken to find the maximum design for the conservation of time, labor, materials, waste, or virtually any other parameter. You can use this to devise the shortest schedule, when that is what the client seeks, or any other parameter of effectiveness and efficiency. And to that end, there is a useful technique you may use to develop FAST or any other kind of diagrams with greatest convenience and efficiency. A case history will illustrate this, while it also illustrates the utility of VM to conserve schedule time.

AN EPA PROBLEM

EPA, the Environmental Protection Agency of the federal government, was having trouble spending all the $10 billion it was authorized by Congress to give away in grants to communities whose water systems needed to be repaired, improved, and/or updated. There was a time limit on the program, but there were also requirements for qualifying each grantee, engineering/ technical requirements, and a Vermont engineering firm had been retained to help the communities make the engineering studies the program required with each grant application. Still, each grant application was taking far too long to get through the system, and it was almost a certainty that unless something was done soon the money would not be spent within the statutory time limit set for it by Congress.

Something had to be done to prevent the program from foundering. The Vermont firm was expert enough in the technical work that had to be done, but they did not have the kind of capability required to help EPA speed the program up. Consequently, EPA decided that this was a case for VM, and assisted the Vermont firm by arranging for the services of three VM experts to help the firm streamline the grant process.

After three days of work the team—the firm's engineers and the VM specialists—reached the point where they had identified all the functions of the entire grant application process. At first they simply listed each function. Then they wrote each one out on a card. And finally they arranged the cards on a board, as a FAST diagram, in the order in which they occurred in the grant process, where all could study them.

That is a useful technique during the study phases of either or both existing designs and projected designs because it enables you to move the function cards around until you are sure they are in optimum order. That means that you need write each function up only once, instead of numerous times, using them as building blocks, while you design the FAST diagram.

In this case, once the cards were arranged in order on the board, the leader of the VM team began to question the engineers as to how long each step—function—of the process took, for the objective of this VM study was to reduce schedule time, not dollars. (Remember that the VM discipline can be applied to optimize any parameter.)

It was not long before it became apparent that the bottleneck and the chief problem lay in the many months it took the engineers in each community to write up the technical reports which were required by the grant regulations. In fact, they were taking from 90 to 180 days to write reports that should have been done easily within 30 days after the engineering work was completed, if they kept good logs and/or worked at their drafts while doing the engineering work, instead of wasting time later gathering data that should have been easily at hand.

Once the problem was identified, the solution was apparent and not difficult to synthesize and implement. Obviously something had to be done to aid the engineers in speeding up their report writing and get the reports done with reasonable facility, but this was no longer difficult to perceive. And, once the specific problem—cause, that is—was identified, it was not too difficult to develop a solution.

PROBLEM DEFINITION

Note what happened in this case: Once the problem was properly identified and defined, the quest for solution was already well advanced. In principle, at least, the solution was defined by the identification of the problem: Some measure to speed up the writing of the engineering reports was necessary. What remained was to identify and list the various options available to do this—and there are several possible approaches to this—and then decide which was the best option to select and implement. These are the chief options available that are suggested by logical evaluation:

☐ Arrange for professional technical writers to work with the engineers and write the reports.
☐ Train the engineers in report writing.
☐ Design a system which includes a standardized report format and requires the engineers to begin drafting their reports earlier and maintain them, with firm deadlines.

Of course, the most practical of these choices and probably the only one which is reasonably certain to work out satisfactorily is rather obviously the first one, although the idea of a standardized format for the reports is an excellent one and would probably facilitate their completion on schedule, if incorporated in any measure taken.

THE PROBLEM IS THE SOLUTION

The fact that the accurate definition of the problem contained the seeds of the solution was not a fluke. It is, in fact, typical. In most cases, when the problem is truly identified or defined it requires no great amount of additional analysis to identify the options available or to decide which of those options is the most practical and desirable one to select. Even in those cases where more than one solution appears to be completely viable and some further analysis is required to make the best choice, that is a relatively small task; the major task is done when the problem has been firmly identified.

The converse of this is that if a problem definition arrived at or offered does not point to the solution or at least suggest it rather plainly, you may be almost certain that the problem has not yet been identified or defined properly. That should serve you as a guide in problem analysis, to help you to avoid confusing the symptoms or trivia with the true problem definition, so that you are guided to continue the analysis until you do perceive the solution or the direct approach to it.

Confusing the symptoms with the problem is an easy thing to do, and we are frequently not conscious that we are doing so unless we have some distinct methodology to help us make the appropriate determination. Referring again to the EPA case cited here, to the federal agency officials the problem was that of how to get all the grant money allocated (spent) in time. That was the problem as they saw it and they turned it over to the Vermont engineering firm and the VM specialists assigned as consultants to the Vermont engineers to help them solve the problem.

On the other hand, that statement of the problem was not satisfactory for the VM consultants because it did not even hint at the cause of the delay in making the grant awards. (In the VM analysis, the first revelation was that the applications were taking too long to complete, which then led to the study of where the bottleneck was in the application process.) It was therefore not a statement of the problem at all, but it was the statement of a symptom, which demonstrated that there was a problem yet to be defined. Before the consultants could solve the problem they had to know what the problem was, so problem definition was 99 percent of the task requirement.

That also points up that a problem definition often depends on the orientation and the special interests of the individual offering the def-

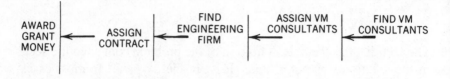

Figure 16. EPA's (Environmental Protection Agency's) FAST diagram for problem discussed in the text. VM, value management.

inition. Obviously the problem viewed by those who address it by hiring someone to solve it is different than the problem viewed by those who must develop the specific solution. The interest of the EPA officials was to comply with the will of Congress and get the grant money allocated before the statutory deadline. That was all that really concerned them, so they cast their problem definition in those terms—in terms of their own need, that is. The mission EPA set for itself, therefore, was simply to find someone to solve the problem and turn the search for solution over as a contracted project. A FAST diagram explaining that, from EPA's viewpoint, would appear as in Figure 16. The main function was to provide engineering support to the grantees to help them accelerate the application and award processes, but the engineering firm required the VM support, so EPA had to supply both, including the VM support as a secondary function that was in direct support of the main function.

This demonstrates that someone else's "problem" is likely to be a symptom to you. The client is quite likely to cast the problem definition in terms of the desired result, as EPA did (speed up the grant applications so we can get the program completed in time), whereas you must cast it in terms of the solution to the problem—what is required, specifically, to achieve that result.

This condition or situation is not confined to clients who have problems that require technical analysis and study to develop solutions. It is equally relevant in those cases where there appears to be no question about the solution—where, for example, the client wants a number of technical or professional temporaries to work on the client's premises and help develop a training program or a marketing presentation. Frequently such clients can use help in determining what their true need is; it is not always what it appears to the client to be, and you should never accept the client's view of the need or problem without examining it and giving it serious study. Part of your responsibility as a proposer is to analyze the requirement as stated and render an opinion as to what the client needs.

There is always some element of risk in telling a client that he or she is wrong, of course, no matter how tactfully you say this, but you can gain a great deal of marketing leverage if you convince the client that you are about to save him or her from a disastrous mistake. It has been my personal conviction for some years, based on the experience of my own mistakes, that while you should be as diplomatic as possible, it is a great mistake to be less than honest with a client, especially about what you believe is in the client's best interests. It is almost always possible to do so without arousing hostility, if you handle the matter discreetly in your proposal.

CHAPTER 8

WRITING, COMMUNICATION, AND PERSUASION

Writing is among our most ancient arts, the proof of civilization, in fact, and despite our best efforts it has remained far more an art than a science.

THE ROLE OF WRITING

The role of writing in proposal development has been downplayed in these pages until now. The sole reason for this was to place proper emphasis on the importance of sales and marketing skills and prevent them from becoming eclipsed or overshadowed by the role of writing skills in the proposal process. For successful proposals are not merely "written," in the conventional sense in which that term is used, but are developed as part of a lengthy sales/marketing process, in which writing, together with its many directly related functions, is properly the final phase of the process and not the central arena of the action.

At the same time, the importance of writing skills should not be overlooked in recognizing the central role of sales and marketing, for while it is sales and marketing that are represented by the basic strategies and arguments of the proposal presentation, writing is the implementation of those strategies and arguments: Because of that fundamental truth, brilliant strategies and powerful sales arguments are seriously weakened by ineffective writing, whereas relatively unimaginative strategies and pedestrian sales arguments are often made quite effective when skillfully presented in the written proposal.

WHAT IS WRITING?

We have become a communication-conscious society, and we tend strongly to equate writing with communication. In fact, many of those who write and lecture on the subject of writing appear to regard *writing* and *communication* as virtually interchangeable terms, or at least to regard communication is the sole objective or purpose of writing. Massachusetts management consultant Jeffrey Geibel, for example, freely acknowledges the role of the proposal as "essentially a marketing device," but also observes that consultants need to use proposals because ". . . communication is critical in the marketing of an intangible. Also, people are imperfect communicators, and correct communication (understanding) is critical to the success of the consulting process and the consultant."

Geibel is, of course, quite correct in his observations. However, it is only fair to note here that if most of us are, indeed, imperfect communicators, as he puts it, that is not necessarily due to the lack of language skills in expressing ourselves. It is also a reflection of the shortcomings of language itself as an unambiguous and unequivocal means of communication. But the question of language and words as effective means of communication itself depends, to at least some degree, on just what we mean by "writing." Do we use that word to refer strictly to the use of words on paper? Or does the word have some broader meaning or more far-ranging frame of reference? Or does that make a difference? But before we get into that question, let us consider communication itself.

WHAT IS COMMUNICATION?

Like the word *writing*, *communication* is a word with many implications in today's world of jet air travel, radiotelephones, computers, and communications satellites. It is with reference to communications that we speak of the world having "shrunk" to such relatively small dimensions, and we consider travel itself part of what we refer to as communications. But we use the term here only with respect to the development of effective proposals. For our purposes, communication shall mean the conveyance of specific meanings from one mind to another, and in most applications and references here it will mean the conveyance of meanings via those written presentations and/or related appurtenances that we call *proposals*. That is a general definition, but it is still not precise enough for our purposes because it does not truly define what is meant by the "conveyance of meanings." In fact, its chief deficiency is that it implies a unilateral action, that communication takes place when something is conveyed from a sender to a receiver, without considering how accurately or effectively that transfer of information was accomplished. It thus neglects to acknowledge the bilateral nature of the process (and *communication* is a process, not merely an action or event): It is not completed until the receiver gets the message sent, and it has not taken place until and unless the receiver gets the same message as the one sent.

Therein lies the difficulty. We have ample evidence that only rarely do senders succeed in placing in the receiver's brain the identical meanings intended by the sender. This is even more the case with verbal messages than with written messages, and this is at least partially what so many of us have in mind when we stress the need to "put it in writing" or "get it in writing." However, even the most carefully drafted of written materials rarely succeed totally in achieving the conveyance of the precise meaning that writers intend.

We must recognize, therefore, that communication is not a one-way process, but is a two-way process, involving both sending and receiving and requiring success at both ends—success in formulating and sending messages "in the clear," and success in interpreting the messages as intended.

THE RESPONSIBILITY FOR CLEAR COMMUNICATION

As a result of work by behavioral psychologist B. F. Skinner and others, modern educational theory and philosophy no longer place the total burden for learning on the learner, but compel the instructor or instructional system to bear the major part of the responsibility (unless, of course, the learners are not individuals with normal learning capabilities). The modern educational theory holds that it is the instructor/instructional system that is defective and has failed when the learner does not learn.

Very much the same philosophy ought to be applied to writing. It is, or ought to be, the responsibility of the writer to write clearly, unambiguously, and unequivocally. Given a reader of at least average abilities to read and comprehend, and despite the frailties of language as a means for clear and unambiguous communication, it is the writer, not the reader, who has failed when the reader's brain records a substantially different message than the writer thought he or she sent. The reasons for that position will become increasingly apparent as we proceed.

PERSUASIVENESS IN WRITING

It can be argued logically that the purpose of all writing is to persuade. (In fact, an especially effective and successful sales manager of my acquaintance many years ago insisted that whenever an exchange between two people took place a "sale" was made, and he presented a convincing argument to support that assertion.) At the least, the writer wishes to persuade the reader to believe what he or she has written, and strives to be credible. However, that generalization aside, it is the obvious and admitted primary objective of all sales presentations to persuade readers to believe and do whatever the sales presentation urges and advocates. We have, therefore, both persuasion and communication as primary proposal objectives.

There is a direct linkage between these two goals. Of course, it is necessary to communicate, if you are to present those motivators and arguments which, you hope, will bring persuasion about. But there are other considerations that show the close linkage between these.

Belief Versus Understanding

Our garden variety brand of commonsense logic explains to us that we tend to believe that which we have come to "understand." Thus the somewhat naive theory that a logical explanation will bring about understanding, and through that, belief. And ergo the "sincere" kinds of proposals that attempt to sell the proposer's services on the basis of pure logical rationale. Alas, this simply does not work because the cause and effects are reversed. People come to "understand" that which they have been persuaded to believe, and logic has nothing whatsoever to do with understanding unless the individual is prepared to first believe. Thus we have those who still stubbornly maintain that humans have not traveled to the moon, but that the U.S. Government has perpetrated a gigantic fraud for purposes of propaganda, and we still have those who cling to their belief that the earth is flat, and many others who cling to beliefs that fly in the face of massive evidence to the contrary and defy what is commonly accepted as demonstrated fact. They can never "understand" what most of us do because they are unable to believe what most of us believe. And, of course, all "understanding" is founded in belief somewhere in the chain of logic and reason for we cannot verify everything personally. None of us have ever seen an atom, few of us have been to many of the more exotic places in the world, and even fewer of us have ever been to the moon. We accept these and many other things "on faith," which means that we find the individuals and/or organizations who report these things credible, and we *believe* their reports.

Those who reject that which almost all of us accept and believe are among those characterized as part of what is termed "the lunatic fringe," those individuals who are grossly and massively irrational by the logical standards most of us agree on and accept. To that extent they are extreme examples. But most of us are also irrational, albeit on a far less extreme scale. Most of us know very well the dictate of logic that belief arises from understanding. But emotional forces within us tend to demand that we "understand" that which we believe, and to believe that which we prefer to believe because it satisfies some need within us. We thus have a rather profound ability to refuse to "understand" that which we prefer not to believe, as almost any argument on politics or religion will demonstrate rather quickly.

This is again testimony to the truth that we are far more creatures of our emotions than of our reason where our personal lives and desires are involved, and this is the critical truth for sales and marketing. Every truly knowledgeable marketer knows that there is an easy way to persuade prospects to believe what you want them to believe: simply tell them what they want to hear. They will always believe that, and they will require evidence more in proportion to the desire to believe the promise than to the logical difficulty in accepting the promise with belief.

That is more than sardonic observation. It is a pointer, once again, to the fundamental truth that the promise of great personal benefits is by far the one easiest to believe. That is, the motivators are invariably emotional appeals. (Of course there are exceptions: a relative handful of people are coldly logical, virtually human calculators and all but immune to emotional appeals, but their numbers are so small that it is not worthwhile to worry about the exceptions.) The most widely used motivators are promises of success, money, prestige, love, security, protection from life's harsh realities, and other "apple pie and motherhood" sweet dreams. But do these appear redundant? Are they all addressing the same *basic* motivation—security? Of course they are. Nothing is more basic than the need to feel secure, whether security is represented by money, prestige, career success, love, avoidance of disasters, or other concrete item. In the end, the drive for security is *the* motivator, possibly the only one. The difference is merely in what represents security to the individual prospect. Find that for your own set of prospects and you have the key to your own sales/marketing success.

Does This Apply to Proposals?

Many people find this easy to understand when applied to goods and services offered to the consumer for personal uses, but find it difficult to believe when applied to the business world. Are managers rational, impersonal, and unemotional when they buy for someone else—for an employer, that is? Or do they respond to the same motivators—are they influenced by consideration of their personal interests—when they are making purchasing decisions for their employers?

The answer to that second question is *yes*, of course. Most people in positions of authority and responsibility perceive their personal interests very much involved in any decisions or actions they take in connection with their positions. In fact, executives are frequently far more emotion-driven when acting for their employers because they perceive their prestige and security to be even more immediately at stake than when they are acting as consumers. In that latter case, perhaps no one else will know of any fiasco resulting from a mistaken judgment. But in the case of acting for an employer a mistake may have direct and potentially severe consequences to one's career. That concern can thus be a most powerful motivator.

Of course, there is the other side of this coin, too: An executive is an individual motivated by the desire for gain, as well as by the fear of consequence. Therefore the possible career benefits of doing well and becoming a local "hero" in a wise and highly satisfactory procurement are necessarily possibilities to be considered most seriously.

The proposal writer should consider these factors when devising strategies, bearing in mind that all organizations, whether small business, huge corporations, or government agencies, are made up of people and that those people are motivated in their decision-making by the same fears and desires as are others.

It is, of course, always dangerous to generalize, and there is no intention here to suggest that there is any single truth about the most effective motivations—that any single motivation is equally effective in or appropriate to all applications and all individuals. To devise successful strategies and make effective appeals, especially those that hinge on judging the best personal motivators of those making the final judgments and decisions regarding your proposal, it is absolutely essential to know something about those individuals personally, as well as about the circumstances surrounding the requirement in general. The motivator that is effective with one individual—fear of failure if an innovative and therefore presumably risky approach is proposed—may fall flat with another individual who wants to gain the attention of the corporate hierarchy by buying an innovative approach, thereby launching a dramatic initiative in the company. The ability to assess personal motivations accurately is often the basis for proposal success.

Credibility

Important although it is, the promise alone is not enough. The promise is what the client wants to believe but cannot accept without some basis for believing, for accepting the promise. The matter of credibility thus arises.

There are actually two aspects to credibility. On the one hand there is the matter of proof or evidence, discussed earlier. Although we are emotional creatures and far less rational than we prefer to believe, we are not entirely irrational. No matter how much we want to believe the promise of some much to be desired benefit, we still demand at least a modicum of evidence to support a promise and give us a basis for accepting the promise. Thus proof, or at least evidence, is one necessary element of credibility. The other element is the technique of presentation itself. Just as powerful strategies are weakened by ineffectual writing and uninspired strategies are strengthened by skillful writing, so the impact and the subsequent credibility of any evidence offered is dependent on the skill with which it is presented. The language has its own profound psychological effect on the reader. And there are many traps for the unwary in this area of concern alone, including hyperbole and generalization as hazards to be avoided.

Hyperbole

There are perhaps uses in which hyperbole is an aid to the purposes of the writer. This is rarely the case in proposals. Here the claim of "many thousands," when it is obvious that the actual number must be only hundreds, is a disastrous faux pas. Here the use of Hollywood-style superlatives—*magnificent, enormous, sensational*, and others of that stripe are deadly for your purposes. Such obvious exaggeration for effect is understood by moviegoers and tolerated, often even with amusement, because it does not affect the individual greatly and because there is little at stake, except the price of a ticket and an hour or two of one's time. On the other hand, the aura of insincerity is the diametric opposite of the effect to be sought in a proposal, and is not easily tolerated by executives to whom a proposal and the consulting project are serious business matters. It is therefore wise to avoid hyperbole and be as precise as possible in offering evidence of any kind in your proposals.

Generalization

Almost as deadly as hyperbole in its effect is the all-too-popular practice of generalization. This can stem from either of two possible weaknesses in the proposal effort and in writing technique generally: Often it is simply a technique of laziness and evasion. Rather than undertake the labor of searching out the specific and even minute details, the writer resorts to generalization as a convenient expedient. But sometimes it is an act of desperation. The writer has no real facts and does not know where or how to seek them out, or what to do as an alternative to generalization. And that is also the result of a lack of imagination, for there are many things one may do to cope with this.

Following are several examples to illustrate what one can do with a bit of resourcefulness and enough energy, for which the moral may well be: Don't reinvent the wheel.

In some cases, where the client wishes to have the consultant make many purchases as the agent of the client, the proposal request will require that the consultant include a description of his or her purchasing procedures and policies. The small consulting organization may very well not have a formal purchasing manual or written procedures, and thus some consultants are inspired to meet this proposal requirement with vague generalizations and philosophical ruminations. (Surprisingly enough, even some rather large organizations do not have formalized procedures and written policies for these functions, other than a typed memorandum or two.)

In other cases the proposal request may include a requirement for a copy of the proposer's personnel procedures and policies, quality control directives, and/or other such formal documents. Again, the unwary proposal writer often responds, unsatisfactorily, with evasive pontifications that tend more to reveal than to conceal the lack of such formalized policies and procedures.

The sensible approach to meeting this requirement in such circumstances is to *create* the requested document spontaneously for the proposal. That document need not be a slick, bound manual, as it would be in a large corporation. It is perfectly acceptable for it to be a typed document bound with a staple or a standard report binder. Nor is it even always necessary to create such a document from scratch. You can often pick up another organization's manual or procedural/policy document and adapt it to your own situation and needs. It is wise to be alert for opportunities to acquire such resource documents for your own proposal library, where the document will be available when needed.

Sometimes a client will want some quantified data by which to assess your experience qualifications. In one case a client seeking a technical writing consultant asked for an account of qualifications on a quantitative basis of technical documents produced—numbers of documents of each type, numbers of pages, and other such figures, rather than of years of experience.

The consultant who wrote the winning proposal in this case did not have project histories recording those figures, but he did have a good recall of specific projects. He made a series of estimates, using a procedure which he believed produced results that were reasonably accurate, and reported the resulting figures. He was also careful to report the exact figures produced by the estimating method and did not round them off, a wise precaution.

In proposing a large training project, for which the details of proposed curricula and supporting materials was a requirement, the consultant who wrote the successful proposal sent for the catalogs of textbook publishers, bought a copy of a government publication listing several thousand training films and other audiovisual training materials, and borrowed a dozen reference books from the nearby public library. Careful scanning and a large cut-and-paste operation soon produced a meticulously detailed proposed program that left virtually nothing to be desired.

The client was more than impressed with the magnitude of the documentation that appeared in the proposal, which was far more voluminous and detailed than the client had expected: He admitted to being "overwhelmed" and even awed by the enormous effort the consultant had apparently expended on the proposal. Ironically, because the consultant had been so resourceful the required effort was not very great, and it was that very factor that permitted the consultant to include such a great volume of painstaking detail. That would not have been possible had he been forced to gain the details by chasing down each item individually.

Again, this illustrates the principle that there is always an easier or better way to get something done if you allow your imagination some freedom from conventional thinking and if you remember that injunction to avoid reinventing the wheel. Even if the idea or information you find readily available is not precisely what you need, it is almost always far easier to modify what is available, adapting it to your needs, than to start from scratch to create an original that is probably a pale copy of something already in existence.

Nouns and Verbs

Hyperbole results from the too-enthusiastic use of superlatives—adjectives and adverbs. Restricting function descriptions to nouns and verbs enforces a discipline and compels the value analyst to make a firm commitment to a precise definition. This principle should be applied to writing generally and to proposals particularly. A rigid economy in the use of adjectives and adverbs forces a discipline of thinking on you as a writer. That, together with a careful avoidance of generalizations and philosophical ruminations, invigorates your writing style and, more importantly, lends your writing an air of authenticity and authority lacking in writing that violates these principles. The result is a greatly enhanced quality of believability.

WHAT IS "BAD" WRITING?

Writing "well" has more than one meaning, depending on application and kind of writing. Certainly it means something different when applied to the novelist than it does when applied to the scientist and philosopher writing in their respective fields. And it means something else again when applied to the present application, the writing of proposals. Therefore, while some of what is said here might have some application to writing in general, that is pure coincidence, for we are concerned here only with what is "good writing" in proposals and/or related presentation and marketing materials.

Mechanics

We will not dwell on the mechanics of using language—grammar, spelling, punctuation, etc. The assumption here is that you can use the English language with reasonable fluency, that you know the basics of sentence structure and other basics of using our language, and that you will turn to a dictionary for guidance in using words correctly and spelling them as they should be spelled. However, there is at least one observation that should be made on the subject of usage: What is acceptable usage in "creative" writing is not always acceptable in proposals. For example, the "creative" writer—novelist, for example—may use sentence fragments—phrases lacking the essential sentence elements of subject, predicate, etc., and even single words—as sentences, as well as perhaps many other violations of the "rules." Creative writers do these things to achieve special effects, and readers understand that. But in the formal business atmosphere of proposal writing such uses are not normally acceptable. Proposals should be straightforward narrative expositions, conforming with normal principles and practices of usage.

This is not to say that there is no need to achieve special effects, such as dramatizing certain points, in proposals. But there are ways to do this without violating accepted usage, and we will discuss these at the proper time. "Bad" writing, as discussed here, has nothing to do with the mechanics of usage.

Content and Organization (Not Grammar and Punctuation)

The chief proposal writing fault that can be characterized as "bad" writing is not linked to usage, but to something far more serious. Even if the proposal turns out to be a little shaky in the matter of usage, a competent editor can fix that rather easily. But this other problem is another matter, not so easily repaired. It is the matter of essential content and organization. Editing cannot repair serious faults of content and organization, and even rewriting often cannot repair it, for the problem stems too often from the lack of substance.

The Lack of Substance

"Lack of substance" can mean any or many of a great variety of faults, and conveys to the client such impressions, whether true or not, as the following:

1. The proposal shows little understanding of the problem. It appears that the consultant began to write without having first done a proper analysis and without having reached a true understanding of what the client wants and needs.

2. The consultant has done only a superficial research job in gathering data and organizing a plan to be proposed. It lacks the necessary detail to permit a proper evaluation.

3. The consultant really does not know what he or she is talking about because he or she appears to be insufficiently expert in what is needed or in the claimed field of technical/professional specialization.

4. The proposal ignores what the client has requested and offers a plan that is inappropriate and perhaps is even an off-the-shelf plan offered to every client, no matter what the client asks for.

5. The plan has good elements but is not well organized, perhaps not even wholly coherent, and is thus all but impossible to understand, much less to evaluate.

6. The proposal is spotty, having some excellent parts, but then having some sketchy and vague areas too, often in important matters. The impression this lends is that the consultant is expert in only some of the relevant areas, lacking competence badly in others.

What all of this adds up to is serious deficiency of content. It says to the client that the proposer is not responsive, for one reason or another—does not understand the problem, is not qualified to solve the problem, was unwilling to make a serious effort to study the requirement and develop a plan to propose, is incapable of developing a plan, cannot think well, or suffers other serious deficiencies.

Unless the client happens to be acquainted with you from some past relationship, you will be judged primarily on the impression your proposal makes. If your proposal conveys an impression of one of the above deficiencies, it is unlikely that you will ever be favorably regarded by that client.

A SIMPLE DEFINITION OF BAD WRITING

Note that the postulate of a client's opinion or reaction is based entirely on the client's perception of truth. In fact, for our discussion here, bad writing is simply writing that fails in its purpose. Even if your proposal contains an excellent plan—perhaps even a brilliant one—it is the impression your proposal makes on the client that will influence him or her. Poor writing of itself, in the sense of awkward usage and dull rhetoric, may cast you in an unfavorable light in general terms of your professional image. But entirely aside from that, there is the potential disaster of failing to bring the client to complete comprehension of everything your proposal says. Obviously, even the most brilliant plan and most impeccable credentials will avail you nothing if the client does not understand and perceive them. Ergo, the importance of logical and coherent organization and the other essentials of clear writing. And that includes the use of every legitimate communication device you can muster in behalf of delivering your messages with absolute precision, such as an abundant and free use of well-conceived and well-executed graphics, tables and matrices, explanatory titles, headlines, and captions, and any other aid to understanding that you can conceive.

WRITING IS MORE THAN WORDS

It is important to perceive in this that "writing" does not refer to the use of words alone, and that touches on one of the common faults exhibited by some writers. They seem to use tables and matrices only when the data to be presented appears to be that which is usually offered in tabular or matrix presentations—when tabular and matrix representations fairly force themselves upon the writer—and they often turn to graphics only as an afterthought, tacking them on to the manuscript in what is sometimes referred to as "outboard" design. (Unfortunately, this is quite often all too apparent to the reader.)

To use these various communication aids effectively you must make them integral to the proposal, conceived as part of the basic vehicle of communication. A later chapter will present many specific examples, which may be borrowed to use as models, but some guidelines covering their use and evaluation are presented here, after a brief discussion of organization and some methods for organizing your information effectively.

Organization

There are a number of classic patterns in which to organize information, including these basic ones:

1. General to the particular, usually in a pattern of growing focus on specific detail until the final point is made, in a kind of deductive-reasoning process, establishing the principles and then applying them to a specific case.
2. Particular to the general, in a kind of inductive-reasoning process, discussing the specific data and inferring the principles or main message from that.
3. Chronological, from beginning to end (or present) or from end (or present) to beginning, tracing the course and process.
4. Order of importance or priority, lesser to greater or vice versa.

It is even possible to mix these methods, although unadvisable if it can be avoided because it is simpler to be coherent and easy to follow if you pursue an unbroken pattern of organization. Mixing them successfully—without causing confusion—calls for some rather expert writing skills and careful control of the reader's orientation.

Each of the methods has its pros and cons, according to the circumstances and objectives of the application. Explaining how you've arrived at a given approach is often best accomplished by a chronological presentation that describes how you evolved the ideas for your approach over some series of experiences or earlier achievements. On the other hand, sometimes it is best to trace the history of your approach by describing it and presenting the chronology in reverse, from the present to its origin.

Similar considerations apply to all other methods: You, as the writer, must be the judge of the best method of organizing discussions. But note this: Each discussion (sometimes that means each section or chapter of a proposal, but it may mean a discussion within a section) itself must be organized along some logical path. You need not use the same method for each discussion (and probably will not wish to do so) as long as you make clear to your reader what the pattern of presentation is to be. You must be careful to never "leave your reader behind" as you move on with your material. This means that you must observe a few absolute basics of what is taught in formal classes as "composition."

Composition Basics

You must create and maintain a unity of thought in each element—sentence, paragraph, subsection, or other. A sentence deals with one main idea, and another sentence is required to present or discuss another, different idea. Similarly, paragraphs and other elements are each about some single subject or thought.

You must keep the reader posted on what is to be the subject of the paragraph, subsection, etc. The paragraph opens with a topic sentence which telegraphs the meaning. (Study any of these paragraphs as examples.) For a larger element, you probably require an introductory paragraph, although in some circumstances that may be a single sentence. A book, on the other hand, generally has an introductory chapter, as does a formal proposal of any size.

When you are through with the subject and ready to go on to another one, you must begin another paragraph (or larger element), with its own topic sentence (or introductory element). But you must provide a transition or "bridge," as many writers call it. That is a device that indicates the logical connection between the elements to maintain the continuity of thought. Otherwise, the reader is almost sure to become confused—disoriented, in fact—and find it difficult, if not impossible, to follow your argument. Study these paragraphs as examples and note that there is more than one way to create those bridges. Probably the best way is to prepare the reader in advance for each transition by ending each element with an introduction to the new subject to come, using some linking word or term (one that the reader will immediately recognize in the next paragraph) to make the connection. But you can also do this in reverse, beginning a new paragraph with a reference in your topic sentence to the preceding one. Headlines, titles, and captions can be used to help with this also, and we will discuss those, too.

Headlines and Captions

It is often painful for me to observe the missed opportunities resulting from the failure to use headlines, titles, and captions freely enough, and especially from their unimaginative use, so that they do rather little to help the writer even communicate, much less persuade. Headlines and captions, such as titles of figures and tables, offer you many special opportunities to communicate and to persuade, as well as to help the reader follow the transitions of discussions from one subject to the next. And they should be used to help create that logical transition, but not as the main or sole vehicle of transition. For the headlines, titles, and captions can be employed to do a great deal more to help you create a proposal presentation of great impact and powerful persuasion.

Briefly, a headline is used to introduce each major new subject, titles are used to characterize and introduce new chapters or sections, and captions are used to introduce figures, tables, matrices, and other such special presentation devices. (At least, that is how we shall define those terms here, although some people refer to figure and table captions as titles.) By their very existence they aid the reader in following the continuity of thought and perceiving the main topics. And, at least in theory, they also help the reader find his or her way back to specific portions of the presentation which they wish to read and review again. (In fact, the array of chapter titles, headlines, and captions in the table of contents ought to offer a fair, if approximate, outline of the proposal.)

Unfortunately, too often writers are satisfied to demand nothing more than the most general of descriptions or categorizations of their titles, headlines, and captions. This results in such unimaginative headlines as "INTRODUCTION" and "GENERAL," and captions such as "Table of Characteristics." And aside from the failure to exploit the titles, headlines, and captions in some positive way, such unimaginative uses often fail even in their most basic purpose of serving as guideposts for the reader simply because the words are so trite that they do not register with the reader.

At the minimum, strive to use fresher words for your titles, headlines, and captions, to stimulate the reader's attention, making the reader aware of them and of what they say. Find fresher words to say "introduction" and "general background." Find something more imaginative than "schedule" to introduce a milestone chart or table. Find words that not only explain and telegraph major topics and presentation aids, but also *sell* them by stressing the positive aspects—the benefits they promise the customer and the evidence that validates the promises. (A later chapter will offer some specific for-instances.)

Tables and Matrices

Tables and matrices are basically devices for listing items that have some coherent interrelationships among the items included. This makes their presentation in a listing or cross-listing a more efficient and more useful presentation than a mere verbal description would be. The difference between the two is simply that the term *matrix* refers to a tabular presentation in which items are so related that some correlation among them exists, whereas a table may be a simple listing of items with something in common among them, as illustrated by Figures 17 and 18.

Something more than mere identification of the table or matrix should be reflected in the captions. Remember the nature of a proposal: It is a sales presentation, and every opportunity to sell should be exploited, as the specific examples in a later chapter will explain.

Graphic Aids

Illustrations are a must for most proposals. One of the cardinal and most basic rules of selling is to make things as easy as possible for the prospect. Bear in mind that the client is probably faced with a number of proposals to review, perhaps as many as 30 or 40, in fact. While there may be some psychological leverage in what appears to be a substantial proposal, one of many pages, the client does not look for-

EVALUATION ITEMS	POINT VALUES
Understanding of requirement	10
Approach	
Analysis	5
Viability	5
Success probability	5
Qualifications	
Staff	20
Organization	10
Management	
Project organization	15
Methods and procedures	20
Costs	10
Total:	100

Figure 17. Simple table.

PROCUREMENT METHOD	NUMBER OF ACTIONS	TOTAL $(000)	PERCENT TOTAL
Fixed price	345	7,653	11.6
Cost plus	123	12,565	19.7
Two-step	12	1,645	3.6
Sole source	4	983	1.8
Setaside	3	765	1.3

Figure 18. Matrix-type table.

ward with any great pleasure to studying a great many words to evaluate what you are offering. Most clients are appreciative of anything that relieves the necessity to read a great deal, and that is precisely what a good illustration must do.

The purpose of an illustration is to convey meaning, and an illustration should be used whenever words alone are not really adequate, that is, when an illustration can convey meaning more accurately or more efficiently than can words alone. In writing a proposal you must often present both concrete ideas and abstractions, which means that you must present both images and concepts. Words rarely convey an image as well as an illustration can because words are merely symbols, and most words must be interpreted by the reader. It would require a great many words to convey the image of a piece of furniture or a communications satellite, and then they would not deliver as accurate an image as a single drawing or photograph would. When an accurate and precise *image* of the object must be conveyed, words simply won't do; an illustration is required. On the other hand, words will suffice to convey the *idea* or concept of the chair or communications satellite, if that is all that is required.

Abstractions present a more difficult problem in communications, sometimes. The idea of a vector, for example, which is the result of two or more forces acting in different directions on an object, is quite difficult, perhaps even impossible, to explain properly without an illustration. And the vector in electrical applications is even more difficult to explain than is the vector in mechanical applications. (In fact, the subject is generally introduced first via mechanical theory for that very reason.) For abstract ideas, analogies that employ illustrations are often the only practical solution.

The quality of an illustration is linked directly to and may be judged by the amount of text it displaces (makes unnecessary). The illustration that requires a great deal of textual explanation is not doing its job at all, and perhaps is not worth having. You may judge the virtues of an illustration in that manner, by the weight of text it replaces, as well as in the absolute terms of how effectively it delivers a message or conveys a meaning.

Analogies, Metaphors, and Other Imagery

Illustrations are not always drawings. There are also verbal illustrations, illustrations by referents, or by textual analogies that the reader can easily visualize. In describing the earth as shaped somewhat like an orange, round but flattened slightly at the poles, the writer takes advantage of the fact that the word *orange* is a familiar referent: everyone in the western world knows what an orange is and how it looks, so it is safe to assume that a drawing of an orange is not required to explain the concept. Nor is it necessary then to offer a drawing of the earth, if explaining its oblate shape is all that is desired.

The use of imagery reaches its peaks in fiction and in popular nonfiction, but ought to be used judiciously in proposal writing by restricting it to that which is absolutely necessary to present concepts. It is far too easy, when employing imagery, to become fanciful and be carried away into that very hyperbole and other exaggeration cautioned against earlier.

Purple prose—use of obscure words found only in unabridged dictionaries (and even then often archaic terms no longer in popular usage), banalities, pompous verbal posing, and the deliberate use of relatively unknown words when simpler words are readily available— is bad writing. A study of such prose—some of the kinds of prose that have become known as bureaucratese, for example—often reveals an interesting fact when it is translated into simple English (which is itself often no mean feat). The fact referred to is that such prose often says absolutely nothing, and only the fact that it is in such convoluted expression conceals that lack of substance from the casual reader. Ironically, the deception is usually not deliberate. Some writers appear able to conceal even from themselves the fact that they have nothing to say, as they offer a storm of obscure words and pontifical prose which, they manage to convince themselves, has some significance.

The causes of this are usually any of several, but include at least these:

☐ The failure to truly think out what he or she wants to say—the main point or objective of the writing—or what the presentation strategy is to be.

☐ The failure to plan ahead by outlining, preparing notes, gathering the data, and, as noted above, truly *thinking* about the subject before attacking the keyboard.

☐ The failure to do adequate research, an absolute must. You cannot write a really good 5,000-word proposal by researching and gathering 5,000 words of information. You must usually have gathered

25,000 or more words of source data, from which you garner the 5,000 words you need.

☐ The belief that glib writing can substitute for substance.

☐ The fear of making clear and unequivocal statements, dreading the possibility of being challenged and, even worse, proved to be wrong. (If the writing is sufficiently ambiguous and tortuous, especially if it is such that it is by no means clear what it actually says, there is less possibility of being challenged successfully. Ergo, consciously or unconsciously, the writer who is lacking in confidence tends to write badly.

The federal government, because it is a huge bureaucracy and bureaucrats often tend to be insecure and reluctant to take the initiative, is a frequent offender. Seeking to do something about the many thousands of pages of paper governing federal procurement, Congress set up an organization (the Office of Federal Procurement Policy, within the Office of Management and Budget) to do something about it. A team of people spent over five years combining, reorganizing, and rewriting some 60,000 pages of regulations, bulletins, and memoranda, creating a single unified and allegedly simplified set of procurement regulations, the Federal Acquisition Regulations. Those who were employed in this effort were required to undergo a full week's special training course in writing. One resulting regulation, typical of the entire result of all that enlightened labor, repeats an earlier one that says that a contractor may not charge the government twice for the same thing, but it takes a full page of small print to say it, which is an almost verbatim repeat of the regulation that was to have been simplified. That kind of writing is always bad writing.

The late Bertrand Russell, a British theoretical physicist, mathematician, and philosopher who was one of the world's great thinkers, was also a prolific writer, and often a sardonic one, reporting his observations with great amusement. He observed in one of his philosophical writings that it was his great good fortune that everyone knew him to be an educated man so that he had no need to impress anyone and could afford to write in the simplest of English, which he did, of course. His many writings are, indeed, a model of clear and simple English, written solely to inform the reader, with no thought of self.

That is the lesson to be learned about writing simply and clearly: Keep in mind your reader and your reader's needs only, and give no thought whatsoever to yourself and your image.

THE SPECIAL PROBLEM OF LETTER PROPOSALS

Writing the letter proposal is a special problem in several ways. The reason for writing a letter proposal is that the project is a small one or the possibility of the prospect actually making any award is an unknown—you are writing an informal letter proposal as a follow-up marketing activity, perhaps entirely for the purpose of qualifying the prospect (trying to establish whether there is enough probability of an eventual contract to merit serious marketing and sales concentration).

In either case, the investment of a great deal of time and dollar cost is not justified. And yet, if the proposal is to be seriously received and to do its work effectively, it is just as necessary to make all the major points and present all the sales arguments here as it is to do so in a large, formal proposal. The scale of the presentation does not change any of that.

To further complicate the problem, it is far more difficult to be concise, while still making all necessary points and delivering the proper messages. In short, it is quite difficult to be as effective in a letter proposal as in a formal proposal because the medium imposes its own restriction. Do not make the mistake of believing that it is easier to write a letter proposal than it is to write a formal proposal. It is not. At least, it is much more difficult to write an *effective* letter proposal than it is to write an effective formal proposal.

For that reason, do not impose unnecessary restrictions on yourself when writing a letter proposal. I have suggested in these pages that a typical letter proposal is likely to be two to four pages or thereabouts, but that is not a rule of any kind. First, you may include appendices and/or exhibits with your letter proposal, as you may with any proposal. Second, you are not by any means limited to two to four pages; you are at liberty to make your letter proposal a dozen pages, if you find that necessary. And third, you are certainly at liberty to use graphics—illustrations—here, as you are in formal proposals. Moreover, there is no reason to inhibit yourself from taking advantage of the opportunities to employ headlines, titles, captions, and other presentation devices in your letter proposals, as you do in formal proposals.

On the other hand, if you do find it necessary to so expand the letter proposal, it might be wise to consider making the proposal a bit more formal, with a title page, table of contents, and other such refinements, binding it in one of those patent report binders you can buy in any stationers or office-supplies store.

You might regard that as a small formal proposal, as an oversized letter proposal, or even as hybrid—perhaps a semi-formal proposal. It does not matter. What does matter is that you do a proper job of preparing an effective proposal, of whatever size, but keeping it in proportion to the several considerations of the circumstances.

CHAPTER 9

SPECIAL PRESENTATION
GUIDES AND STRATEGIES

The objective of a proposal is not truth but persuasion.

SALES STRATEGY VERSUS PRESENTATION STRATEGY

Successful presentations do not happen by chance. They are the result of successful presentation strategies properly implemented. The proposal is itself a presentation, of course, a *sales* presentation. Sales strategy, however, should not be confused with presentation strategy. The two are not identical. And although inevitably the presentation strategy is intended to be in direct support of the sales strategy, it is essential to differentiate the two in conceiving and implementing them.

Defined as briefly as possible, the sales strategy is that concept which, you hope and expect, will persuade the client to accept your proposal and award the contract to you. The presentation strategy—or strategies, for more than one is possible and more than one may well be embodied in a proposal—is designed to give the proposal maximum impact in several respects. However, while the sales strategy may be identical with cost or technical (program) strategy, in some cases, it is most unlikely that it will ever be identical with the presentation strategy. That is, you would almost certainly be deluding yourself to hope that even the most clever presentation strategy would of itself win the contract. Rather, you should expect a successful presentation strategy to help make your sales strategy an effective one by achieving the following for you and your proposal:

1. Capture the reader's (client's) attention.
2. Generate and sustain the client's interest.
3. Make it easy for the client to read and understand everything your proposal has to say.
4. Inspire respect for your professionalism.
5. Make your promises and proofs totally believable.
6. Make your appeals persuasive.

Although these are separate and distinct objectives to be pursued, they are not totally unrelated to each other. Quite the contrary, some of them are closely related to each other, even to the extent that in some cases they act as constraints or defining boundaries for each other. That shows up immediately when we consider these items, as we do in the following discussions. For example, when we consider item 1 we find that it must be constrained by consideration for items 4 and 5 but it is also not unrelated to item 2.

First we will discuss these six items briefly and in general, and then we will consider the specifics of employing them in typical proposal applications.

Capturing Attention

Obviously you cannot get your message across effectively if you do not have the client's attention, and that means the client's full attention. Otherwise, the client may very well go through the mechanical motions of reading your proposal, out of an accepted moral obligation to do so, but with considerably less than full awareness of what you say. Even more significant, the client will read your proposal without paying special attention to those things to which you need to direct the client's special attention. That is, your strategy may fall flat and fail simply because it lacks the impact on the client's consciousness it must have, if it is to do the job for you.

TV commercials offer many object lessons in using opening "hooks" to grab the prospect's attention. Movies and TV plays, for example, open with some exciting or curiosity-arousing scenes to capture the viewer's attention, and only then switch to the commercials, titles, and other less fascinating material, hoping they have now made the viewer captive.

There are a great many ways to capture a reader's attention, but not all of them are desirable ones, especially in a proposal. Certainly you would not want to resort to some of the more bizarre devices that might capture a client's attention, for you must command the client's respect for you as a professional, and your representations must also be credible, of course. The bizarre ploy, while effective for some purposes, involves a great risk to your professional image. Therefore, while you must find ways to command attention, you must do so in ways that are entirely in keeping with your profession and the serious image you must maintain. For example, while it is perfectly acceptable to use simple line drawings to help present a message and/or gain attention, there is some potential hazard in using cartoons for the purpose, and you would probably be wise to refrain from doing so. But that is by no means the only factor of importance to consider, in connection with getting attention; there are several others.

Sustaining Interest

Getting the client's attention is only a first step in getting your message across and supporting your sales strategy—giving it a chance to succeed. Having gotten the client's attention, you must do whatever is necessary to hold it. That is called, in the "AIDA" concept, arousing interest or keeping the client interested. The relationship between the two, getting attention and holding it, is so close that it is difficult to separate the two, and this discussion does so only to dramatize the futility of getting attention without really arousing interest.

That is one of the practical arguments against the bizarre attention-getter. Aside from the potential hazard to your image as a serious professional, getting attention through some novel device usually does nothing to help you hold the client's attention, especially when it is an attention-getter that does not arise from the material.

You can see that and other common mistakes made frequently in commercial advertising and sales presentations. Nor are these mistakes confined to the small organizations and the inexperienced individuals; some very large and successful organizations make these same common mistakes over and over. Following are some of these other common mistakes.

Irrelevant, Trivial, and Even Cryptic Attention Getters. Frequently some clever device is used to get attention, but too often the attention-getter is something that has no direct relationship to the main subject matter (or, even worse, to the prospect's interests) and so the prospect's attention is gained only momentarily and interest is not even genuinely aroused, much less sustained. One advertisement, for example, that is supposed to appeal to meeting planners and persuade them to book their business meetings into the advertised conference center uses a modest-sized headline that urges the reader to set the highest standards for his or her conference and then identifies the hotel and conference center by name, with a wood-cut type of drawing, saying very little else. Actually, it is stretching things to even class this as an attention-getter, for it is not that at all. It doesn't do anything to command attention and does even less to arouse the reader's interest with its almost meaningless hints of quality and prestige.

Even worse, perhaps, is the advertisement of one of a well-known supercorporations which tells you that your computer "should look you straight in the eye." Only with careful reading of the body copy do you discover that this refers to the dubious benefit of having the monitor mounted on a swivel, so that you can change its angle for your comfort. This is a useful feature, but hardly a major one, and certainly not one important enough to be the focus of the sales strategy, as this advertising headline forces it to be.

Reverse Orientations and Empty Claims. An even more serious and more common mistake is the offering of items intended to command attention that do not succeed in doing so because they offer the prospect no inducement to pay even slight attention to the message. Instead of being oriented (appealing) to the interest of the prospect, they are oriented to the interests of the advertiser. Typical of these are those appeals that stress how great the advertiser is, how long the firm has been established as almost a tradition, and other such self-laudatory irrelevancies as the reason to favor that advertiser with patronage.

In a specific case a professional speaker advertises his services by headlining the claim that no other speaker has his credentials. He features his picture prominently in his advertising literature too, but fails to give the reader even a hint of what he speaks about, much less what his speaking does for the client or even what those vaunted credentials are.

Another firm offers what it claims are "high quality, low cost data switches," going on to pile a few more unsupported claims on top of that, but offering not a shred of evidence to support the claim of high quality, although it does offer what appears to be a rather reasonable price.

The Deadly Sin of Cleverness. The irresistible urge to be clever and to parade one's cleverness is the force underlying many of these disastrous approaches to presentation strategy. And puns appear to be the most tempting Loreleis that attract copy writers. For example, one presentation that is aimed at selling a sophisticated laser printer promises that "with the right tools you can nail the competition," and then supplies a photo of an assortment of worn hammers and other hand tools, along with an assortment of nails, to complete the pun. Still not satisfied with the display of his or her cleverness, the writer goes on to beat the pun over the head a bit more by showing the reader how to "hit the nail on the head." If the reader can find the patience to plod on and endure more of this heavy-handed humor, the reader finally discovers what the advertiser is selling and learns of some promised benefits, but they seem rather anticlimactic by now.

All of these are guilty of the most common sin of sales presentations: They are so busy being clever, boastful, and self-congratulatory that they forget to sell the product or service. They forget to think in terms of the customer's interests—of what they can do for the customer.

Nothing else counts, as far as the client is concerned. The client is not interested in how clever you are, or in being entertained, or in any of the many elaborate, but unsupported, claims you might make. Forget these.

Even the evidence of capability, dependability, honesty, and other attributes necessary to make the sale are of interest only if and after you have presented the one thing the client really wants to know about: what you are going to do for him or her.

That is what captures the client's attention and interest, and that is the only thing that will sustain the client's interest long enough to enable you to present your entire sales argument and employ your sales strategy.

One fallacy responsible for such disasters of presentation, which are found in proposals as well as in other sales literature, is the mistaken notion that claims alone are sales arguments and will be perceived by the client as promised benefits. In fact, some writers of sales copy appear to believe that the more extreme and "louder" the claims of excellence are, the more powerful and persuasive those claims will be. Of course, the opposite effect usually results: The more extravagant the claim, the more unquestioning credulity, even naivete, it demands of the client. Even if the client were to be swayed by your eloquence and claimed excellence, rather than by some specific promises of benefits, you would have to prove that your claims of excellence were justified before the typical client would even accept them, let alone act on them.

Readability and Clarity

One of the cardinal principles of selling is that everything connected with the process of making a buying decision and placing the order should be made as easy as possible for the prospect. Anything the prospect finds difficult, troublesome, or inconvenient in any way discourages the sale. It is for this reason that so many sales appeals include preaddressed, postage-free response envelopes and order cards, many of which require only the recording of a credit card number, along with a name and address, to place the order. (My own mail order office-supplies vendor asked only for the name of my bank and my account number to open my charge account, for example, and we have done business together for more than a half-dozen years since.)

Many examples used here to illustrate the principles of sales presentations were drawn from conventional advertising because they were convenient and obvious examples, but everything illustrated has equal application to proposals. However, probably nowhere is the application to proposals more significant than in the case of making the presentation easy to read and understand. A prospect might fight through a few hundred words of less-than-crystal-clear prose if the interest aroused were great enough, but asking the client to struggle through several dozen pages of stilted and difficult copy is another matter. Many clients faced with that prospect will give it up with a sigh and turn to the next proposal in the stack.

But even that is only one consideration with regard to readability and clarity. There is the matter of communication per se. Your text can be quite accurate and thorough, although difficult to read. But prose can also be easy to read, while failing to be clear. For the client to be either puzzled by your meanings or misinterpret them is just as deadly to your purpose as discouraging the client's reading entirely. You can hardly sell something to the client when the client does not understand what you are selling or precisely what your arguments are.

Therefore, we are actually talking about two separate matters regarding writing per se, and they are not directly related to each other. You are well advised to keep your organization of material, usage of the language, and chosen vocabulary as simple as possible, for ease of reading, but efforts to achieve this must not be permitted to degenerate into a failure to be comprehensive and accurate—to include all necessary detail and to get the facts straight. Both are necessary.

In this respect, you should know, if you do not already, that most of us have several personal vocabularies: We speak with one, we read with a second one, we write with another, and we even think with still another.

The size of individual vocabularies varies quite widely, from as few as 5,000-10,000 words to as many as 40,000-50,000 words. If you are one who is blessed with a large vocabulary, don't permit that blessing to become a curse by trying to utilize all of it in your writing. The real blessing of a large vocabulary is that it is an enormous asset to your reasoning powers: People with large vocabularies tend to be superior thinkers. Reserve most of that large reserve of words to help you reason well, and try to keep your writing vocabulary within that 10,000- to 20,000-word range. You won't be writing down to anyone, in so doing, but you will be helping yourself develop a brisk and highly readable style.

Promoting and Maintaining Your Professional Image

"Professionalism" has probably as many meanings as "consulting" does, varying according to the individual's bias. Some individuals believe that only physicians and lawyers are truly professionals, but we also make reference sometimes to "professional plumbers" and other tradespeople as professionals. However, inasmuch as consultants normally provide their services on a custom basis, are often entrusted with the client's proprietary and confidential information, and are often given almost carte blanche freedom on the client's premises, the relationship must be based on great respect for and trust in the consultant.

Accordingly, it is essential that you develop and maintain a highly professional image, and I will define that here for our own purposes without regard to how others might define it. Here the term will mean that you must maintain an image that goes beyond mere competence. It must be one of authority in your field of specialization, but must reflect also dignity, integrity, and dedication to your profession.

Should your proposal undermine that image in some way, it will represent a peril to your prospects for success. To protect your image, and even to enhance it, you must use the language well and, at the minimum, avoid such faux pas as misspellings, ungrammatical constructions, and unintentionally humorous misuses of language. The latter types of error convey a strong image of a semieducated individual, which is hardly what you would wish. Here are two examples of such unintended humor detected in proposals that had a deadly effect:

☐ One consultant was attempting to explain that the proposed design for a piece of equipment that would serve a critical function would have a "backup" set of duplicate components. Unfortunately, he referred to this feature as the "duplicity" of the design, which the client found highly amusing but not reassuring as far as the image of the consultant's professionalism was concerned.

☐ Another consultant wished to explain in his proposal the system by which identifying numbers would be assigned to a large array of terminals in a complex equipment design. He introduced the subject with a headline that announced the subject to be discussed next as the "assignation" of the terminals, again with disastrous damage to his image as a presumably well-educated professional.

Such blunders can be avoided. For one thing, it's a good idea to have someone edit or review your copy to detect errors and do something about them. But it's even more important to avoid trying to sound impressive through the use of language. The way to be impressive in your writing is in offering clear expositions and ample details. You can prove your competence through offering the detail, for anyone can generalize and philosophize, but the presentation of accurate and comprehensive detail demonstrates that you know what you are talking about. The words will not impress the client; the information will, if it is adequate, to the point, detailed, and easily understandable.

Make Your Presentation Believable

The offering of comprehensive and accurate detail is itself a powerful influence in making your arguments credible, but there are other elements that contribute to credibility. One is the avoidance of hyperbole and superlatives generally as discussed earlier. Another is frankness, such as ready admission that problems may be encountered (as compared with the "soothing syrup" of bland but unsupported promises that some proposal writers offer). And still another is either avoid making your promises appear too extravagant or, if you believe that you can deliver truly remarkable results and wish to promise them, be sure that your proofs do justice to the promises and are in proportion to them.

Make Your Appeals Persuasive

Persuasiveness of your appeals has been an underlying theme throughout this chapter so far, and is a general objective in all those other discussions. However, it is useful to single this out and establish it as a special objective to remind yourself that all sales presentations have persuasion as their ultimate objective, and that everything in the presentation must contribute to that ultimate goal.

GENERAL ADMONITIONS ABOUT WRITING STYLE

Part of the image you should be trying to develop and nourish should be that of being thoroughly businesslike, which means alert, efficient, and direct. And to encourage that image in your writing you should develop a crisp and vigorous writing style. Here are a few tips to help you do that:

1. Use active voice, rather than passive voice. This sentence is itself an example. "Proposals should be written in active voice," on the other hand, expresses this idea in passive voice.

2. Use frequent stops in long sentences—colons, semi-colons, and dashes—especially for interjections. Long sentences with stops are the same as a series of several short sentences and are as easy to read.

3. Get to the point. Ideally, telegraph the point when you introduce the subject. Or, at the least, march directly to the point without detours.

4. Make positive statements as often as possible, and avoid over-qualification of statements. Even when you are not certain of the point

or for some reason cannot state something as an absolute fact it is possible to present it without sounding fearful and indecisive. (Perhaps President Jimmy Carter was not as hesitant and indecisive as he appeared to be, but he might as well have been for that was the public perception.) For example, instead of hedging a statement around with many qualifications, often found in research papers in such expressions as "The indicators tend to suggest the possibility that . . . ," say something such as, "The possibility indicated is . . . ," which commits you no more than the first version does, but makes you appear far more authoritative and confident in what you are saying.

There is no doubt that to the sensitive and perceptive reader (and you must assume that the client is that kind of reader) your mental set manages to come through between the lines of what you write. Unless your writing reflects confidence in what you are saying and what you are proposing, it is unlikely that the client will have that confidence. Confidence—or the lack of it—is something you share with your reader, whether by intent or not.

The need is for balance: confidence; promises of desirable results; desired, clear expression; easy readability; and positive statements balanced by reasonableness, accurate detail, and substantial evidence to support all promises and claims.

APPLYING THE IDEAS

But now let's begin to look more closely at how you can apply these ideas to the specific proposal elements. The suggested general proposal format, with brief notes explaining the main section titles and subheads, is presented in Figure 19. This is, of course, a generalized format, and must be adapted to each specific situation, for some situations may require large, formal proposals offering entire teams of specialists and their services, whereas others will be one-person projects. Still, whether you offer only your own resume or those of a dozen associates or employees, the principles are the same: The client wishes to know how well you understand the requirement in its essence, what your management philosophy and procedures are to be, what your technical/professional qualifications are, what your specific experience is, whom to call to verify your experience and competence, and other such matters.

SECTION I: INTRODUCTION

ABOUT THE OFFEROR	A brief introduction, with your basic qualifications; scene setting; explain that details come later
UNDERSTANDING OF THE REQUIREMENT	The requirement in essence, with obscuring trivia stripped away for a clear view of the central need or problem; sets stage for next section

SECTION II: DISCUSSION

THE REQUIREMENT	Elaboration of the understanding, bringing in of related considerations, establishment of basis for analysis
ANALYSIS	Exploration of all possibilities, surfacing of probable problems (potential "worry items"), pro and con discussions of alternatives
APPROACH	Logical conclusion of analysis, pointing to synthesis of design; identifying approach opted for and justifying decision; scene setting for next section

SECTION III: PROPOSED PROJECT

PROJECT ORGANIZATION	Description of team and/or task organization to implement approach opted for; logic of organization explained
MANAGEMENT	Principles, quality control, cost control, other controls and administration
PLANS AND PROCEDURES	Procedures, forms, standards, criteria, liaison with client
STAFF	General description of self, associates, and/or others
DELIVERABLE ITEMS	Qualitative and quantitative specifications in detail
SCHEDULES	Chart, tabular, or milestone presentations
RESUME(S)	Employees/associates who will provide services

SECTION IV: QUALIFICATIONS AND EXPERIENCE

RELEVANT CURRENT AND RECENT PROJECTS	Tabular data, brief descriptions, names, phone numbers of clients
RESOURCES	Facilities, equipment, personnel, other relevant resources
REFERENCES, TESTIMONIALS	Supplement to project histories, including certificates, letters of appreciation, other such evidence of merit

MISCELLANEOUS

FRONT MATTER	Title page, table contents, response matrix, executive summary
APPENDICES	If/as needed

Figure 19. Each proposal section and subsection and brief definitions.

THE MATTER OF HEADLINES

The format shown here uses generic titles and headlines, rather than those that should be used in specific cases. A presentation strategy must be developed for each case, according to the merits and circumstances of each individual case, but there are some principles that should be followed for all cases. One of these is that to maximize the effectiveness of the presentation strategy, everything, including titles, headlines, figure captions, and table captions, should be conceived and composed for maximum contribution to the selling process.

The first section or chapter of a proposal is normally introductory, introducing both the consultant and the consultant's understanding and preliminary appraisal of the requirement. Almost everyone therefore titles it INTRODUCTION, GENERAL, or by other such generic title, thereby missing an early opportunity to make an important point. To get the maximum benefit compose a title that reflects some important benefit, theme, or virtue of what you are offering. Work at making this an attention-getter, while it still relates directly to your offer. And if you can tie this in to somehow support your main strategy, so much the better.

Here are a few examples, some hypothetical, some drawn from real-life case histories:

A NEW BROOM . . . (the proposer was bidding for an ongoing contract and had gotten word that the client was dissatisfied with the incumbent and wanted to make a change.)
A DIFFERENT KIND OF SERVICE (you have something new and different to offer, especially when that is central to your strategy.)
A FRESH VIEWPOINT (the proposer believed that he could offer an entirely new and far better approach to solving the client's problems.)
SOLUTIONS DESIGNED TO MATCH PROBLEMS (a proposer who wishes to stress the custom-designed nature of his services.)

The subheads, listed generically for the first section as ABOUT THE OFFEROR and UNDERSTANDING OF THE REQUIRE-MENT, should likewise be tailored to the situation. ABOUT THE OFFEROR might become SCIENTIFIC PROGRAMMING SPE-CIALISTS, WE'RE SMALL ENOUGH TO MAKE YOU OUR

(MOST IMPORTANT CLIENT), or whatever suits your situation and your strategy. (The idea expressed by that latter example of a subhead is a reminder that large consulting firms often tend to treat small contracts, especially from small clients, rather casually. It is thus a powerful strategy to not only overcome the possible liability of being a small consulting firm, but even convert that into an asset. (Of course, you might go the other way and say something such as WE'RE LARGE ENOUGH TO HAVE ALL THE RESOURCES TO SATISFY YOUR NEED, if you are a sizable firm and want to make that a sales argument.) And UNDERSTANDING OF THE REQUIREMENT should likewise be changed to something more pungent, such as A CLOSER LOOK AT THE REQUIREMENT or THE ESSENCE OF THE REQUIREMENT. However, although those are improvements over the generic subhead, even those can be further improved by composing a subhead that is more directly relevant to the individual proposal. If the proposal were in response to that hypothetical client with a problem of unreliable reports coming from the computer, the subhead might dramatize the requirement in its essence along the lines of THE TRUE REQUIREMENT: FIND THE *CAUSE* OF UNRELIABLE COMPUTER-GENERATED REPORTS. That, of course, is almost ideal for laying the groundwork to discuss the requirement in the second section of your proposal, which might then get a title following up that idea, such as SEVEN POSSIBLE CAUSES FOR UNRELIABLE COMPUTER-GENERATED REPORTS or THE MOST EFFICIENT WAY TO TRACK DOWN THE TROUBLE and even a subtitle, such as A DISCUSSION OF ANALYTICAL TECHNIQUES AND TROUBLESHOOTING METHODS. The various headlines in your discussion section would then guide the reader through the main points and main logic of the approach and the methodology you propose there.

Of course, if you happen to have a special technique or special resources, such as a proprietary program, perhaps, to help you do this job more efficiently or more effectively than anyone else is liable to be able to do it, by all means strengthen those by working direct references to and indications of those into your headlines and titles.

How Long Should a Headline Be?

Some of those headlines and titles can become fairly long, even two or more lines, as some of the examples used here demonstrate. That should not stay your hand. First of all, there is nothing wrong with lengthy titles and headlines, popular belief to the contrary. Book titles, which themselves serve as headlines when well conceived, furnish many examples of lengthy titles that did not hamper the sale of the books and probably contributed to their success. Here are titles of several highly successful books, some of them even best sellers:

HOW TO PROSPER IN THE COMING BAD YEARS
HOW TO FORM YOUR OWN CORPORATION WITHOUT A
LAWYER FOR UNDER $50.00
HOW TO SUCCEED AS AN INDEPENDENT CONSULTANT
HOW TO WRITE, PUBLISH AND MARKET YOUR BOOK
HOW I TURN ORDINARY COMPLAINTS INTO THOUSANDS
OF DOLLARS

The supposed rule about keeping titles and headlines short is not even conventional wisdom; it is pure mythology, perpetrated and perpetuated by individuals expressing their personal biases. The almost unlimited number of successful "exceptions" reveals that rather clearly. It is, in fact, in the same class as that bias that created the myth of the need for lots of white space around advertising copy, under the misconception that the reader will refuse to read lengthy copy in an advertisement.

The simple fact is that experience refutes this entirely. Among the most successful advertisements, including many that ran for years without change, are those that consist of nothing but a simple headline and a full page of solid text. Such copy itself has often used fairly long headlines, which is itself revelatory. Here are some of those headlines, some still in use today:

I WANT YOU TO HAVE THIS BEFORE IT'S TOO LATE
THE LAZY MAN'S WAY TO RICHES
DO YOU MAKE THESE EMBARRASSING MISTAKES IN EN-
GLISH?
THEY LAUGHED WHEN I SAT DOWN AT THE PIANO, BUT
WHEN I STARTED TO PLAY!
TO PEOPLE WHO WANT TO WRITE—BUT CAN'T GET
STARTED

GREAT NEW DISCOVERY KILLS KITCHEN ODORS QUICK!—MAKES INDOOR AIR "COUNTRY FRESH"

Even if there were any validity to the idea that titles and headlines must be short and "punchy," the goal of making them so would have to be subject to a rule of practicality. The title or headline that fails to do what you want it to do is worthless, no matter how short and punchy it is. So if you cannot devise a short title or headline that suits your needs, you've little choice left, logically, except to use a longer one.

The idea that the title or headline must be short to be effective is nonsense. The simple fact is that if your headline or title captures the client's attention by appealing to his or her own interest—i.e., if the client perceives that it is in his or her own interest to read what you have to say—wild horses will not stop him or her from reading your headline and as much body copy as you care to offer. For that and for no other reason, those books and advertisements cited here as examples were and remain successful, some of them after running continuously for many years. Only when and if the client ceases to identify his or her personal interest in what you say will he or she stop reading and go on to something else. It's as simple—and as complex—as that. Go back and study the several examples of titles and headlines listed here and see if they do not appeal directly to the self-interests of many potential readers.

How to Develop Titles and Headlines

There is only one really sensible rule for judging how long titles, headlines, and copy generally must be: The titles, headlines, and copy must be exactly long enough to do the job, and not one comma longer. Of course, that leaves us with the problem of determining just what that means: How long is "long enough to do the job"?

The answer is clearly implied in one of the many observations about the editing process. Someone who is obviously quite familiar with the processes and problems of writing and its related functions has stated that editing is most typically a function of reducing the bulk of a writer's copy, probably eliminating about one-third of the average manuscript.

Like most generalizations, this one has too many exceptions for it to qualify as anything resembling a rule or principle, but it does reflect (1) the common problem of excessive verbosity on the part of a great many writers and (2) the fundamental truth that even the most skilled writers usually overwrite (sometimes deliberately) in their first drafts and then tighten their manuscripts up in revision through boiling out a great deal of non-essential material and/or finding more efficient ways to express their ideas.

This latter idea is especially appropriate to writing advertising and sales materials, such as proposals, including titles and headlines. The best practice, for most of us, is to write a first draft that says everything you can think of that is relevant. In that draft you concern yourself primarily with including everything that contributes to the client's understanding of what you propose and to persuasive arguments for your proposal. It is more urgent, in this draft, to see to it that you have not left out anything important than it is to be eloquent and efficient in your language.

Once you have satisfied yourself that you have included all the necessary and relevant information, you can begin the self-editing process to edit out extraneous material, tighten expression, and polish your language generally.

With titles and headlines the process often has to be varied somewhat because quite often the headline or title you select proves to be entirely inappropriate to what you have written. Therefore, you must maintain an open mind about titles and headlines and be prepared to edit and revise them ruthlessly, or even to scrap them entirely and make a fresh beginning at coining an effective combination of words.

In recognition of this truth, my own practice is to go a step beyond rewriting original titles. Instead, I generally use generic titles and headlines (some of us call those "working titles") that I do not intend to keep, but plan to scrap later, when I edit and revise my manuscript and prepare a final draft. At that time, I study the copy first to identify the most appealing benefit promised or evidence provided in each discussion. Having decided what that is I begin to work on headlines and subheads for each discussion. And when I have formulated those, I work on titles for sections and captions or titles for illustrations and tables, working these over until I believe that I have polished them for maximum effect and minimum number of words, each consistent with achieving maximum effect.

THREE BASIC KINDS OF PRESENTATION STRATEGY

The strategic objective we have been discussing here has been that of getting attention, and we have been examining one general strategy that is always available in pursuit of this: devising titles and headlines that command attention through appealing to the client's self-interest and, whenever possible, dramatizing the message. But there are other ways to get attention and capture interest. But before exploring the several other ways, let's recognize that there are at least three basic approaches to this, each of which represents a different kind of presentation strategy:

1. The copy itself: what your proposal says and how it says it.
2. Cosmetic effects and special elements of the proposal.
3. Special devices related to, but not integral parts of, your proposal.

THE PROPOSAL COPY

More About Titles and Headlines

We have already discussed a major element of your proposal that gives you an opportunity to capture attention and sustain interest: the titles and headlines. To get maximum benefits from these not only must give a great deal of thought to composing these but you must use them freely. Used well, they do more than dramatize and stress important points in your presentation generally and sales arguments especially; they guide the client through your proposal and lighten the burden of reading by serving as guideposts so that the main messages come through, even if the client does not read every word with deep consciousness. (Remember that rule of advertising that you must sell it in the headline, which then renders the body copy far less important.)

In recognition of this, it is important that you have a title, headline, subhead, or caption for every important point in your proposal. Titles and major headlines should summarize or draw attention to major points you wish to make but all points, including lesser ones, should be covered, in the philosophy that even if the client were to read only the titles and headlines he or she would have gotten most of the main message. (This alone justifies the titles and headlines, and the effort to develop them.)

Test the entire array of your titles and major headlines (they should be in your table of contents) by scanning them to verify that they accomplish three things:

1. They provide a reasonably detailed outline/abstract of your proposal.
2. They present and point out every important point in your proposal.
3. They offer a good sales argument for your proposal by providing promises and proofs.

Section I: Introduction

The introduction is brief, and yet it is quite important. If you are submitting a requested proposal, as distinct from an unsolicited proposal, you can expect the client to read it as a necessity. But if you want the client to read with interest, you must do something *immediately*—in the introduction—to capture that interest. Capturing the client's attention and interest—"hooking" it, in the vernacular—should be your main objective here.

About the Offeror (First Subsection)

One way to capture the reader's interest immediately is to introduce the most attractive, novel, and/or dramatic element of your proposal immediately. Ordinarily, you use the ABOUT THE OFFEROR opening discussion to furnish your business name, a few words to qualify and explain your interest and qualifications, summarize your credentials briefly, and advise the client that all of these will be offered in greater detail later.

These summary explanations should be dramatized here for their greatest effect. If you happen to have something impressive or novel to say about any of these things, by all means do so here. Otherwise, search out the most impressive, novel, dramatic, or appealing promise/evidence/fact in your proposal and introduce it here on page 1.

Obviously you can't do this until you have written your proposal and decided precisely what to offer and how you would do the job. Therefore, the introduction is written last—when you know exactly what it is that you are introducing—as introductions generally are. If you are the type of writer who needs to work with a "lead," as I do, you will probably need to draft a working introduction, which you expect to scrap later, when you write the final introduction and introduce that interest-capturing jewel you have extracted, usually that item which is at the heart of your program strategy. Here are a few examples of such items:

☐ A promise of extraordinary results, with only a hint of why and how you can offer this and the promise of details to follow shortly.

☐ Ditto the above for remarkably low costs or speedy results.

☐ Hints or even brief identification of a serious problem and the promise of a soon-to-come explanation of how it will be solved.

☐ Some extraordinary resource available or searched out especially for the project, such as a well-known authority persuaded to serve on the project or the pledged assistance of some prestigious organization.

The strategy underlying such tactics as the above is fairly obvious. Most of these items are teasers, arousing the client's curiosity and interest through promising that full revelation will be made in later pages, but all bear some direct suggestion that the client will benefit directly from the proposed program.

Understanding of the Requirement (Second Subsection)

This, too, should be brief, but it is an outstanding opportunity to capture client interest early. Always remember that the client may not be expert in the work required and presumably is not, since he or she is seeking help. Therefore the client may very well be not only intensely interested in your view of the problem, but may be greatly influenced by it. At the least, most clients read your feedback analysis of the requirement as a first indicator of your capability.

The "understanding" portion of your proposal's first section is therefore an opportunity to help the client gain a better understanding of the true problem, while you can "score points" here, as you get down to cases (down to the true *essence* of the requirement). Keep this discussion short, since it should identify and focus entirely on the core issue of the requirement. (Otherwise, you may blur the focus and obscure the client's view of your main point.) Show here that you are not distracted by side issues, but are capable of keeping your eye firmly on the ball. However, this subsection should also introduce something to help hook the client—build interest—even more firmly. First make it abundantly clear that you are deliberately focusing here on only the essential or core problem and will analyze and discuss the requirement overall more discursively in pages to come. If at all possible, raise a worry item here and promise to have a great deal more to say about it soon. Or, as an alternative, suggest some technical boon or special asset you will provide, again with the promise of fuller discussion soon.

The purpose is, of course, to build suspense and desire to learn more about these questions you raise. Accordingly, for maximum impact you must link these to something important to the client, and the most important thing at this point is the overall success or failure of the entire project. Therefore, don't waste time and energy on items that affect relatively trivial matters, but seek out those that bear directly on and seriously affect the probability of overall success or failure.

Section II: Discussion

Section II is the section which is usually the key to the entire sales effort. Here is where you must do the bulk of your selling, for while it is ostensibly the technical discussion that explains your understanding and approach to satisfying the requirement, it is also your principal sales argument. If you fail to convince the client here that yours is the most desirable plan or set of services, it is unlikely that you will be able to do so elsewhere in the proposal or by other means than the proposal, no matter how well you reinforce your arguments with other proposal sections and/or other related sales activity. In doing so you should include at least the following subsections.

The Requirement

The understanding summarized in the first section bridges directly into this section, where you unfold your program strategy after first elaborating on your understanding to explore the requirement more fully. Here you must continue and expand the discussion, especially those elements about which you have raised questions or made promises. Here you should present your analysis, "thinking out loud" so that the client can fully understand the logic of the process and develop a full appreciation of the validity of the worry items you project and the results you promise.

Analysis

It is in this subsection that you develop and employ your competitive strategy by (1) demonstrating greater insight than your competitors do into the problems and needs of the client, (2) revealing greater wisdom than others in responding to those needs and problems, and (3) unveiling your special methods for being less costly, faster, more reliable, or better than others in some way. Here, too, is where you try to persuade the client to make specific comparisons of your offer with that of others. The ways already suggested for doing this are relatively subtle, however, and depend on the chance that the client will make specific, point-by-point comparisons, in addition to the inevitable general comparison. But subtlety is totally out of place in most sales presentations; you need to be "unsubtle" without being crude. One way to do this in a proposal is to make an actual statement of the qualifications you believe necessary for success in satisfying the client's requirement. This, if it is persuasive, virtually compels the client to make that point-by-point comparison that is usually an effective competitive strategy when handled well.

Approach

To introduce this idea of listing specific qualifications required to handle the assignment successfully, you must somehow demonstrate the logic of (prove the validity of) your analysis, and this is best done in some striking manner that focuses sharply on that logical progression of ideas that builds the argument to a desired climax and conclusion, your approach to the project. (Many government RFPs announce that the government will evaluate each proposer's approach as part of an assessment of the technical quality of each proposal.) An excellent way to dramatize this idea and draw special attention to it is by giving it special treatment, such as by making it a figure, with suitable introduction, of course, rather than including it in the main text. Figure 20 suggests a format for doing this, using the example cited earlier of the Postal Service requirement calling for materials for on-the-job training of maintenance technicians for bulk mail plants.

Note the head data and, especially, the "most critical task" item. In this case, as in many others, there is a task that is not only critical to success of the project, but is not well recognized. In this case, it was not readily apparent that the consultant would be required to identify the maintenance requirements and design the maintenance programs (electrical/electronic and mechanical), before designing the training programs themselves. The client had furnished no information on course content, evidently completely overlooking the need for this, and this really changed the very nature of the qualifications required. The request had been issued apparently with the thought that consultants specializing in training design and development would be the chief respondents, but this consideration raised a question as to consultant qualifications necessary, as the figure shows. It argues and presents evidence supporting the position that competence in training-system development is not enough, and that the consultant must have technical/professional qualifications in understanding of electrical/ electronic and mechanical technology and systems, and in the design and development of maintenance programs for such equipment and systems.

Of course, to achieve maximum impact in designing this strategy of specifying your own qualifications as the necessary ones for successful performance you must have some idea who you are competing against and what your competitors' own strengths and weaknesses are. However, bear in mind also that you are always dealing with the client's perception of truth, and you must assume that the client knows about each proposer only what each proposal says. Therefore, if your competitors fail to grasp all these points and thus fail to describe and list all those special qualifications (a common shortcoming in many, many proposals) they might as well not have them at all, for the client will assume then that they do not have such capabilities. And even if they are able or willing to say, "me too," in later followup presentations, they are in seriously weakened positions, to your own resulting advantage.

This kind of presentation is in itself a major competitive strategy in situations where you believe that the client has overlooked some important point that you can make capital of, as in this case and in many others. (Remember the point made much earlier that it is often possible to actually persuade the client to accept arguments which are actually your own modification of the requirement?)

Figure 20, then, turns out to be a summary integrating the most important points of the client's request with your proposed approach and main strategies, presented in a small package that is virtually an abstract of your entire proposal, while it focuses on key issues and points. It can only be developed as you build up your proposal generally, and most of it is a reflection of the substance of the Section II discussions and presentations, although it can be used on a much wider basis, as a result of its broad scope and comprehensive coverage.

In many cases this tabular figure is such a powerful tool that it can be used effectively in additional and possibly even more important ways than in support of your Section II discussions. In fact, you might do well to introduce this figure quite early in your proposal, in your introductory section or even in the front matter, and use it as an attention getter and interest-arousing hook on its own. It is quite suitable as a basis for frequent references throughout the proposal and can thus become a major tool for exploiting your strategies. It can, in fact, be the chief marketing weapon for your entire presentation, along with the functional flowchart, as an effective means for aiding the client in following your arguments and understanding the logic of your approach to satisfying the requirement.

Section III: Proposed Project

In some respects this is the true essence of your response, for this is where you truly commit yourself to specific actions and end items to be delivered to the client. The main objective here is to deliver the true proof of your offer: what you propose to *do*, in totally specific terms. Previous sections of your proposal have theorized and philoso-

Basic Requirement: Develop on-the-job materials for bulk-mail maintenance technicians to be trained for work in 21 bulk-mail centers.

Most Critical Task: Design and develop maintenance data and maintenance program for each option.

Most Important Secondary Problem: High turnover (attrition) rate of technicians leaving Postal Service and going on to other employment after heavy Postal Service investment in individual's training.

- -

Special Problem: Much of the equipment is new, virtually prototype, with no maintenance history on which to base development of curriculum and weighting of course content.

- -

Important Design Objectives and Approaches to Them

1. Design maintenance program especially for bulk-mail equipment: Research, compile list of and technical data on all bulk-mail equipment; analyze and project estimated maintenance needs. (Devise and perform failure-probability analyses.)
2. Structure training to minimize turnover of trained technicians: Avoid overtraining, to minimize turnover of technicians. (Confine course content to Postal Service equipment and provide technical coverage only to depth/extent required for Postal service maintenance.)

- -

General Qualifications Required

1. Technical knowledge/experience in electrical/electronic and mechanical equipment and typical maintenance needs and practices.
2. Experience in design/development of sophisticated maintenance systems for electrical/electronic and mechanical equipment.
3. Capability for gaining access to and using technical data on Postal Service bulk-mail equipment.
4. Capability for development of maintenance-needs projections on as well as qualitative, basis, drawn from research.
5. Capability for translating of data into comprehensive and suitably weighted training specification.
6. Knowledge/experience in training-systems design generally, including development of all documentation necessary, and in on-the-job systems especially.

Figure 20. Major strategies implemented in a single presentation.

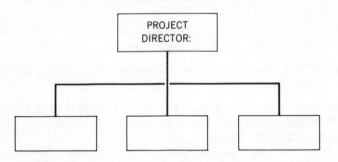

Figure 21. Typical organization chart.

phized. This section must be a specification of what you pledge your-self to do and what you commit yourself to deliver. This is the essence of the contract you offer to sign.

Management Subsection

Management is often a prime concern with clients. The elements that many proposal writers neglect here include, especially, quality control and specific procedures. Specificity and detail are the key elements here, and that applies to all elements of management, including orga-nization, controls, deliverable items, and schedules, as well as those two elements already mentioned.

Here again you can gain an advantage over competitors by the mere fact of being entirely specific, where many proposal writers are defen-sive and unsure, and so they do whatever they can to avoid specific commitment.

Graphics Elements

Graphics are as helpful here as they are elsewhere. If the requirement is such that it requires a staff of several people, you must have an organization chart of some kind, as in Figure 21. Schedule commit-ments may be made by a tabular schedule (Figure 22) but is often more useful if presented as part of a milestone chart, (Figure 23), since this kind of schedule presentation aids the client in visualizing the interdependence of the various events. And resumes may be of-fered here or in the next section, but wherever they are offered, the almost inevitable question of format arises.

ITEM	WORKING DAYS AFTER AWARD
Preliminary meeting	1
Report of initial analysis	10
Client review, comments	20
Submission of revised plan	30
Work begins	35
Draft of final report	90
Client review, comments	120
Revision, submission of revised report	150
Client signoff	180

Figure 22. Tabular schedule of events.

Working days after award →

```
              0   20   40   60   80  100  120  140  160  180
- - - - - - - - - - - - - - - - - - - - - - - - - - - - - - - - -

First meeting _____

Report initial analysis _____

Client review, comments _____

Submit revised plan _____

Work begins _____

Draft of final report _____

Client review, comments _____

Submit revised final report _____

Client signoff _____
```

Figure 23. Milestone chart as schedule.

Resumes

In the question of resume formats, many proposal writers have the deplorable tendency to confuse the resume requirements of a proposal with those of a job-seeking enterprise and to make at least two basic mistakes in the presentation of resumes in the proposal. One is to structure the resume as one would for a job application, and the other is to use a boilerplated or standard resume for all proposals, without regard to the specific needs of each requirement and each proposal seeking a contract. If you are to invest the time and money in a proposal, which is usually a significant investment, it is foolish to try to save an insignificant part of your investment by using a standardized resume. The resumes should be customized for each proposal, using a format along the lines of Figure 24.

The format suggested there is such that it is possible to revise resumes rather easily for each new proposal, especially if you are using a word processor. The logic of the format is rather obvious, of course, tailored to the individual proposal and the requirement to which it responds.

Priority in presenting information in a resume should always be given to accomplishments first (patents, awards, outstanding achievements of any kind, as long as they are somehow relevant to the requirement), to experience second (previous positions, most relevant and important ones first), and then to education and educational achievements (degrees, honors, awards).

The customization of the resume to each proposal is thus primarily in the position proposed and the introductory paragraph. The remaining data—which is entirely amplifying detail—can usually be kept unchanged. This makes it fairly easy to customize resumes for each new proposal, especially if you use a word processor, the magic of which greatly simplifies copying a file and revising it quickly.

One presentation that belongs in this section of many proposals is a tabulated estimate of tasks, assignments, and hours (Figure 25). There are several reasons for including such a chart or table in this section:

1. It is risky to fail to do this, for constructing the chart compels you to plan in detail, rather than in broad terms, and thus makes you calculate effort and costs realistically. (It's quite easy, otherwise, to persuade yourself to take the easy way out by "ballparking" your es-

Name

Normal position

(e.g., President, Systems Analyst)

Proposed position

(e.g., Project Director)

Summary introduction: General qualifications in narrative format—most relevant achievements; experience; education; special training, including current employment; in order of importance/relevance to project without regard to chronology. (Keep brief for maximum focus and impact.)

Experience details: Chronology of positions/functions/assignments in current and previous employment. (Precise dates not required; approximate time periods satisfactory.)

Education, other details.

Figure 24. Suggested format for resumes in proposals.

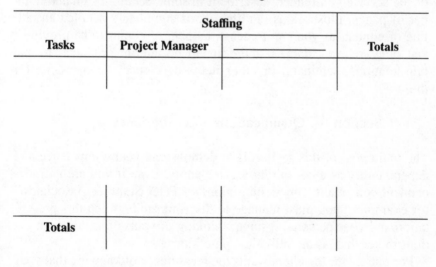

TASKS, ASSIGNMENTS, AND EFFORT REQUIRED

Tasks	Staffing		Totals
	Project Manager	——————	
Totals			

Figure 25. Suggested format for presentation of task/labor estimates.

timates, with the attendant hazard of badly underestimating or over-estimating the cost and effort required, unless you force yourself to the discipline of some detailed planning. This gives you confidence in your estimates.

2. The chart is excellent evidence of your mastery of the requirement and what is needed to satisfy it, on the basis that this represents planning detail, and that is itself evidence of capability for designing and managing the work. It usually gives the client the same confidence in your estimates that you feel. In general, moreover, an abundance of detail in a proposal is almost always favorably impressive.

3. It demonstrates the validity of your cost estimates.

4. It is a silent but eloquent commentary on the proposal of any competitor who is less frank and less thorough.

It is wise to be equally thorough in all other areas of this section. Strive to present as much detail in your qualitative and quantitative descriptions or estimates of deliverable items, for example. If you are going to develop a manual or report of some kind as the end product of the service you render, describe it in some detail—estimated number of pages, illustrations, and tables; as completely detailed an outline of content as you can forecast; number of copies to be provided; and other relevant data. If there are to be interim products, formal presentations, seminars, or other items developed, do the same for those.

Section IV: Qualifications and Experience

The main goal of this section is to demonstrate your competence and dependability as a consulting service entity. Even if you are an independent consultant, functioning alone—"Peter Smith & Associates," for example—you must manage to discriminate between this presentation and your personal resume, thinking of yourself as an organization, rather than as an individual practitioner.

For one thing, the client wants the reassurance of knowing that your services have been and are acceptable to others, that you are capable of carrying out the proposed program in both technical/professional knowledge and abilities and in the practical sense of having the resources to do so: relevant experience/accomplishments, physical facilities, staffing resources, and anything else required.

Some clients become concerned that the consultant may be straining his or her resources to cope with the requirement, and that even a relatively small problem or small miscalculation could cause the program to abort. So one objective in writing this section is to point out that you have adequate resources for the program, so that you can fall back on a reserve of whatever is needed, as a kind of insurance.

In previous sections you have worked at selling the client on and building client confidence in your plans and personal credentials. Now you must sell the client on and build client confidence in the capabilities and reliability of the professional entity you represent, whether that is simply you alone as an independent, sole practitioner or a larger business entity. Following are descriptions of the kinds of information you must provide here to achieve the objectives listed for this section of your proposal.

Relevant Current and Recent Projects

Whether the client requests it or not, a presentation of current and recent relevant projects and clients is a useful item. Of course, many projects are confidential, and many make you privy to confidential and proprietary information. Many of your clients may not wish to have even the mere fact of some of their projects revealed without their express permission. It is usually wise to request that permission before identifying clients or revealing information about current and recent projects.

Within whatever constraints that may impose—to the extent that those constraints permit you to—this is the kind of information this subsection should include:

Name, size, type of project.
Relevant details.
Name of client.
Brief contract history: degree of success, adherence to schedule and budget, other indicators of success.
Contact person (individual who can verify data), with telephone number.

The specific project descriptors should be presented in order of importance and relevance to the proposal. Therefore, like the resumes, this table should not be boilerplated, although possibly many of the individual project descriptors may be. They are probably most efficiently presented in a tabular format, but a new table should be organized to suit each proposal. Again, if the descriptors are written up as elements of one or more computer/word processor files, reorganizing them into a new table for each proposal is relatively simple.

Proposing Organization(s)

Clients are usually interested in the specific organizational unit offering the proposal. If you are a department or group within your company, explain this and show it with some kind of organization chart. Show, also, where and how it reports in the organization, especially to reflect the degree of control the proposed project directory is likely to enjoy in the organization. (Show the client that the project is important enough to you to merit some priority of staffing by assigning a senior person to head it and direct the work.) If you are an organization made up of more than a single subdivision within a corporate entity, it is appropriate to explain this, illustrate it with a corporate organization chart, and show where the proposing entity fits into the overall structure.

Facilities and Resources

A description of available physical facilities—office space, office equipment, computers, laboratory resources, warehouse space, or other—is often relevant and appropriate. This, again, can be a simple tabular listing, but it can be supported with drawings and/or photographs.

Software resources—a library, files, computer programs, or other such facilities.

Staff resources not described earlier, such as other staff persons who could be made available to support the project, if needed.

Access to additional facilities and resources, beyond those that are integral parts of your own organization, so that you can provide additional insurance against the program becoming crippled in any way. Those might include resumes of associates available to you, of laboratory facilities you have made preliminary arrangements with, or of other organizations who have agreed to back you up, if necessary.

References and Testimonials

The names of current and recent clients appearing in your table of relevant current and recent projects, if you have been able to list a few, are references, of course. But it is always useful to present a list of references generally (again, with permission of those listed) and especially useful to include such testimonials as laudatory letters of appreciation and complimentary remarks in forms rating your seminar and other presentations.

It is usually not difficult to get such letters, after you have been in business for a time, but clients rarely think to send them on their own initiative. On the other hand, many clients will cheerfully furnish such letters if you request them, and you can gather an impressive set of such testimonials in a short while by remembering to ask for them.

Miscellaneous

There are several other parts of the typical proposal, all of which should be at least introduced here, to be discussed in more detail later, although they are "miscellaneous" matters at this point. Some of these fall into the general classification called "front matter," which means that they customarily appear before the first page of text; others are appended or loosely attached to the proposal.

Response Matrix

Without a doubt the most important and most useful piece of front matter in a proposal which is a response to a formal request for proposals is a device I refer to by that title "response matrix." Some discussion will help explain the usefulness of this item.

It was pointed out earlier that clients usually do not have an easy time evaluating proposals on a comparative or even on an absolute basis because each proposer employs a different format and different philosophy of presentation and response to the request. The response matrix helps the client evaluate proposals by offering a guide to each item the client wishes to see covered in the proposal. It is, in fact, a virtual "map" to the proposal, in that sense.

The response matrix is developed along the general lines of Figure 26, which presents a suggested format and a few sample entries. This guides the client's review so that you get "credit" for responding to all requirements, including some that may not have been explicit, but that you deduced from your own study of the client's needs, as stated and as you inferred them from your analyses.

This matrix is useful for all proposals, but is especially valuable when proposing to government agencies, for they make actual numerical evaluations of your proposal's technical merit. It has been amply demonstrated by experience that this type of presentation almost invariably maximizes the technical scores achieved by the proposals in which they are used.

The items are rather easy to gather, if you have made up the checklists at the beginning, as suggested, for they contain the items that go into this matrix. That, in fact, is one of the several reasons for the checklists.

Be sure, in making up your matrix, that you direct the client's attention to your various graphics devices, as well as to textual passages, for the use of the matrix also helps you bring more impact to your presentations in this way—that is, by directing the client to the specific places in your proposal where you make your best and clearest arguments.

The blank right-hand column is for the client's convenience so that he or she may verify and check off your responses and make notations, as well.

Executive Summary

A number of years ago, when I wrote proposals at Philco's Communications and Weapons division in Philadelphia, a standard section of our proposals bore the title "Why Philco Should Be Awarded This Contract." This plainly stated the objective of this section: It was a section in which we summed up the principal selling points of the proposal and asked the client to focus sharply on our main arguments. Today that practice and intent is reflected in most formal proposals in a portion of the front matter entitled "Executive Summary."

REQUEST FOR PROPOSAL	PROPOSAL RESPONSE	
pp. 3, 4: Understanding of the requirement	pp. 1–3	
p. 12: Current/recent experience	pp. 1, 5, 15–18	
p. 14: Facilities and resources	pp. 19–22	

Figure 26.   Format for response matrix.

Nominally that bit of text is intended as an abstract of the proposal, and yet it is not so entitled. It is titled so as to suggest that this is intended for those top-level executives who would not normally read the entire proposal—really have no need to spend time poring over details which are usually of interest to only the technical/professional staff specialists and technical managers. (Of course, despite this, everyone reads the Executive Summary.)

The Executive Summary should summarize the proposal, of course, but it must focus primarily on the benefits and proofs—the reasons for favoring the proposer with the contract. This is its purpose in life, and it should appear in each proposal, whether the client has requested such a summary or not.

Appendices and Exhibits

An appendix is a place to present information that you expect to be of interest to some but not all readers of your proposal. It's the way to avoid burdening readers with details they do not wish to wade through, without denying that information those who will find it useful and do want to see it. That includes such things as additional resumes (although some proposal writers put all resumes in an appendix), drawings, papers from technical journals, reprints of articles, and other such matter.

In some cases, particularly when it is impractical to provide more than one copy of the item (and many proposal requests require multiple copies of the proposal), the term "exhibit" is employed, and the item is not an integral part of the proposal but is an exhibit of the proposal. (However, some people label such items as illustrations in the proposal "exhibit.")

A FEW OTHER DEVICES

There are a number of other devices and ways to strengthen your presentation. These are not truly new or novel as editorial and publications devices, for the most part, but are not used as often as they should be in proposals because proposal writers are usually not familiar with them. In fact, some organizations use what they call a *story-board* approach to proposal writing, which makes use of these devices.

Storyboarding

The term *storyboard* springs from the audiovisual and movie industries, where the storyboarding technique is used as a planning and presentation tool. In its simplest form it consists of a series of simple sketches and accompanying text, somewhat like a cartoon strip. These are organized into logical sequences.

Adapted to proposal writing, the storyboard becomes a bold headline or title at the head of a page, followed by a "blurb" or "gloss," followed by amplifying text. The goal is to present a new topic, in this format, on every page. But even if that is not always possible, as it often is not, every new topic does begin on a new page, with its headline and blurb.

Blurbs and Glosses

The gloss is a rather time-honored device, found even today in many formal textbooks, where it appears as a marginal note in small print, summarizing the text alongside which it appears.

A blurb is just a bit different. It is a brief statement, such as the summary of an article or some intriguing element of an article, which usually appears under the title of the article in a periodical, although more than one blurb may appear in a given text. (Significantly, however, the term is also applied to brief advertising messages and/or brief text used as standard descriptors of some item.)

In the storyboard technique, the blurb appears under a bold headline at the top of the page, and the blurb has as its purpose summing up some important substance of the page, almost as an explanatory subtitle or abstract of the page. However, its purpose is to sell, and it is used to make the greatest contribution possible to that function.

Used together, all these many devices, tactics, and techniques can double your chances for success. And even if you have a truly outstanding offer to make, you need to do these things to get a fair reading and fair consideration of your offer.

GRAPHICS

Graphic aids—illustrations—are more than a convenience; they are a necessity. The consultant who tries to write a viable proposal without using adequate graphic aids is working under a self-imposed handicap that is likely to prove crippling, if not fatal.

WHY GRAPHICS ARE A MUST IN PROPOSAL WRITING

The Three Basic Sales Problems/Objectives

Unfortunately, a great many, if not most, proposal writers tend to use too many words and too few graphics. The purpose of a proposal is persuasion, of course; the proposal is a sales presentation. That means inducing someone—a client—to decide that he or she wants something, which in the applications we are discussing is a service that you wish to provide. But the sales problem is not always a simple one, nor is it always the same. It may, in fact be any of three basic sales situations and problems, as summarized in the following:

1. In many cases, particularly when you are submitting an informal and/or unsolicited proposal (which usually means a noncompetitive one), you are probably simply trying to persuade the client to want the kind of service you offer, since you are the only one offering it to this client.

2. On the other hand, if the client has already decided to buy the kind of service you offer, your marketing problem and main objective of your proposal is to induce the client to buy that service from you, rather than from someone else.

3. However, in some cases, you may have the double task of persuading the client to both need buying the service, and to buy it from you. (Some sales presentations succeed in only the first of these tasks and so create a sale for a competitor!)

Understanding Must Precede Persuasion

Whichever the sales mission you must carry out, you must somehow induce the client to understand your arguments, specifically the promise(s) you make and the evidence (sales arguments) you provide to support and validate your promises. And you must do so in such a way that it does not become an intolerable burden for the client to study your proposal, understand your proposed program, and grasp all your sales arguments. To so burden the client is, in effect, asking the client to sell himself or herself, and this approach rarely works. The client expects you to do the selling, and a most fundamental sales principle (enunciated earlier) is to always make things as easy as possible for the client. But that means easy to follow your presentation, easy to understand what you promise, and easy to find your evidence credible, as well as easy to place the order with you.

Words Versus Graphics in Communication

Words are the principal and most used means for communicating among ourselves as a matter of pure necessity. Over the centuries humans developed more and more sophisticated and efficient means to transmit words to each other, in both terms of mass communications (printing and movable type) and communications over long distances (telephone, telegraph, radio, and TV).

Still, there is evidence that the earliest communications, other than vocal sounds, were via graphics. Throughout the world we find artifacts attesting to this, from crude prehistoric drawings on the walls of ancient caves to sundry forms of art (paintings and sculptures of every kind) created by every civilization and society we know of since homo sapiens emerged from the caves and began to build shelters.

It is significant also that movies and subsequently TV were immediate successes, and that worldwide TV transmission and reception were among the earliest and most popular applications of satellite communications systems. Moreover, the utilization of computer systems for the generation of graphics also proliferated rapidly, with the translation of spreadsheet data into graphic representations (e.g., charts and graphs) the primary goal of many sophisticated software programs.

Why Graphics?

Illustrations of all kinds, and especially graphic illustrations, facilitate and improve communications for more than one reason:

Pure Efficiency. A good illustration is simply more *efficient* than words are in getting a message across: A simple drawing, when conceived and executed properly, gets an idea across to a reader with barely more than a glance, and it usually requires less physical space than equivalent text would.

Less Effort Required.   Less effort is required of the reader to absorb a concept or image presented graphically than is the case when the reader must read and translate words. The illustration presents the desired image directly, eliminating the need for the reader to try to translate the language into images or concepts that can be visualized. (Once again, this is the principle of making things as easy as possible for the client.)

Greater Accuracy.   Even with the greatest effort by readers it is rarely that words are so translated as to create the precise image you wish to transmit. That is because words are merely symbols, and require the reader to search for a referent—something familiar to see as a guide or aid to understanding a description—so that the ways in which readers translate language is largely dependent on their own vocabularies and mental "reference libraries" of personal experiences. We all tend inevitably to introduce our personal memories and biases into our interpretations of what we read. Ergo, it is not surprising that each reader's interpretation of the meaning of any given textual passage is somewhat different than anyone else's interpretation. A drawing or photograph of an object, on the other hand, tends to be seen the same way by every reader.

There Are Various Degrees of Complexity

All of the foregoing is true for even the simplest communication needs, such as helping the reader visualize the appearance of an object. But it is even more true for more complex cases of communication, such as those cases where it is necessary to assist the reader in perceiving and understanding an abstraction or a complex relationship. You cannot expect the reader to find it easy to grasp the concept of phase relationships in an electrical or electronic circuit, or the Theorem of Pythagoras, for example, unless you offer some graphic devices to facilitate understanding. But it is not only in technological subjects that the problems of conveying abstractions and complex relationships arise. The problems obtain in many presentations that are not technological in any sense. Presenting and explaining business problems, societal relationships, professional functions, political processes, and many other subjects can be equally complex and challenging to present in easily understood explanations. Moreover, it is often necessary to create explanations that are understood easily by lay people.

The use of graphic devices is not always simply for aid to the writer in making the presentation and to the reader in following the explanations. In some cases it is simply not possible to make a sensible presentation by words alone. In such cases, graphic aids become an absolute necessity, rather than merely a convenience. So we must consider all these cases and the many ways to cope successfully with the presentation problems of each case.

A FEW UNDERLYING PRINCIPLES ABOUT GRAPHICS

The Sales/Marketing Consideration

What has been and will be said here about the logic and practices of using graphics properly is true for all applications of writing and publications work. However, remember also that these ideas become even more important when they are applied to the preparation of proposals. That is because the proposal is a sales presentation, and while the reader of a book or report might struggle through difficult text passages that could and should have been made easier through graphic aids, the client reading a proposal is under no compulsion to do so and is likely to discard the difficult-to-follow proposal. Therefore, in addition to every other guideline, principle, rule, and/or caution offered to help you judge where, when, why, and how to opt for a graphic aid, always consider also the possible contribution an effective graphic aid may make to sales persuasion—to winning the contract, that is.

Relative Costs

Graphics used in proposals—drawings and photographs, normally—are relatively expensive. It is possible today to create many, if not all, your own drawings at professional or near-professional quality by turning to the many ready-made artist's aids which anyone can use. Any well-stocked art-supplies emporium and even many large stationers can supply such items as templates, paste-down lettering and graphic material, stencils, and other such items, which even the professional artists use today. Moreover, there is the possibility of generating thoroughly acceptable drawings with your own personal computer and suitable graphics software. And even without special software, with a little imagination you can use your word processor to generate many useful drawings. (Some graphics used in developing the manuscript for this book were generated in this manner, and some are reproduced in this book as examples.) But even when you generate the drawings yourself, creating a drawing can be costly in time, if not in dollars (although the old "time is money" cliche is still as true as ever). And where special art departments are used to generate highly professional finished drawings, there is a definite dollar expense involved.

Consequently, it is understandable that the complaint is sometimes raised in publications groups that graphic illustrations, especially detailed drawings that are generated for one-time use, are too expensive to be used in any case where their use is not an absolute necessity. The argument used most commonly is that a "page of illustration" costs several times that of a page of straight text.

This reflects a lack of understanding about the economics of using graphics, and is one of the deterrents to the use of graphics, leading to the impoverishment of product quality (of the quality of your proposal, that is). What the originators of such objections do not take into account is that the comparison is faulty: The cost of a "page of illustration" should not be compared with the cost of a single page of straight text, but with the cost of several, perhaps many, pages of text. For unless the illustration eliminates and makes unnecessary at least several pages of text, the illustration is a poor one. It fails in its mission and should not have been created.

Why Many Graphics Fail

There are three common reasons for the failure of a graphic illustration, with only one of them a reflection on the illustration per se: This is where it is a poorly conceived illustration that simply does not do the job it ought to do. The other cases are those in which the illustration is either an unnecessary one and used where no illustration is helpful or where the writer fails to take advantage of the illustration and insists upon using a great deal of unnecessary language to explain what the illustration itself already makes quite clear.

Relevant Rules and Principles Inferred

All these types of failure point to more than one basic rule or principle, the first and most general of which is that a graphic illustration is not or should not be a supplement to textual presentation but is itself as primary and independent a means of communication as are the words. Each has some dependence on the other, of course, but the interdependence is incidental, and each must stand on its own, for the most part. And to do that, each must be used where it is the right medium to meet the need. ("Right" medium to meet the need may mean *best* medium or it may mean *only* medium that meets the need.)

This means that as a writer of proposals you must think and plan in terms of *what* you wish to communicate before you you consider *how* you will do so. First of all, bear in mind that everything you must communicate is either concrete or abstract information. More basic, perhaps, is the consideration of whether you are trying to communicate an image or an idea. We think in both images and words, and even when we are trying to understand and digest abstract ideas or concepts we tend to conjure up images in analogizing the concepts. Obviously, when the reference is to some common object or idea it is rarely necessary or profitable to employ a graphic illustration; the reader will furnish that mentally. The judgment of need for an illustration should be based entirely on judgment of what is to be communicated and how that is most effectively and/or efficiently accomplished.

Remember in this connection that efficiency has a somewhat different meaning here than it might in another application. That is because here we are talking about sales presentations, and efficiency refers here to more than efficiency in communicating information; it refers to efficiency in persuading the client to your arguments. In many cases a graphic aid will be more persuasive than words, even when it might not communicate information any better than words would, and so it adds efficiency in achieving the primary objective of the proposal. So we must also consider the impact of graphics in terms of persuasiveness, as compared with the persuasiveness of words alone.

GENERAL TYPES OF GRAPHICS

There are many types of graphics, and they vary widely in costs, time required to execute them, skills required to create them, applications for which they are most suitable, and other parameters by which they may be compared with each other. A first broad discrimination might be made between photographs and drawings.

Photographs have rather limited use in proposals, generally, although there are exceptions. In the case of a proposal for a project which required the proposer to offer a warehouse site with ready access to a seaport and all facilities necessary to dockside operations at such a port, at least one proposer offered photographs, including an overall aerial photo of the proposed site, with appropriate "callouts" (arrows and labels surprinted on the photos) indicating the various facilities.

One great advantage in using photographs, rather than simple drawings, in such a case as this, is the much greater credibility of photographs. In fact, in such a case as this, where the question of suitable facilities bears on the client's final decision, drawings purporting to show the facilities are claims, whereas photographs are evidence. Even elaborate and costly "artist's conception" types of drawings (often developed by architects to depict the final building planned) are a reflection of what the proposer conceives and promises, while photographs invite the client to view with his or her own eyes what actually *exists*, a far more persuasive alternative, obviously.

There are many special cases, such as this, in which a photograph is critically important as the most effective and even the only way to get the information across to the client as proof, rather than claim. However, in general, photographs may be used to show clients your own facilities and equipment, where that is relevant—offices, library, data processing system, and/or whatever else is evidence of your suitability for serving the client's needs well. (Some consultants use photographs of individual staff members, but it is to be doubted that that helps very much as sales support.)

Photographs are usually less costly for this application if you have them prepared in printed form in sufficient quantity to simply bind them into all your proposals or, as a practical alternative, to include them in a standard capabilities brochure which you use as part of the "qualifications" section of your custom proposals.

General Types of Drawings

For proposal purposes, drawings to be considered are almost always of the general type known as *line drawings*. That general category includes all types of graphs, charts, and pictorials that do not include subtle shadings, as do renderings in oils, water colors, charcoal, and other such artistic interpretations. (Although some shadings or "tones" are achieved even in line drawings, they are created via mechanical means or special ready-made materials that anyone can use.)

It is, in fact, rather difficult to draw up a complete list of types of line drawings, for there are a great many classes and subclasses, according to both the characteristics of the drawings and the applications to which they are put. Even the following list does not convey a complete profile of all the possible types of line drawings, but does serve to establish that there is a broad range of types from which to choose that type which is most suitable for a given application:

Pictorials	Bar charts
Flowcharts	Pie charts
Networks	Plots
Graphs	Milestone charts
Logic trees	Organization charts
Matrixes	Block diagrams
Cartoons	Clip art

Even within these types many broad subdivisions are possible. Note, also, that this list includes matrixes, which are more like tables than drawings, but are functionally in the same class as line drawings. Again, this will be borne out in the following discussions, some of which will include examples of types of line drawings, although a more complete set of samples and examples will be offered in an appendix as reference material for your use later in preparing proposals.

A simple pictorial diagram is shown in Figure 27, which depicts a local area network in a ring configuration. This network is also presented and explained in the block diagram of Figure 28.

These illustrate quite clearly the difference between the two methods of graphic presentation. Both offer the same information, but obviously the pictorial drawing is somewhat more effective in demonstrating the system suggested. And it is more effective in more than one respect: First of all, the pictorial is far more effective than the block diagram in reflecting the general idea of the system. It requires hardly more than a glance to understand the system, at least in general terms, whereas it takes at least a brief study of the block diagram to

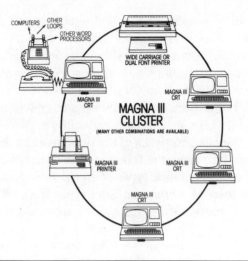

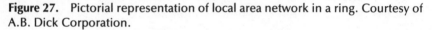

Figure 27. Pictorial representation of local area network in a ring. Courtesy of A.B. Dick Corporation.

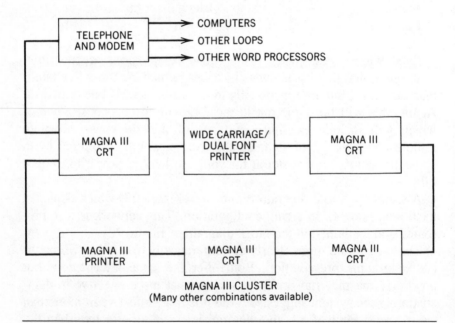

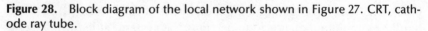

Figure 28. Block diagram of the local network shown in Figure 27. CRT, cathode ray tube.

grasp the overall idea, even with the various labels and identifiers. That is the key to the principal difference: A reader can recognize instantly such familiar items as desktop computers and telephones, even before reading the labels. The labels are almost entirely merely supportive. On the other hand, the labels in the block diagram are the only means of communicating most of the information, requiring the reader to make the translation from words to images.

But that isn't the only difference. The pictorial conveys the idea of a ring configuration much more efficiently than does the block diagram, and would do so even if the block diagram was arranged in a circular or oval pattern. That is an important part of the concept here because there are several other possible configurations for local area networks. In addition to that, however, since the reader is not required to translate the words of the block diagram into the the images of the equipment but is shown a good representation of the equipment as it actually appears, the writer is in far better *control* of the communication.

That is perhaps the most cogent argument for the use of pictorials whenever and wherever practicable: it does offer you far greater control of what the reader sees and "hears" in reading your proposal.

Unfortunately, pictorial drawings tend to be more expensive than many other illustrations because they usually require the services of professional illustrators. (There are exceptions to this, which we will explore later.) They also tend to require more lead time to prepare. For both reasons, it is usually impracticable to use them indiscriminately, and so their use should probably be confined to the most important messages you wish to deliver to the client, and perhaps to broad and general overviews of complex projects. They often prove especially useful in this application, for they are often the key to brushing aside the trivia and the distractors, and focusing, at least for the moment, on the real essence of the problem.

On the other hand, even disregarding cost entirely, pictorials are not always the most effective graphic illustrations to use. For some applications other graphic representations, such as networks, are more effective in helping the client grasp the concept easily.

Networks are especially useful for showing serial and parallel relationships, interdependencies, alternate paths, and numerous other absolute and relative characteristics of the assorted elements. The network used as an example here (Figure 29) is a simple one, showing

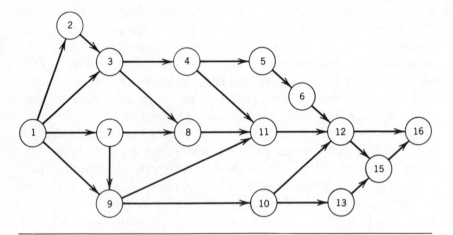

Figure 29. A simple network.

the basis for such sophisticated networks as CPM (Critical Path Method) and PERT (Program Evaluation and Review Technique), used for large and complex projects. The figure, however, demonstrates that there are several paths to the ultimate goal or objective of the project, and facilitates showing the client the validity of premises underlying of a discussion of viable alternatives. In Figure 29 item 1 represents the starting point of the project, and item 16 is the objective. The ideal path from the start to the objective is the shortest one, a straight line from 1 to 16, via 7, 8, 11, and 12. However, since it is rare that any project goes that smoothly, you have anticipated possible forced detours of the project or, better yet, planned the various alternatives which you will have ready, in the event problems materialize.

Thus, this figure helps you explain what is necessarily a rather sophisticated and fairly complex project plan, while it also demonstrates the high caliber and thoroughness of your planning and preparation.

In such drawings as this you can label each of the nunbered elements or you can simply prepare a set of notes—a legend, in fact—explaining each numbered element.

In a simpler presentation, an illustration such as that of Figure 30 may be used. The boxes in which the various steps and functions are explained can be any shape—rectangular, circular, or other (Figure 31). Several different shapes are shown in the figure to illustrate this,

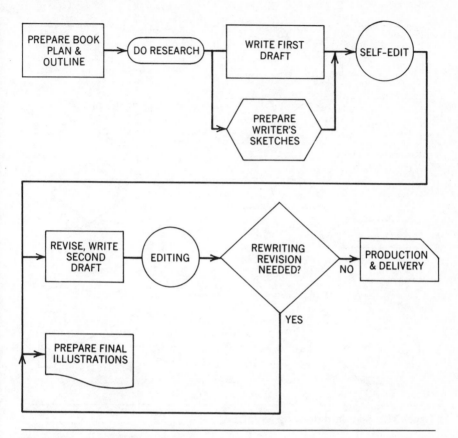

Figure 30. A simple flowchart.

and many people use an assortment of shapes in such illustrations, as a matter of trying to make the illustration interesting and pleasing in general appearance, as well as informative. In some applications, such as computer program flowcharts and logic diagrams, the shapes of the boxes have individual and distinct meanings—specific shapes are used for specific applications, as illustrated in the figure.

All of these were drawn with standard drawing templates, which are readily available in artist supply shops and at many well-stocked stationers. Templates have been designed for a quite enormous variety of applications in all kinds of professions—all the engineering fields, architecture, mathematics fields, and many others. You can have a choice of literally dozens of different kinds, many of them in a number

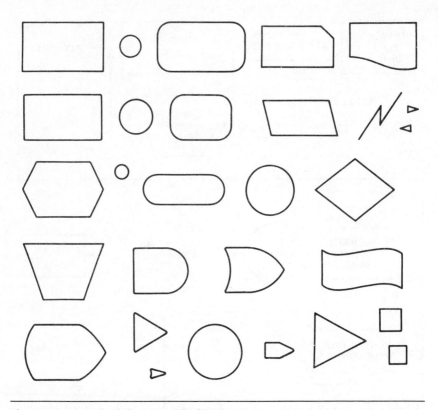

Figure 31. Standard drawing templates.

of sizes, too. However, templates are only one kind of drawing aid; there are many other drawing aids available, including boxes, arrows, borders, symbols, and other such devices in paste-down (self-adhesive) and transfer (decal) forms. And again, the variety is broad and applicable to many fields.

There is also "clip art," which is material available especially for use as illustrations, which can be purchased in sheets and/or in booklets at supply stores. Some of these are illustrated in Figure 32.

"Logic trees" are another useful idea to illustrate a kind of binary or Aristotelian logic: the progression of yes-no, high-low, go-stop, or other mutually exclusive states to reach a conclusion. A simple example of this is shown in Figure 33.

Figure 32. Paste-down and decal drawing aids.

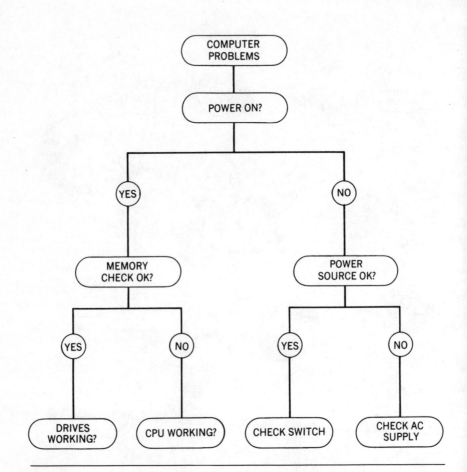

Figure 33. A simple logic tree. CPU, central processing unit.

CHAPTER 11

THE EXECUTIVE SUMMARY (AND OTHER FRONT MATTER)

Used properly, the executive summary often proves to be the most important element in the proposal. At the least, it would be a serious error to underestimate its importance and so fail to utilize it effectively. But there are other elements of front matter, too.

FRONT MATTER

In any formal publication certain elements appear before page 1—before the presentation begins, that is. There are usually a title page and a table of contents, at the minimum. But there are often other elements, as well—prefaces, forewords, abstracts, and notices of various kinds.

Formal proposals are not an exception to this, although they generally include in their front matter elements not normally found in most other formal publications.

The title page and table of contents are de rigueur; they are found in just about every formal publication of every kind, including formal proposals. Other elements normally found in formal proposals include an abstract, executive summary, a foreword or preface, and/or in some cases other special elements, such as one very useful one I refer to as a response matrix. That and the executive summary are probably the most important elements of front matter in proposals.

WHAT IS AN EXECUTIVE SUMMARY?

Many things are not quite what they appear to be, and to some extent that may be said for the executive summary. The term itself suggests that it is a kind of abstract of the entire proposal, offered to help executives absorb the main thrust of a proposal with a brief reading. And that is true in a most general sense. But there is a great deal more to the matter than that. An executive summary is far more than an abstract, or it most certainly ought to be in the hands of an astute marketer. It is, in fact, probably the most important element of the front matter and one of the most important elements of the proposal overall.

The executive summary is, in principle, particularly appropriate in proposals that are highly technical. In fact, it was the growing complexity of technical detail presented in major proposals, along with the massive and unwieldy size of many proposals (literally thousands of pages and several volumes, for many large contracts) that inspired the idea of the executive summary and all but mandates its continued use.

The rationale underlying the idea is, of course, that in a great many cases it is impractical for executives on the client's staff to read or attempt to read entire proposals. They will not normally read the main text of the proposal for more than one reason: They, the executives, may or may not be in a position to appreciate and appraise the technical detail, but even if they are, it is an inappropriate and inefficient use of their time to read the entire proposal, even when that is a practical possibility. The typical executive needs and wishes only to get a general overview and thus a broad appreciation of each proposal. There are usually specialists on staff whose duties include studying proposals in depth, including the technical details, and making their evaluations and recommendations to management.

From this it might be concluded that only management—the executives—read an executive summary, since it is to management—to the organization's executives—that the executive summary is addressed. Experience shows clearly, however, that almost invariably everyone who reads any portion of the proposal reads the executive summary. The summary serves the useful purpose, from the reader's viewpoint, of providing an advance orientation and thus a road map to help the reader grasp the proposal overall. And it represents several things from the proposer's viewpoint, as well.

The executive summary is therefore an element that everyone reads ordinarily, and that should suggest to anyone responsible for proposal preparation some uses to make of the executive summary.

THE USES OF AN EXECUTIVE SUMMARY

Everyone writing a proposal presents arguments in his or her own behalf, just as the Philco organization (and other companies) did when they included a special proposal section entitled "WHY PHILCO (or other company name) SHOULD BE AWARDED THIS CONTRACT," as described in an earlier chapter. This final proposal section recapitulated and summed up all the major sales appeals and arguments that had appeared in the earlier pages of the proposal. Each of these organizations was not the least bit coy about their desire for the contract and their conviction that they were by far the best-qualified proposer for the job. They were at pains to assure the client that they did, indeed, sincerely wish to win the contract and did believe that it was in the client's best interests to make the award to them.

It is still perfectly proper tactics to include in your proposal some element that makes that desire and conviction plainly apparent to the client by stressing it and drawing special attention to it. (Remember that the proposal is a sales presentation.) Today, however, the convenient and popular mechanism for doing so is almost always that executive summary, as a result of frequent requests by government agencies to include such a section in proposals. The inclusion of such an element in proposals has become virtually a de facto standard. But it appears in the front matter of the proposal, rather than as a final section.

The executive summary thus becomes a major sales tool, perhaps the most important one in your proposal. It becomes the opening argument of that sales presentation you offer a client as a proposal, and in so doing it provides certain distinct strengths that can prove decisive:

1. You get an unusually good opportunity to get attention and arouse interest immediately—even before the client comes to page 1.
2. You gain the benefit of being able to establish that important first impression favorably.
3. You can condition the mind of the client—"position" yourself and your offer—advantageously.
4. You can focus the client's attention on the key points and, in so doing, greatly increase the impact of those key points when the client reads them in the main text.

For these reasons it is important that you do not underestimate the importance of the executive summary, but expend enough effort on it to use it to your greatest advantage.

WHAT TO CALL AN EXECUTIVE SUMMARY

For discussion purposes, I use the generic and descriptive term *executive summary* here, but only for those purposes. (In some cases another name for it might be more appropriate.) On the one hand you want to persuade the client to read this section as a time-saver that will offer a quick appreciation of the entire proposal. On the other hand you do want to take advantage of all opportunities to persuade the client to your cause—to *sell*, that is. In the interest of making all the titles, headlines, and captions work for you in selling by stressing the benefits and proofs you offer, you should choose a title for this element that helps sell your proposal, while also persuading the client to read this curtain raiser.

Following are some suggestions for such titles, offered as idea starters. (Probably you can come up wth better ones.)

SUMMARY OF LEADING FEATURES
SUMMARY OF BENEFITS
WHY _____(YOU) SHOULD BE AWARDED THIS CONTRACT
WHAT _____(YOU) PROPOSES TO DO FOR YOU
THE BENEFITS OF _____(YOUR) PROPOSED PROGRAM

A FEW RELEVANT PRINCIPLES

Since the client will expect the executive summary to provide an overview and abstract of the proposal, it is important that it does offer an abstract of at least your key points. However, your goal is to accomplish that without sacrificing or even compromising your marketing goal of making the executive summary a principal selling tool. Therefore, every item listed in the executive summary must be couched in positive terms, as a sales argument. In fact, it is helpful to think of the executive summary as being a miniature proposal in and of itself, with the following objectives:

1. Introduce yourself briefly, but in highly positive words, words that demonstrate the advantages you offer.
2. Focus on the most critical or important aspect(s) of the requirement and demonstrate that you have the necessary 20/20 insight.
3. Sum up, in clearly focused and to-the-point delivery, the benefits and proofs—the sales appeals and arguments.

A CASE HISTORY AS AN EXAMPLE

Nothing makes all of this quite as clear as an actual example from a case history. The successful proposal of North Atlantic Industries, Inc. for a large and important Navy procurement of a computerlike item of equipment (a teleprinter) owed at least part of its success to an excellent executive summary. A description of their executive summary, along with an outline that includes the actual headlines they used, is presented here to help illustrate these principles and practices:

The Proposer: Supplier of the AN/USH-26(V)

North Atlantic Industries (NAI) pointed out another Navy program which they were carrying out successfully, mentioned some outstanding achievements in that program, and demonstrated the relevance of that experience and accomplishment to the proposed program. They pointed out, for example, the excellent performance and demonstrated reliability of the cited equipment, and a Navy award for excellence in quality.

Supplier's Commitment

NAI stressed the importance of the procurement, pointing out key elements, compared favorably and point-by-point the needs of the program with what NAI had to offer, and pledged their total commitment to the goals of the program. They observed that the program had an importance larger than might be suggested by its relatively modest size, also pointing out that the program would be relatively small to a large corporation, but was large and important to them, as a small company. This was to stress the advantages of using a smaller company as the contractor, of course.

Basic Premises

Here NAI drew four points, analyzing the requirement and pointing out the four critical considerations they perceived as what ought to be the areas of concern in developing a design, with due regard to the present state of the art and what could be reasonably anticipated as probable future developments, given recent experience in the fields of interest.

A Logical Conclusion

From the above, NAI presented, as a logical conclusion, the indicated prime requirements of any practical design, specifying that these were carefully considered in drawing up the NAI design.

A Logical Solution

Here NAI set forth its specific design objectives, derived from and chosen as the logical outcome of the preceding technical arguments. This was to prove the integrity and authenticity of the technical analyses.

An Advanced Design

NAI provided here some additional data on the proposed design, pointing out that it was truly an advanced design, as promised and suitable to the requirement, and responsive to the capabilities of current technology.

Total Compliance

NAI affirmed here that they were in total compliance with the RFP in their response, as they will be in their performance.

Exceeding Requirements

Here NAI listed nine individual and specific items in which they pledged that they would not only meet all requirements, but would actually exceed them—deliver more than is required, providing the client many special and additional benefits.

Special Feature

This promised feature overcomes to a large extent one of the drawbacks—relatively slow access—inherent in using tape for storage purposes.

Some Examples of Enhancements

NAI described possible enhancements to the design—options the client could elect to include—and listed nine specific items under this headline.

Technical Support Services

Here NAI summarized the required support services and how their organization could and would respond to these.

Geographical Advantage

NAI perceived an advantage in their locale (Long Island, New York), which is a center of relevant industries and resources, and pointed this out.

Upgradability

This paragraph showed how both the system and the individual units proposed could be "upgraded," and done so quite easily, in the field.

Management

Here the proposer summarized its several levels of management—technical/project, general/administrative, and corporate—as they would relate to the program.

Why NAI Should Be Awarded the Contract

This headline should have a familiar ring. You may remember that it was once the title used for an entire proposal section. As used here, it introduced several paragraphs that reinforced briefly all the arguments that had gone before, but then presented the final argument that NAI should be awarded the contract because what was proposed was what the client needed—that is, the design was exactly right for the requirement.

HOW LONG SHOULD AN EXECUTIVE SUMMARY BE?

An executive summary, by its nature (i.e., as a *summary*), should be short. In the case history offered here the summary met this criterion: Despite the length of this explanation and the use of 14 headlines, this entire presentation was not more than about 2,500 words, nine double-spaced pages. In a proposal of nearly 250 pages, that is not excessively long.

There are, of course, no specific rules governing the ideal length of an executive summary. However, aside from the fact that its very name dictates that it must be short, with relation to what it summarizes, a lengthy executive summary defeats its own purpose. It cannot, for example, succeed in focusing the client's attention on key issues and critical points if it rambles on about many other matters or fails to get directly to the point for each item covered. It is therefore largely a matter of individual judgment, but there are some guidelines which can help you form judgments and develop effective executive summaries:

For one thing, the executive summary cited here as a case history represented approximately 3.6 percent of the total proposal. That is a reasonable percentage, although it is desirable to make it even more concise, if possible. Two to three pages of executive summary for every hundred pages of main proposal is a good rule of thumb for sizable proposals, if you can hold it to that.

However, do not misinterpret this as a recommended yardstick by which to measure all executive summaries, for it is not that. A basic rule for length is this: Make the executive summary long enough to present all those points you believe to be decisive, but no longer than that. That is, do not short-change your presentation because of any perceived hard-and-fast rule of maximum allowable size. Far better for it to be a bit longer than it ought logically to be, and present everything important, than to be brief and fail to present important items. Never lose sight of the purpose of the executive summary: It is designed ostensibly to present a brief overview of your proposal, but the chief objective is to make a sharply focused and hard-hitting sales presentation by summing up your most cogent arguments. It therefore needs brevity, but it also needs completeness, to get that job done.

HOW TO WRITE "TIGHT" EXECUTIVE SUMMARIES

Rewriting is Far More Important than Writing

Concise and effective executive summaries are never written; they are *re*written. That is a rule for all writing, in fact: The experienced professional does not expect to get his or her best work down on paper (or on a floppy disk, for that matter) in the first draft. The first draft is (should be) written in complete freedom, getting thoughts down on paper (or disk). In subsequent drafts—and even the best writers often find it necessary to revise through more than one subsequent draft—the writer works a steady improvement in a number of ways.

Rewriting (and Editing) Means Cutting Copy Down

It is something of a writer's platitude that the essence of editing, and certainly the first task of editing in most cases, is to boil down the copy, which is almost invariably overwritten. Many and perhaps even most writers are too verbose, and the editor can often delete as much as one-third of the copy without losing anything important. Recognizing this as an almost unvarying truth, many professional writers simply do not worry about verbosity when they are writing a first draft. They concern themselves only with getting all the ideas down on disk or paper, with the full expectation that they will eliminate the excess verbiage themselves, in the process of preliminary self-editing and rewriting before an editor sees the copy.

This is especially true and probably the best approach for writing an executive summary. First go through the proposal and transcribe all the "goodies"—promises, benefits, proofs, credentials, and whatever else appears to help. Then go through this and begin to sort, determining which are the most important items and which are merely clutter and should be dropped.

Organization of the Executive Summary

Continue this process until you are sure that you have reduced the items to the minimum possible. Then start organizing the items into a logical sequence. That logical sequence is not necessarily the same as that used in the case history cited here. You will have to decide what sequence is best for you—best for implementation of your strategy, that is. Logically, you should lead with whatever is your main strength. In the case of North Atlantic Industries, one of their major strengths was the record of performance they had already established with the client on a previous contract, and they decided to lead with that. Your own case should be decided on its own merits. For example, your main strength might be one of these (or one of many other things, of course):

Special capabilities and/or experience/accomplishments.
Special resources.
Features of your plan.
Insights into the requirement.
Cost-reduction ideas.

Whatever your decision, build your approach around that major item, use it as your lead, and build your case on it.

The Next Stage of Reduction

That first stage was addressed to reducing the number of items to those of greatest importance. It was necessary to gather up all the items first, of course, and then make judgments as to which to keep and which to discard as not being important enough for the executive summary. With that done, it is time to address the second stage of condensation of the summary. That is an editorial kind of stage: Items will not be eliminated—presumably, you have by now dropped all items that were not truly essential—but the presentation will be tightened up by dropping unnecessary words and simplifying expression generally. It is usually acceptable to use special space- and time-saving devices, too, such as telegraphic style (eliminate articles, such as "the" and "a," use briefest verb forms, such as "run" for "running," use bullets for listings, and otherwise get meanings across with greatest possible economies of presentation.

The purpose of all this effort to keep the executive summary as short as possible is not only to conserve the reader's time, but also to achieve a much more dynamic style. These measures add a great deal of vigor to the style. Compare the following two items, for example, which are portions of an executive summary. The first was written in simple but conventional style, and represents the final stage of drafting and polishing the copy before reducing it to the telegraphic, punchy style of the final version:

Original Version

☐ Medical Management, Inc. (MMI) offers to provide a detailed medical management plan that includes a complete set of step-by-step procedures; a complete (8-hour) training seminar for as many of your staff as you wish us to train; complete documentation in the form of procedural, policy, and training manuals; and special consultation services at no charge for 90 days following installation of the MMI system.

☐ MMI offers extra options, at nominal additional costs: (1) MMI will make this a turnkey program—will ourselves install the system: operate it for 90 days and debug it; train your staff; and then turn over the trouble-free and smooth-running system to your own staff. (2) MMI will remain on-call for one year, as needed to help solve problems, deal effectively with new and unanticipated problems, and/or answer questions and provide additional training for your staff. (3) MMI will operate your system for a full year, while providing training and customizing all procedures, policies, and documentation for your own organization.

Final Version

☐ Medical Management, Inc. (MMI) proposes a detailed and specific program:
☐ Complete step-by-step procedures.
☐ 8-hour training seminar for all staff.
☐ Policy, procedural, and training manuals.
☐ 90 days free consultation.
☐ Also, for nominal additional costs, these options:
☐ Turnkey program: we operate, debug, train and turn over after 90 days.
☐ MMI on-call, for full year, as consultant, troubleshooter.
☐ MMI operates system for full year.

Note that the final version is far less verbose, without missing any of the important points, but is far more vigorous, making each point sharply and guiding the reader's attention to focus on the benefit, and not become distracted by irrelevant adjectives and adverbs. The client has no difficulty in grasping immediately the specifics of your offer— and your proposal is an offer, not a pleading.

EXECUTIVE SUMMARY IN THE LETTER PROPOSAL

A small program usually calls for a letter proposal, rather than a formal one. A letter proposal is rarely more than two to four pages, even with a program outline. Obviously, such a brief and informal proposal will not include a formal executive summary, such as that discussed and shown here. Nevertheless, the letter is still a proposal, and it is, as such, a sales presentation, just as a formal proposal is.

For that reason, the philosophy of the executive summary still applies, although it may appear as a simple narrative paragraph or two. On the other hand, it is perfectly proper to make a "laundry list" type of presentation, as in the examples just used, when a number of items are to be featured. Whichever the case, the summary should be as close to the opening of the letter as possible, or even as the opening itself, as in the following examples of each style:

☐ Because Marketing Consultants, Inc. (MCI) has stored in our computer and other files over 200,000 of our proprietary marketing materials, we are able to assemble a custom-designed system for you almost literally overnight and at unprecedented low cost.

☐ And while we will make recommendations, you have the opportunity to review these materials and make choices of your own.

☐ Marketing Consultants, Inc. (MCI) offers clients a unique service:

☐ Widest choice of materials & styles in industry—GUARANTEED.

☐ System completely custom designed for you—GUARANTEED.

☐ Turnaround (delivery) in less than one week—GUARANTEED.

☐ Lowest cost anywhere—GUARANTEED.

☐ MCI can do this for you because our library has over 200,000 proprietary designs and marketing materials in our files. MCI makes recommendations, but you have the right to make choices.

TITLE PAGE

Unless you are preparing a truly large formal proposal and going to the considerable expense often associated with the preparation of such large proposals, your letterhead is likely to serve well as the basis for the title page of your proposal. Figure 34 is an example of such a title page. It includes reference to an RFP. When such a formal request does not exist, for whatever reason, reference is simply not made— that is, the two lines beginning "in response to" are simply deleted.

The notice of proprietary information is likewise not always appropriate. Where it is, however, such a notice should be printed on the title page, and the actual material cited should be identified as confidential and/or proprietary on those pages by suitable notations there.

In the event you are submitting a formal proposal to a government agency, the RFP will normally suggest the wording for this proprietary notice, but it will be along the general lines shown in the figure.

The copyright notice is a good idea for all cases, as further protection for your confidential and proprietary information, as well as for your proposal itself. A great many people are imitative, especially when they observe a success (as in every industry), and there will be those who are likely to plagiarize your exact wording, if and when they manage to get copies of your successful proposals, which happens frequently these days. You are entitled to copyright your proposal, and you need to do nothing more than shown to secure to yourself a common law copyright. (It is only necessary to have that copyright registered with the Copyright Office of the U.S. Library of Congress if and when you get involved in litigation concerning your copyright, and you can register it at that time, if it ever becomes necessary.)

TABLE OF CONTENTS

The table of contents of a publication lists, as a minimum, the titles of chapters or sections and the page numbers. Some writers choose to list for each chapter all the major headlines, thus offering almost an abstract of each chapter, probably an exceptionally good idea for a proposal presentation. (See table of contents for this book as a general example.)

HRH COMMUNICATIONS, INC.

P.O. Box 6067
Silver Spring, MD 20906
(301) 460-1506

PROPOSAL

Offered to Hardesty & Hardesty, Inc.

in response to RFP HH-86-001

dated June 22, 1986

NOTICE:

Information contained in pages 33-37, 45, 49, and 76-82 is confidential and proprietary to HRH Communications, Inc. and should not be disclosed to anyone not a recipient or reviewer of this proposal. However, in the event of award, this information may be disclosed to and will be used in behalf of and according to the interests of Hardesty & Hardesty, Inc.

July 15, 1986

Copyright June 1986 by HRH Communications, Inc.

Figure 34. Typical title page of a formal proposal.

Among other refinements possible for the table of contents, although not universally practiced, are the inclusion of additional sections in the table of contents headed by such titles as LIST OF FIGURES (or ILLUSTRATIONS) and LIST OF TABLES.

FOREWORD OR PREFACE

Unlike books, proposals do not often carry prefaces or forewords, although there is no good reason why they should not do so, except that the executive summary serves at least part of the purpose generally served by a preface or foreword. (Moreover, many proposers bind a copy of their letter of transmittal into the proposal, and that often serves as a preface or foreword.) However, there are other purposes that can be served by such introductory remarks. For one thing, in the large consulting organization the CEO (Chief Executive Officer) may utilize this to address the client with assurances of his personal concern and his pledge of conscientious effort. (This is otherwise conveyed in the letter of transmittal, but conceivably may be far more effective in an element identified as a preface or foreword.) But a preface or foreword may be used to carry any special message or preliminary remarks deemed suitable and helpful.

RESPONSE MATRIX

The item I call a response matrix is an especially important element of the front matter. It's a device to help ensure that you do respond to all matters of concern, but even more important, it helps the client verify that you have done so, and that your proposal is completely responsive.

The response matrix is derived from the request for proposals and, more specifically, from those checklists you made earlier in analyzing the requirement and what the client wished you to respond to. It may be several pages long and usually is, for any proposal of size. Figure 35 is part of a single sheet from one such matrix. Note the column titles: SPECIFICATION refers to the RFP and what it specifically

MATRIX TABLE SHOWING COMPLIANCE WITH ELEX-T-551

Specification				Proposal Reference		
Par.	Title/Subj.	Compliance?	Exceeds?	Par./ Graphic	Page No.	Title/ Remarks
3.5.8	Printer copy	YES	—	2.3,1, 2.3,2	2–14, 2–46	
3.5.9	TEMPEST	YES	—	3.1	3–1	
3.5.10	ELEC. DESIGN	YES	YES	2.3, 4	2–14	
3.5.11	THERMAL DESIGN	YES	—	2.5, 6, 8, 9	2–16, 2–17	
3.5.12	TEST MEASURE.	YES	—	2.13	2–18	
3.5.13	TEST PROVISIONS	YES	YES	2.15	2–20	
3.5.14	CLASS A TEST	YES	—	2.15	2–21	
3.5.17	CLASS B TEST	YES	YES	2.16	2–22	

Figure 35. Sheet XIV from a many-page response matrix.

calls for. COMPLIANCE WITH SPECIFICATION calls for a "yes" or "no." EXCEEDS SPECIFICATION also calls for "yes" or "no." PROPOSAL REFERENCE refers to the proposal, listing the page and paragraph numbers (where paragraphs are numbered, as they were in this case), and leaving a rightmost column blank for the use of the client in checking off the compliance with all specifications.

Of course, this form should be modified and adapted to your own needs, which are likely to be less formalized than this one was. For example, you may not have numbered paragraphs, and you may even not have a formal specification to refer to, and so you may wish to substitute other column titles, such as NEED for SPECIFICATION.

This is an important element, and should be developed carefully and introduced with a brief explanation that it is provided to assist the reader in locating specific responses to required information, as well as to ensure that the author of the proposal has made all necessary responses.

LETTER OF TRANSMITTAL

Informal or letter proposals are complete in and of themselves, usually. Formal proposals normally have three elements:

Technical proposal (may be more than one volume)
Cost proposal (often required to be a separate document)
Letter of transmittal

The letter of transmittal is a courtesy, but it is more than that, too. Many consultants believe that the letter of transmittal is of great importance, although others think it is a mere formality and of little significance in making an award. The truth falls between the extremes, of course, as truth usually does. But the importance of a letter of transmittal—or its lack of importance—is at least partly the consequence of its treatment. Obviously, if you treat it as a pure formality, that is all it will be. However, you can compel it to assume greater importance if you design it to be more important.

The matters that a letter of transmittal ought to cover are these, as a minimum:

1. Confirm that the proposal is a response to some specific RFP (hereby identified), an informal request, submitted as agreed to earlier, or citing whatever circumstances led to the proposal.
2. Make brief mention of the requirement to which it responds and the chief characteristics or features of the proposal (but especially of any major feature).
3. Confirm that you are authorized to make the offer, and that it is a firm offer.
4. State the period of time for which the offer made in your proposal is firm.

5. Make an offer to provide any additional information desired in any form desired, including in writing and in face-to-face discussions, with or without formal presentations.

The letter of transmittal is addressed to the client or to whomever issued the request for proposals, such as the client's purchasing agent. (In the case of proposals to the government, it is normally addressed to the contracting officer.)

It is a common practice of many consultants to bind a copy of the letter of transmittal inside the cover of each copy of the proposal, so that every reader of the proposal can read the letter also.

The following sequence is recommended for the front matter:

1. Copy of letter of transmittal (inside cover).
2. Title page.
3. Executive summary.
4. Preface or foreword, if used.
5. Note introducing response matrix.
6. Response matrix.
7. Table of Contents.

THE COST PROPOSAL

Everything discussed in this chapter has so far been front matter. The remaining two items to be discussed here are not front matter, but require only brief discussion and can be fitted here as well as anywhere else. One of these items is the cost proposal, where a separate cost proposal is required.

The reason for making the cost proposal a separate item is to withhold from evaluators all knowledge of costs. This is done to encourage evaluators to make their evaluations of technical proposals uninfluenced by cost considerations.

Governments almost invariably require separate cost proposals, and usually provide forms upon which to list costs and explain how the proposer has arrived at the bottom-line figure. Usually, the cost proposal is only a few pages, at most, although there can be exceptions to this.

APPENDICES

The remaining item to be considered is the appendix. This is a simple item also, and is a place where you include material which will be of interest to some readers, but not to all. That might include additional resumes, drawings, professional papers cited in the body of the proposal, sample materials, or other items qualifying to be appended, but not included in the main text.

CHAPTER 12

COMMON PROBLEMS AND
IDEAS FOR SOLUTIONS

A marketer's "positive thinking" platitude is that when someone hands you a lemon you make lemonade. It's a trite expression, but the idea is valid and it is almost always possible to
make lemonade.

SOME OF THE MORE COMMON PROPOSAL PROBLEMS

The problems consultants encounter in writing proposals are probably more common ones than you think. Following are a few typical ones, to illustrate this. In fact, these examples reflect questions I get again and again from attendees at my proposal-writing seminars and from readers of my basic book on consulting as an independent practitioner. (*How to Succeed as an Independent Consultant*, John Wiley & Sons, Inc., 1983.)

> I am a very small business, and I can't list a half dozen qualified specialists as staff employees for those projects that need a half dozen or more professionals. How should I handle that?

There are several variants of this question. Some of the questioners are independent consultants, having no employees. Some are partnerships without other employees. Some are even part-time consultants. But all address the same question: Will it be disastrous to admit that they do not now have all the staff necessary and/or will it be disastrous to stipulate that they will hire employees or use associates, in the event they are awarded the contract?

More often than not it is the case that the problems exist in various forms and degrees, as the following sets of related questions show:

> I am just starting out, and I really have no experience to describe or other clients to list. How do I answer a requirement to list current and recent projects? Or: I have only a little experience. Or: I have a little experience, but sometimes it is not the right kind for the project, although I know that I can do it.
>
> I work at home. Do I need a downtown office in a building so that I look as though I am a real professional? Is having my office at home unprofessional? What do I do if the client wants to see my facilities for handling the job? I can arrange to use a friend's office as a kind of "front." Would that be a good idea or a bad one?
>
> How do I avoid using long and difficult words, as you advise, when I am in a field that communicates in such jargon? Won't clients think I am unqualified or inexperienced if I don't use the right jargon or "buzz words"?
>
> Should I be incorporated to make myself look more important in

my proposals? Doesn't being a corporation add prestige? And related to this: Does it help to have an important-sounding name,
such as International Marketing Associates, Inc., instead of John
Smith, Consultant or John Smith and Associates?

Akin to this latter set of questions are these: "Should I have my
proposals typeset and printed, with printed covers and professional
artwork? What about that statement in some government requests that
warn readers against elaborate proposals? What does that mean exactly?"

Let's take these up, one by one, as well as several other problems
that are likely to trouble you now or in the future, and you will see
that the picture is not as bleak as you might fear.

THE (APPARENT) PROBLEMS OF SMALLNESS

It's quite amazing how common it is for independent consultants and
other small consulting organizations to see their smallness as a handicap instead of recognizing the ways in which being small offers advantages. And smallness does offer advantages, even in the marketing
of your services. But before we talk about how to take advantage of
being small when you write your proposals, let's examine the reasons
you see smallness as a drawback and consider generally some of the
benefits of smallness. We need to understand the problem before we
can solve it.

The conviction that being small is a weakness in your competitive
position as a consultant is a manifestation of insecurity. It's born entirely out of fear, fear of what appears to be the overwhelming advantage of your large and (apparently) well-established and entrenched
competitors.

The humans employed by your large competitors are no less fallible
than you and in all probability no more talented or experienced generally as individuals. Their advantages are primarily in having some
kind of "track record"—experience—and resources to draw on. In
some cases they can offer a cost advantage as a result of size. (The
cliche here is "economies of scale.") Where and when that is the case
it is almost always because there is an optimum size for an organiza-

tion, that size at which they can operate most efficiently and that usually means at lowest overhead rates.

On the other hand, the direct rates—principally the direct cost of all labor before overhead enters the cost picture—tend to run considerably higher in larger organizations than in small ones, especially in the case of independent consultants. That tends to counterbalance any overhead advantage the large organization might have, so that the small organization can usually be cost competitive.

In fact, if you are an independent practitioner, you can afford to make some sacrifices, such as working overtime without charging yourself for it, as one means of competing. This is a special advantage when you are in an early stage and need special advantages to get started and begin to build your own track record.

One of the major advantages of smallness in marketing via proposals is being able to point out tactfully to clients that what is a small and not very important project to a large corporation is a very important project to you. Therefore, while the large organization would quite likely use other than its most experienced and most qualified specialists on the projects, you would give the project your full and undivided attention and see to it personally that every detail is attended to properly.

That latter, properly handled, can be a telling blow in your own behalf. And "properly handled" means getting the point across effectively to the client while being tactful, which means avoiding giving the appearance of making a direct attack on competitors. (You can compare yourself favorably with your competitors, but it is always a bad tactic to openly "knock" competitors and best to never mention them by name.)

An excellent way of making this statement diplomatically is to point out that there is an optimum size for handling the project in question and make the technical arguments for this view. Explain the potential hazard of a relatively small project becoming lost among large projects. That is the point at which you explain that this cannot happen with you because your operating philosophy is to focus on small, specialized projects. When you put the argument this way the client will get the point quickly enough.

You can also use the successful approach made popular a few years ago by the car rental firm, Avis: "We try harder."

But your concern may go well beyond smallness in general. It may be that more specialized problem that is related to smallness, such as pursuing a contract that requires a half-dozen consultant professionals, while you have only yourself or only one or two others on staff or even as associates. But even so it is possible to make lemonade of this problem, to actually finesse the problem by seizing it and making a strength of the weakness.

DEFINING AND REDEFINING THE PROBLEM

Consider the case of our space program, in which reentry was an early problem that appeared insurmountable to some. There was (and is, at least so far as we know today) no practicable way for a space vehicle to reenter the earth's atmosphere at any but extremely high speed. That means almost unimaginably great friction, with the resulting heat great enough to melt and even vaporize any metal or alloy we know of, not to mention what such heat would do the interior of the vehicle and its occupants.

Since we did not know of any way to avoid this problem of speed, friction, and heat, our choice was to give up the program or find a way to succeed *in spite of the problem*. That is, we had to accept the great heat as a condition to live with.

Once we accepted that, we changed the nature of the problem: Instead of being a problem in how to avoid the heat, it became a problem in finding a way to shield the vehicle and its interior from the heat. And that quest resulted in the *ablative* heat shield—a ceramic shell on the surface of the reentry vehicle (ceramic tiles, in the case of the space shuttle) *designed deliberately* to burn off during reentry.

Charles Kettering faced a similar problem in designing an automobile self-starter. He knew, as every automotive engineer did, that any starter motor large enough to crank an automobile engine would overheat if it were not as large as the engine. Since making it that large was impractical, and since he had already decided that he must and would create a workable self-starter, he changed the problem from one of trying to design a practicable self-starter that would not overheat to a problem of how to design a practicable self-starter that could endure overheating without being destroyed by it. Of course, he did so successfully, as we all know today.

Remember the earlier admonition that a proper definition itself points to the solution or to more than one possible solution. That means that if the problem is insoluble, as defined, it must be redefined. Redefining the problem means first accepting the condition that is unavoidable, but appears to be a barrier to solution. Then create a new definition which is such that it accepts the unavoidable condition as a given, but points to a solution that is workable despite the given condition.

In the case of not having enough key people on staff or as associates to man the proposed project properly, there are several possible ways to approach this, each way based on redefinition of the problem. The original problem is conceived as being one of appearing to be totally unqualified for the project as a result of being disastrously undermanned. The fact of not having the necessary staff on board is the unavoidable condition.

The redefinition is simple enough: The problem becomes one of how to appear well qualified in spite of not having the necessary staff on board. And, aside from "hanging paper"—misleading the client by offering resumes of people you don't even know and pretending that they are on staff or associates—you have only the alternatives of proposing to hire new people after award, proposing to seek out other consultants to act as subcontractors or associates, or offering resumes and letters of agreement from such people, verifying that they are professional associates and will work on the project with you. That, however, might still be regarded as an expedient, to compensate for a weakness in staffing capability. Something more is needed to solve the problem satisfactorily. Otherwise, these expedients appear to be just that, and they appear also to be apologies for not being fully qualified, with pleas for mercy.

That is always a tactical mistake, for it is an admission of weakness, and you can win only by attacking from strength. You must take the bull by the horns and say, in effect, "Here is what I am going to do for you," as you finesse the problem. And one way that has worked well in turning this apparent weakness into a strength has been to state boldly that the special nature of the requirement indicates to you a need for certain specialists. You have therefore sought out the most notable and outstanding such specialists in the field and gotten their agreement to work with you on this worthy program. Of course you must do more than make that kind of general statement. You must prove your case with suitable technical arguments.

In general in all such situations, never appear to be apologetic and defensive, and never lie about real conditions. In this case, you need never admit that there is only you or you and one or two others, for you never address the matter of the size of your staff at all. Instead, you bore in aggressively with resumes of these highly specialized new associates and their letters of agreement to work on the project with you. And if the question of your staff and its size ever does come up, you can easily say that you handle all projects with hand-picked associates because a significant feature of your consulting is exactly that: seeking out and employing on behalf of your clients the precisely right specialists. In fact, you can make that kind of positive argument in your proposal, if you wish to make an issue of it there and establish it there as a basic premise upon which you base your entire approach to satisfying the requirement. That would be a direct attack, and probably a novel approach.

QUESTIONS OF EXPERIENCE

Two kinds of experience are in question when writing a proposal, the direct and personal experience of any whose resumes are offered and the experience of the proposing organization. If you are an independent consultant working alone, there is a certain ambivalence about this. On the one hand the client wants to know about your experience and achievements as an independent consultant serving clients under contract. On the other hand, all your "organization" experience is your own personal experience. Practically, they are the same. Technically and philosophically, they are not. Serving your employer's clients, with your employer bearing the ultimate responsibility, is not quite the same as winning the assignment on your own and being totally responsible in all respects for the work. So if you are only recently established as an independent consultant, you are in short supply of that latter kind of qualifying experience as an "organization."

Many consultants get around this problem by careful wording that does not specifically claim individual experience as organization experience, but encourages the reader to so interpret it. That is an expedient that works for many who are skillful enough and careful enough in writing to bring the idea to reality.

A second approach, which I am convinced is more effective and should be used whenever practicable, is to meet the issue squarely, head on. Argue the case of fresh ideas, an open mind uncluttered by conventional ideas, technology transfer resulting from your diverse earlier experience, and other such bold tactics as they fit your own experience. And if your earlier experience included working with some prestigious firm, a university, or other impressive reference, by all means capitalize fully on it.

Again, avoid at all costs any appearance of defensiveness, apologia, or other self-deprecation. Those are defeatist tactics, and defeat is the result of such tactics.

The same philosophy applies to those cases where you are in pursuit of a contract to do something a bit out of your usual field, but something you are sure you can handle well, despite your inability to point to directly related experience. In such cases it is important to dwell at length and in detail on your specific program designs and plans. Demonstrate the technology transfer or whatever basis you have built your program strategy on. Show, in as much detail as possible, exactly what the technology transfer is and why it is not only appropriate, but advantageous to the client. Remember in all cases that the client's number one concern is what he or she thinks is in his or her own interest. The more what you offer appears to be in the client's interest, the less proof of anything else you need to offer. Always seek the argument that indicates what you propose as best for the client's personal interest.

HOW "PROFESSIONAL" DO YOU HAVE TO BE?

When I gave up my own costly suite of offices in downtown Washington in favor of a comfortable office and conference room in my own home, I did so with some trepidation. The move was very much in my own interests in many ways, but I feared its psychological effects on some of my clients. Particularly, I had misgivings about how one particular client would react to this move. This was a prominent and prestigious corporation with approximately 20 companies, very well known in the business and financial worlds, and I was dealing with people very near the top of the corporation. So it was with some trepidation that I announced the change to the corporate vice president with whom I had most of my direct dealings.

To my relief and pleasant surprise the reaction was along the line, "Cutting overhead, eh? Great idea. Smart move."

In the years since I have worked with people from this corporation and others in my own home conference room, although the nature of my consulting work is such that I do not often have need to receive clients in my own office. Having my office and conference room in my home, in a quiet residential neighborhood near a shopping center has never proved a disadvantage or, as far as I can tell, caused me any loss of respect by my clients.

I do not believe that it is necessary in all cases to have an office in an office building, as far as it concerns your credibility, image, or prestige as a consultant. There may be very good reasons for renting an office in an office building, but those would be the wrong kind of reasons to do so. Nor should you ever fake it by using someone else's office. To do so is not only deceit that will harm your image—who will trust you after discovering that subterfuge (and it will eventually be discovered)—but is totally unnecessary.

On the other hand, if you have your office at home or in a suburban business district and must meet and confer with a client in town, it is perfectly legitimate to make temporary arrangements. But don't deceive the client; be "up front" about it, and you'll suffer no harm for it. In fact, most clients will be appreciative of your action in making things more convenient for them.

ON INCORPORATING

Incorporating yourself is today extremely easy to do. In most states you can do so for $40 or $50 by filling out a simple form or two. (In Maryland the form is a single page, and the fee is $40 plus $6 for a certified copy of the approved form.) It is so easy to do, in fact, that for that reason alone there is no special prestige attached to being a corporation. There are good reasons for many consultants to be incorporated, but gaining prestige is not one of them. It will not make your proposal more impressive.

Very much the same philosophy applies to the name you choose for yourself. One executive I know who reviews capability brochures and proposals quite often has remarked more than once, "The bigger the name, the smaller the company," whenever he encounters a lengthy company name in his reading.

Here are the names of a few of the most prominent and successful consulting companies, and this is probably the best answer to the question of how helpful is a lengthy and "impressive" name:

Ernst & Co.
Price Waterhouse
Arthur Young & Co.
Peat, Marwick, Mitchell & Co.
Booz Allen & Hamilton, Inc.
Coopers & Lybrand

HOW ELABORATE THE PROPOSAL?

Proposals ought to be "professional"—neat, clean, grammatical, spelled correctly, well organized. They may be typeset, but composition by electric typewriter or computer printer is quite acceptable. They may be printed in an offset print shop, but duplication by office copier is quite acceptable. They can be bound in printed covers, but binding in a patent report binder is quite acceptable.

RFPs issuing from federal agencies often include injunctions against "excessively elaborate" proposals, warning the respondent that the submittal of proposals meriting that description may be interpreted as lack of cost consciousness, to the discredit of the proposer. Many consultants worry about this. Those admonitions refer to a day when the Department of Defense was spending billions recklessly (although *that* does not appear to have changed very much) and defense contractors were going to such extremes as binding multi-volume proposals in morocco leather with specially built cases to hold the several volumes, and some of the illustrations were of the ultra-costly process-color type, a la *National Geographic* magazine. *That* is considered to be "excessively elaborate." That, however, certainly is no bar to typesetting, printing, and binding according to normal commercial standards, if you wish to go to that expense or happen to be equipped to do such things in-house, as many companies are.

PRODUCTION PROBLEMS

Until now we have been discussing tactical problems, problems of proposal content, except for the question of what is excessively elaborate in a proposal. That latter is a production matter, and you may encounter a few production problems.

"Production" refers to all the details of making up the physical proposal in whatever is the required number of copies for delivery to the client. At the low end of the scale, where only a single copy is required, and especially where that is an informal letter proposal, you need make only a single file copy for yourself and probably require only the simplest kind of graphics if you need graphics at all. (It is likely that you will not in such cases.)

On the other hand, as the proposal becomes more formal and larger the practical production requirements change considerably, and related problems may arise. This is especially the case if you are an independent consultant with typically limited resources.

Today, with the ease of using modern office copying machines and the high quality of the work most produce, it has become common practice to "print" the required number of copies in this way. In fact, even photographs may be reproduced with fairly good quality on many modern office copiers.

In terms of cost it is usually less expensive to reproduce proposals this way than it is to print them because proposals are usually produced in only a handful of copies. (The economies in offset printing are not realized until the number of copies begins to mount up into hundreds.)

If you wish to include photos in your proposal, you may be able to make reasonably good copies on an office copier. That failing or if you are not satisfied with the admittedly less than perfect xerographic reproduction of a photograph, you can have a printer screen your photos and print up enough copies for your needs or you can bind the actual glossies into your proposal. Frequently, if you are duplicating only a few copies of your proposal, it is least costly to do this, since glossy prints of photographs are relatively inexpensive today. (However, if your original is a printed copy of an original photograph and is sharp and clear, you can probably copy that quite well on an office copier, since it is a reproduction of a screened photograph.)

You can, as has been noted already, prepare most and possibly all your own graphics with the aid of templates, paste-down symbols and type, and other modern artist's aids, and achieve nearly professional quality in doing so. Or, if you prefer, you can hire someone to prepare your graphics, either a freelance illustrator or a local graphic arts shop.

One problem that arises is that of large drawings. If you do develop functional flowcharts and other such drawings, they can easily grow to sizes well beyond that of a single page. The usual practice for using such drawings is to make foldouts of them—lengthy drawings folded down to page size with a binding edge left free so that the reader can extend the drawing to its full size. And such drawings can easily become several feet long, which poses a special kind of problem: How can it be reproduced inexpensively, as it must be when you must deliver more than one copy of your proposal? (In any case, even when you need deliver only one copy, you still need a file copy for yourself.)

The alternatives are (1) have a printer print several copies for you; (2) reproduce the drawing in sections, on an office copier, and paste the sections together to make complete drawings; and (3) use another process, such as ozalid copying.

The first alternative is one sometimes used by large corporations turning out major proposals that require a large number of copies. It's an expensive alternative because a large printing press is required, and a large negative and plate must be made. Moreover, it is not always easy to get the job done quickly this way, and that alone is often a bar to using this method, given the tight, often "impossible" schedules that are typical of proposal preparation. The second alternative is tedious, time-consuming, and not too pleasing aesthetically.

The third alternative is often the most practical approach. Ozalid is a process used by most large blueprint shops. Most shops of this type can make copies of a large drawing economically and quickly.

The process is such that it can copy anything drawn on a transparent or translucent medium, such as vellum and mylar. If possible, have your original drawing on such a medium. Otherwise, a negative of the original must be made first. (Most large blueprint shops are equipped to handle that for you, however.)

The question of where to bind foldout drawings in a proposal arises. Conventional practice regarding placement of graphics in publications of this type is to have the illustration follow the first text reference to it as quickly as possible, which in this case normally means on the next page. For foldouts, however, this can create another kind of a problem: You may wish to make numerous references to the drawing, and it becomes quite awkward for the reader to flip pages back and forth, folding and unfolding the illustration.

A way around this problem is to bind all such drawings at the back of the proposal. This permits the reader to leave the drawing folded out for easy repeated reference.

PAGE-LIMITED PROPOSALS

It has become a fairly common practice of government and some other proposal requestors to ease the burden of reviewing and evaluating large formal proposals by limiting their size. Without such controls the sizes can vary wildly, from a few dozen pages to thousands of pages. The client, in such cases, makes a judgment as to a proper size—the number of pages in which a proposer ought to be able to make his or her presentation—and mandates that as a limit.

When an RFP mandates a page limit it usually specifies minimum type size—usually 10 point (expressed as 12 pitch for a typewriter or printer)—spacing—whether the pages are to be single- or double-spaced—and the size of margins. Frequently, such RFPs except certain elements of the proposal from the limitation. It is not unusual for the RFP to except resumes, some front matter, and sometimes appendices from the restriction. On the other hand, the RFP may fail to state specifically whether there are any exceptions. Or it may warn that appendices and exhibits are included in the limitation and will not be reviewed or taken into account in the evaluation if they exceed the page limit.

Most often this is a general and overall limitation, but not always. In one recent case the RFP limited the proposal on an element-by-element basis, calling out maximum page counts for the executive summary, the resumes, the discussion, and the other major elements.

This is a problem to many proposal writers, but it is also a problem to your competitors and therefore offers you a special and additional opportunity to excel. In fact, such a limitation can be made to work to your advantage by compelling you to do what you should do anyway in writing a proposal. It therefore ought not to be a major problem nor should it require any subterfuge to overcome. For one thing, experience has shown that the clients' estimates of what is necessary to make an adequate presentation are usually quite sound. For another, it is in your own interest to keep your proposal as "tight" as possible, which would be the result of good writing and editing practices in any case. There are two major points to be made here, both guidelines to follow when responding to any proposal request, whether page-limited or not:

1.   Use graphics effectively, and you will eliminate many pages of text by that measure alone. And judge, in reviewing and editing draft, where the presentation could be made more efficient with a graphic illustration, and generate those illustrations, thereby reducing verbiage.

2.   Do not attempt to limit your writing in first draft, but get it all down. Then edit it down to size. That alone should, in the typical case, boil out about one third of the text as extraneous, redundant, covering trivia, or otherwise easily dispensed with. Properly, you do not *write* a proposal to satisfy a page limitation; you *edit* the proposal to comply with that limitation.

In my own experience these measures have proved to be effective in every case, achieving compliance with the size limitation without compromising the effectiveness of the presentation.

PACKAGING

"Packaging," as used here, refers to physical and cosmetic characteristics of the proposal package you will deliver in most cases. Usually, there are at least three elements, the technical proposal, the cost proposal, and the letter of transmittal.

Even in those cases where the client does not mandate that the cost proposal be physically separate from the technical proposal it is a good idea to separate them, to encourage review and evaluation of your technical proposal as objectively as possible.

The original letter of transmittal is normally in a separate business envelope accompanying the package of technical and cost proposals.

Binding may be done in many ways, of which these three are probably the most popular and most commonly used:

Side stitching—stapling the sheets and cover together.
3-hole binder, either a hard ring binder or a report binder.
Spiral binder, using plastic "spines."

Spiral binding requires special equipment to punch 18 or 19 rectangular holes in the sheets and install the plastic spines. (The number of holes depends on what model binding equipment you use.) But such binding does offer the advantage of the proposal lying flat, when opened.

Three-ring binding offers this same advantage, when a hard 3-ring binder is used, rather than one of the stationery store report binders, with its metal clips. However, repeated handling of a document in a 3-ring binder almost always means that some of the pages become detached.

It is possible to buy hard binders to accommodate those 18- or 19-hole sheets and so combining some of the better features of each alternative. There are also some other types of jiffy binders which are easy to use without any special equipment or special preparation, and are usually suitable if your proposal is a small one.

CHAPTER 13

MISCELLANEOUS USEFUL INFORMATION FOR PROPOSAL WRITING

Other consultants' views, overcoming some inherent handicaps to proposal writing, finding more proposal opportunities, and references.

QUESTIONNAIRE RESULTS

In researching and preparing to write this book I sent out a brief questionnaire to a large number of consultants, most of them small companies and/or independent practitioners. My purpose was to uncover common problems in proposal writing, to be able to report factually to you on what other consultants do and how they feel about proposal writing, to validate my own opinions and experience in this field, and to validate (or amend) my own judgment as to what information and guidance should be included in these pages. The questionnaire petitioned the consultants' responses to a series of questions, some calling for factual reporting, some for opinion or speculation, and others for identification of concerns and perceived problems. Additionally, respondents were invited to make any comments they wished to and to send on copies of proposals or related materials they use.

Figure 36 is a reproduction of the questionnaire. I mailed many directly to consultants known to me, but many more responded to a copy of the questionnaire included in an issue of the *Consulting Opportunities Journal*, a bimonthly newsletter published by Steve Lanning, whose generosity made it possible to reach his readers with this questionnaire, many of whom I would not have otherwise reached. Many of the responses reported here are therefore from readers of that newsletter.

A tabulation of results, by percentages, is included here for the factual items reported in each category, with accompanying explanations, observations and remarks, as necessary and appropriate. And, as almost always occurs in surveys of this type, where there is a large element of "opinionaire" to the survey, there are a few anomalies. My purpose in offering this information is to provide whatever guidance you can gain from this admittedly limited survey of the consulting field. However, before presenting those figures, it is useful to have a look at some of the various consulting specialties represented here, since consulting as a profession and industry (for it is both) is remarkably diverse, which itself accounts for many of what may appear to be anomalies in the results of this survey.

The survey did not require respondents to identify themselves, but a large majority, slightly more than 87%, did so, although not all furnished enough information to indicate clearly what their consulting

USE OF PROPOSAL IN MARKETING

[ ] Never   [ ] Rarely   [ ] Frequent   [ ] Always   [ ] Only when requested

[ ] Whether requested or not   [ ] Other: _____

HOW OFTEN REQUESTED

[ ] Usually   [ ] Occasionally   [ ] Rarely   [ ] Other: _____

SUCCESS WITH PROPOSALS

[ ] Over 75%   [ ] 50–75%   [ ] 25–50%   [ ] Under 25%   [ ] Other: _____

TYPE OF PROPOSAL USED AND FREQUENCY

Informal/letter:_____% of time   Formal:_____% of time _____

PROPOSAL PRACTICES

[ ] All original material   [ ] Parts boilerplated   [ ] All boilerplate

[ ] Quotation plus standard brochures and letter

[ ] Other: _____

SECTIONS/MATERIALS NORMALLY INCLUDED IN PROPOSALS

[ ] Statement of problem/need   [ ] Technical discussion   [ ] Resume(s)

[ ] Qualifications   [ ] Descriptions of deliverables   [ ] Schedules

[ ] Facilities & resources   [ ] Price   [ ] Letter of transmittal

[ ] Other: _____

PROPOSAL PROBLEMS, NEEDS, COMMENTS

_____

_____

_____

_____

(Add comments, as necessary [use other side for more room]; attach/enclose samples of your proposals and/or brochures, other materials, if possible.)

Figure 36.   Questionnaire form.

specialties are. However, here is a list of some of the specialties that were identified:

Lecture	Sales
Management	Computer programming
Financial services	Direct mail
Training	Organizational development
Marketing	Proposal development
Digital systems	Polling and surveying
Engineering	Apparel
Conference management	Direct response marketing
Seminar production	Theatrical productions
TV productions	Small business management
Personal grooming	Modeling/models agency
Advertising	Business/personal image
Medical secretary training	management
Telephone usage	Health care cost containment
Communications	Mailing list management

The tabulated results of the questionnaire are as follows:

Use of Proposals in Marketing

Rarely: 6.45%
Frequent: 51.6%
Always: 32.23%
Only when requested: 9.67%
Whether requested or not: 22.58%
Other: 6.45%

Note, first, that no one checked off "never," and fewer than seven percent indicated any rate of use less than "frequent." However, there is one apparent anomaly: It would be reasonable to expect that anyone checking off "whether requested or not" would be those who also checked off "always." Mysteriously, that is not the case: many of those who checked off this item also checked "frequently," in addition, with no explanation for this apparent inconsistency. Those checking off "other" used this as an occasion to make a remark to explain that they used something as an alternative to a proposal. (For example, well known consultant Nido Qubein, remarked that he prefers to use what he calls "action plans," which result from a paid-for needs analysis.)

How Often Requested

Usually: 35.48%
Occasionally: 48.38%
Rarely: 12.9
Other: 3.23%

Success with Proposals

Over 75%: 33.33%
50–75%: 26.66%
25–50%: 26.66%
Under 25%: 13.33%

Type of Proposal Used and Frequency

Forty-five percent of respondents reported using informal and letter proposals more than half the time, with most reporting such usage as approaching 100 percent, and a few as actually reaching that figure. Thirty-two percent reported the reverse orientation, usually using formal proposals. The remainder tended to about an equal or near equal division of formal and informal proposals.

Proposal Practices

Some respondents checked off more than one item in this category, and the results are by frequency of appearance, with no attempt to make correlations:

All original material:	42%
Parts boilerplated:	55%
All boilerplate:	3%
Quotations plus brochures:	42%
Other:	13%

"Other" included qualifying or explanatory remarks, such as "On major applications, full scale business plan," "Depends on level of relationship with client," and "Letter."

Sections/Materials Normally Included in Proposals

Respondents were expected to check off several items in this category, and responses are reported by frequency of occurrence, with no attempt to make correlations:

Statement of problem/need:	97%
Technical discussion:	45%
Resumes:	55%
Qualifications:	58%
Descriptions of deliverables:	74%
Schedules:	77%
Facilities & resources:	58%
Price:	90%
Letter of transmittal:	52%
Other:	10%

"Other" was used to make qualifying remarks or to explain a practice that is peculiar to some given field. Tom Hill, of Drubner Industrials in Waterbury, Connecticut, a commercial real estate specialist, noted in this block that his proposals normally include maps and zoning regulations. Another used this block to explain that he sends clients a statement of contract terms, while still another remarked that his prior checkoffs are provisional and depend on client needs and the specific situation of the moment. JJ [sic] Lauderbaugh, a California image and grooming consultant, advised that she sometimes includes audio and/or video tapes, which is understandable enough in her case. She also noted that in her case clients sometimes require a form of their own to be filled out, which she complies with, of course, even if she has already prepared a proposal.

Among the comments invited are many of special interest. A few are quoted here:

Dr. William Cohen, Professor of Marketing at California State University in Los Angeles, a marketing consultant, a former federal government contracting officer, and author of a number of business books of his own, observed,

> If you've done your preproposal marketing correctly, your audience should find no surprises in your proposal . . . but you must never, never forget that the proposal is a sales document.

Francine Berger, speaker, seminar leader, trainer, consultant, developer of in-house speakers bureaus for corporations, and president of her own firm, Speechworks, of Stony Brook, New York, added this to her response:

> I hate to write them [proposals, she means] much rather discuss the specifics face to face or by 'phone then write a little follow up letter to confirm. Also, whenever I deal with the president, they usually say 'Go ahead' and don't need one or want one. In dealing with middle managers of traditional bureaucratic companies, they do need one.

Another respondent, not identified, opined that a proposal is, in its "best sense," a confirmation of work agreed upon, except when it represents a competitive bid, and the probability of success is only 10 percent, in his opinion.

And still another respondent stated flatly that proposals are very costly to prepare and should be undertaken only when the probability of success is quite high. He cited Peter Drucker on "cost of transactions" to support his view.

Still another viewpoint, one with a great deal of validity, was expressed: "Proposals do not often 'get the job,' but often get the opportunity to discuss and negotiate in person." In fact, it is a legitimate viewpoint that the immediate objective of a proposal ought to be to induce the client to invite you "to the table" for discussion.

Dave Hamilton, Commercial Operations Manager of the Tulsa Division of Quadrex Corporation, reflected his insights into marketing and proposal quality with the valid observation that one "must continually review/rewrite for 'selling statements' inclusion, benefits analysis and promotion," pointing out that too often the proposal is a "straight technical dissertation."

And, finally, Strategies Management Consulting, of Modesto, California, pointed out that their clients are all small businesses and that for their practice the usual proposal is a one page document that is also the agreement between consultant and client when signed by both, but may be supplemented by oral presentations and attachments to proposals. The sample enclosed demonstrates that even though it is a one page proposal agreement it does furnish definition of project or service to be provided, schedule data, estimated time and fees required, and terms.

Many of these viewpoints are worth considering, depending on what your own specialty is, of course.

THE PROPOSAL LIBRARY

There are two common problems in proposal writing for most consultants. One is that it is always an ad hoc activity—something improvised as an interruption to regular daily activities and requiring a special, non-routine effort. Important though proposal writing is, as a marketing and business necessity, it is difficult for most of us not to regard it as an unwelcome, if necessary, intrusion into our daily routine and a disruptive activity for which we never seem to be prepared.

The second problem is that there is virtually never enough time to do the job: Proposals are almost invariably written in haste against a pressing and all but impossible schedule, and the need seems to always fall at a time when we are busy and trying to get some important project completed. Consequently, even when we finally get the proposal writing job done, we often have the feeling that we didn't do as well as we should have and would have, had we had just a bit more time.

Large corporations whose work is almost entirely custom work and who must rely on proposals for all or nearly all their business often establish permanent proposal writing departments, suitably equipped and staffed with proposal professionals specialists in the art. Smaller organizations cannot do this, as a practical measure. But you can do something similar to offset at least some of the difficulties resulting from these two common problems. You can create your own special proposal development resource, a proposal library.

Unless you write a proposal only once in a great while, and the fact that you are reading this book suggests that that is not the case, you are tying your own hands unnecessarily if you do not have a proposal library. The efficiency and effectiveness of your proposal efforts will be greatly increased by the existence of a well stocked and well thought out proposal library. It will be a resource that will give you an organized basis for all your proposal work, give you more time to devote to the task, and make it somewhat less an impromptu or improvised effort. Even more important, perhaps, a proposal library will enable you to steadily improve the quality and the success incidence of your proposals.

Obviously a first requisite for this library is a collection of reference books pertaining directly to your own career field and/or those technical/professional aspects in which you specialize and which are the subjects of the proposals you write. As a consultant, however, you are in the somewhat ambiguous position of all consultants of being compelled to be the master of both your technical and/or professional specialty and of the skills and resources required for your consulting services. And included among those latter required resources are reference and other materials which normally constitute a proposal library.

The term *library* is used here in a rather special sense, referring to far more than a collection of books, although it certainly includes those. But a properly stocked and well organized library also includes many other kinds of on-the-shelf resources to make it easier to write proposals and to make it possible to write better more effective proposals. It can do this in several ways: by speeding up the process, an important consideration in most proposal efforts, through organizing useful materials and making them readily accessible; by storing the special materials, those of proven outstanding merit conveniently at hand; and by providing ready access to those materials that will contribute to the bid/no bid analysis and decision making and to the evolution of suitable approaches and strategies.

To these ends, your proposal library ought to include at least these general classes of resources:

Reference books.
Relevant periodicals.
Special reports relevant to your field, consulting, and proposals.
Your own past proposals.
Stocks of your own brochures and other promotional literature.

Copies of competitors' proposals.
Copies of competitors' brochures and other promotional literature.
Swipe files.

To do the subject full justice requires individual discussions of these classes of materials and the media or forms in which they should be stored and made available for use.

Reference Books

There are at least three general classes of reference books that you can put to good use in your proposal library. One is, of course, those already referred to as those dealing with your technical/professional specialties. A second class is that rather small collection of books that deal specifically with proposal writing and a much larger collection of books about sales and marketing, as they bear on proposal writing. And a third and possibly largest class is that of general reference books that will spare you a great deal of research time by their ready availability. The following are some of the general types. (Some specific suggestions will appear later in lists.)

Books dealing with consulting skills generally.
Catalogs relevant to your field.
Directories, general and specialized.
Relevant how to manuals.
Proceedings of relevant conferences and symposia.

Periodicals

There are an estimated 30,000 newsletters published in the United States, and a large number of other periodicals magazines, journals, tabloids, and sundry others. Few of us have a full appreciation of the huge population of such literature because a relative handful of these appear on the newsstands. Even the most completely stocked newsstand, for example, does not carry on it shelves most of the periodicals published as "trade journals," dealing with and of interest to only those engaged in specialized fields, such as direct mail and business conferences. Even more prominent by their absence are the many periodicals published by associations and corporations of many kinds, both for profit and nonprofit. There are literally thousands of these latter two classes, ranging from simple newsletters to tabloids, to slick magazines in full process color.

A great many of these, especially the trade publications, are distributed free of charge to "qualified" applicants, as "controlled circulation" publications. The qualification is to be part of or have direct business interests in the industry addressed, such that you are a reasonable prospect for those whose advertising appears in the periodical.

That resulting ability to address the publication almost entirely and exclusively to those who are good prospects for the publisher's advertisers makes it worthwhile for the publishers to give free subscriptions to those so qualifying. With the circulation figures verified by an audit agency, as is the case with controlled circulation periodicals, the publisher is able to command premium advertising rates, making the venture worthwhile. (Those who do not qualify for free subscriptions are usually permitted to purchase subscriptions, if they wish to.)

There are several directories that list periodicals of various kinds, including trade journals and controlled circulation periodicals. One popular one is *Writer's Market*, published annually by Writer's Digest Books and available in virtually all bookstores. Another is *The Newsletter Yearbook Directory*, published in a revised edition every few years by The Newsletter Clearinghouse, 44 West Market Street, Rhinebeck, NY 12572. And there are other directories available in most public libraries, so that it is not absolutely necessary to invest in these, if you prefer not to.

The usual requirement for a free subscription to those periodicals that are distributed without charge may be merely an application on business stationery and/or a business card. However, it is an increasing practice of such publications to require the applicant to fill out a brief questionnaire generally consisting entirely of checkoff items and to require requalification every year.

Past Proposals

You should have a complete inventory of your own past proposals, especially those that were successful. They are useful in more than one way: Reviewing them may uncover a previous proposal that has many points of similarity with your current effort and so can save you a great deal of time in all phases of the effort, from research to final writing. You may also be able to save yourself a great deal of time and expense by reusing some of the graphics and other materials from earlier efforts. Keep a tight rein on these; the loss of even one file copy of your past proposals may be a disaster. And "loss" may even mean merely mislaying it, but that is a true loss, nevertheless, at least for the moment. You should probably never dead file old proposals generally, and certainly not old successful proposals.

Brochures and Promotional Literature

As you may have noticed in reading the results of my questionnaire survey, many consultants utilize standard brochures and other sales literature as parts of their proposals. This enables them to develop and submit a greater number of proposals than they would otherwise be able to handle. But even if you do not incorporate the actual brochures and other materials sales letters, reprints of articles by and/or about you, your own newsletters and reports, and other such material they are often handy time savers for the creation (paste up) of rough drafts. And many, especially reprints of articles but not confined to those, are useful as enclosures appendices and exhibits to your proposals.

Competitors' Material

From time to time you get opportunities to acquire copies of competitors' proposals. One way, if your competitors do business with the federal government, is by requesting copies of winning proposals under the Freedom of Information Act. But copies can come into your hands by other means, too, such as via new employees.

Competitors' general literature brochures and other items are relatively easy to acquire, especially at trade fairs, national conventions, conferences, and other such conclaves. Such material is valuable through all phases of proposal development, from the initial bid/no bid analysis and decision making to the development of written arguments.

Swipe Files

Anything and everything in your proposal library is potentially useful to actually borrow ("swipe") and use in your new proposal. But for most cases it is only after spending much time to review many things in your library that you uncover such useful materials and decide that they can or cannot be used without or almost without change readily modified for a new use, that is. On the other hand there are usually certain items that fit so well into most of your proposals that you find them reusable again and again, with little or no change necessary to adapt them to the new uses. Examples include milestone charts, schedules, labor loading matrices, tabular/text descriptions of past projects, lists of resources, and other such items.

It should not be necessary to spend a great deal of time tracking down such universally useful materials; since they will be used again and again they ought to be made more readily accessible. To achieve this, it is necessary only to make master copies of such material and store them in special files, suitably indexed for quick search and location.

FILING METHODS

A library is typically conceived as a collection of books arrayed on shelves, periodicals arrayed in some suitable stand or file, and other materials on shelves and/or in filing cabinets, along with suitable indexes or catalogs to make search and retrieval possible. However, things have changed quite a bit in the past few years, and one change that is affecting libraries as much as its affecting consulting and proposal writing in general is the advent of the personal computer, which is now rapidly becoming as commonplace in the office as the typewriter. Aside from its benefits as a replacement for the typewriter, when armed with a suitable word processor program it offers enormous benefits as a filing system, with unparalleled search and retrieval efficiency far beyond that of manual systems.

If you have such a system, you will find it advantageous to have as many files installed and emplaced on your disks (whether floppies or hard disks) as possible. That applies to a great many, if not all, of your text files, many of which you may very well have originally created via word processing. You may, for example, already have all or many of your past proposals, articles, reports, and other data on magnetic disks. If you are familiar with computer operation you are already well aware of the ease and speed of summoning up files and examining them on screen, as compared with our older, manual methods for search and retrieval of filed documents.

There is no point in keeping paper files of what you have filed on magnetic disks, although it is wise to always have two copies of anything important so that for safety your library copy is "backed up" with an archived copy. (Data on disk are durable, normally, but can be destroyed easily. Backup copies are a sensible precaution against such casualty losses of disk files.)

Swipe files should likewise be on disks. You can create these easily by copying from your various proposal and other files any materials you expect to be able to use frequently and repeatedly. Then set up special files for these materials, along with suitable indexes. (Many catalog and indexing software programs are available, which will help you create suitable indexes to facilitate searches and retrievals.)

One of the many advantages of installing swipe files on disks is that you need not keep other copies of the original, paper or otherwise; you can easily and swiftly make a copy of anything in your disk files. In fact, you should never alter or modify an original copy of anything in your disk files when adapting it to a new use. Make an exact copy, which is quite easy to do, of course, and make your changes to that copy. (And if you run into difficulties or make mistakes that are troublesome to correct, don't even spend the time to patch or make corrections; just make a new copy and start over.) But when you modify a copy of a master file to create something new, always consider the possibility that it might be worthwhile to add that new item to your swipe files as another original. (In some cases the new material may be such an improvement over the old one that you might wish to replace your original with a new original.) In this manner your files grow, not only in their abundance, but in their inherent quality, with resulting benefits to your future proposal efforts.

FEDERAL GOVERNMENT BUSINESS OPPORTUNITIES

If you wish to pursue government business you should subscribe to the Government publication *Commerce Business Daily* (CBD), published daily and listing requirements for various agencies in synoptic form with information advising you where to write or call for the RFP and full package of information. The publication may be ordered from the Superintendent of Documents, Government Printing Office, Washington, DC, 20402, at $160/year, first class mailing; $81/year, second class mailing; $88/6 month trial subscription; first class; and $45/6 month trial subscription, second class. However, the publication is also available as "CBD ONLINE" (via computer and modem, with dial up telephone connections) from the following services:

United Communications Group, 4550 Montgomery Avenue, Bethesda, MD 20814, (301) 656-6666; Data Resources, Inc., 2400 Hartwell Avenue, Lexington, MA 02173, (617) 863-5100, (301) 589-8875; Dialog Information Services, Inc., 3460 Hillview Avenue, Palo Alto, CA 94304, (800) 227-1927.

Figure 37 lists some of the typical consulting requirements of government agencies. In fact, these are probably the most far ranging kinds of requirements to be found anywhere in the world. There are few products or services the U.S. federal government does not buy, and mostly these must be custom services, designed especially for the federal agencies' specific needs. Therefore a great many consulting services are required, although listed under a variety of headings in the periodical.

The CBD does not list all government requirements, unfortunately. In fact, it lists only about 10 to 15 percent of the requirements, while at least 35 percent of government requirements (which total approximately $200 billion annually at the the time of this writing) are filled via open competition among all those interested. The other resources for uncovering federal government RFPs include filing the federal government form 129, Application for Bidders List, which is available from the offices of the Small Business Administration, the General Services Administration, the Department of Commerce, and any government contracting or procurement office. Most of these can be found in the nearest federal office building, and you can usually find them listed in the local telephone directory under "United States, Government of."

There are several other ways to get information and learn more about the federal procurement system and how to learn of business opportunities in the multibillion dollar market it represents. You can also visit the nearest Government Printing Office bookstore, where you will find government publications discussing how to do business with the government, and you can write to the Department of De-

Figure 37. A few government consulting needs synopsized in the *Commerce Business Daily.*

fense, the Small Business Administration, the General Services Administration, the Department of Commerce, and other federal agencies and ask for information. These requests will usually produce a variety of brochures and manuals which will help and which will cost you nothing but the postage stamp for your letter of inquiry. There is, in fact, quite an enormous array of useful literature available via such sources, and you can compile a substantial library from these sources alone.

STATE AND LOCAL GOVERNMENTS

What is true about doing business with the federal government is also largely true about doing business with the thousands of state and local governments (county, city, township, and other municipalities). There are nearly 80,000 of these government entities, and within many of these state and local governments (as within the federal government) are large numbers of subordinate agencies and bureaus who may buy your services independently and who often solicit proposals. In the aggregate we are referring to perhaps a half million or more prospective clients as part of the government establishments, and that is probably a conservative figure. Many of these governments, especially the state governments and the larger city and county governments, publish substantial literature describing their procurement systems and policies, as well as listing dozens and dozens of local government agencies, bureaus, and establishments, so that these too offer a large contribution to your store of information resources.

Most of these governmental entities urge contractors to visit their purchasing offices to become personally acquainted with the various buyers in these offices and to learn at first hand how the systems function. The central purchasing offices and purchasing officials are located in the state capitals, the county seats, and the city or town halls.

Most of these have their own counterpart of the federal Application for Bidders List, and many have literature describing their procurement systems and listing information useful to prospective contractors. Many also, emulating the federal government socioeconomic programs, have programs of their own, offering loans, loan guarantees, and other kinds of special assistance and preference to small business, to minority entrepreneurs, to women entrepreneurs, and to handicapped individuals. And many state and local governments also offer some preference to local suppliers, although all agree to do business with anyone who qualifies. In all, these many governments represent a vast market, estimated at about $565 billion annually, of which a substantial portion is spent for consulting services of many kinds. (The figure depends heavily on how you define consulting, but it is probable that at least 20 percent, well over $100 billion annually, is used to buy a variety of technical and professional services.) Like the federal government agencies, state and local governments and their agencies tend to perceive many of their needs as unique, which therefore inevitably require specialized custom (consulting) services to satisfy.

On the other hand, state and local governments do not have an equivalent of the federal government's Commerce Business Daily in which to announce their requirements and solicit inquiries and expressions of interest from consultants. Maryland, however, does announce at least some of its requirements in the official Maryland Register, the state's equivalent of the federal government's Federal Register, and occasionally a local government has some official publication that is useful for this purpose. But for the most part state and local governments seeking consulting services use their bidders lists but rely primarily on local newspapers to announce their requirements, synopsizing them in classified advertising columns under the heading BIDS AND PROPOSALS. State and local laws generally mandate that requirements be so advertised in the leading daily newspaper published in the locality of the procurement office. (For example, the city of Washington, DC and most surrounding Maryland and Virginia counties and municipalities advertise their requirements in the Washington Post.)

Again emulating the example of the federal government, state and local governments have their own small purchase laws, and permit procurements defined as small purchases in their procurement regulations to be made under limited competition and, for the smallest classes of such procurements, often without competition. Therefore many of the smaller projects are never advertised at all, but are let through direct negotiation, usually following submittal of an informal proposal and/or an unsolicited proposal, formal or informal.

SELECTED GOVERNMENT OFFICES

A few key federal government offices, the central or headquarters offices of the agencies in most cases, are listed here. (Local offices of these agencies are generally listed in local telephone directories. If not, a call or letter to the agency will bring you information on where to find the nearest local office of the agency.) A simple inquiry by mail and a request for information, general or specific, will generally bring you necessary forms, such as the Form 129, Application for Bidders List, and a great deal of useful literature to add to your library. The literature will guide you in finding opportunities to pursue government business and supply information that will be helpful in writing proposals. Included here is the address of the Federal Procurement Data Center, which compiles detailed data on federal procurement and releases periodic reports that are extremely useful to the serious marketer as marketing research tools. Also included is the address of the main bookstore (and plant) of the Government Printing Office (GPO). The GPO is a rich source of books, brochures, pamphlets, and other helpful information that can constitute a valuable resource when researching data for a proposal, and it would be almost surely be useful to know of and resort to the GPO bookstore nearest you. The GPO can, of course, furnish a list of their bookstores.

Department of Agriculture
14th Street & Independence
Avenue SW
Washington, DC 20250

Department of Commerce
14th & Constitution Avenues
NW
Washington, DC 20230

Department of Defense
The Pentagon
Washington, DC 20301

Department of Education
400 Maryland Avenue SW
Washington, DC 20202

Department of Health and
Human Services
330 Independence Avenue SW
Washington, DC 20201

Department of Housing and
Urban Development
451 7th Street SW
Washington, DC 20410

Department of the Interior
18th & C Streets NW
Washington, DC 20240

Department of Justice
10th Street & Constitution
Avenue NW
Washington, DC 20530

Department of Labor
200 Constitution Avenue NW
Washington, DC 20210

Department of State
2201 C Street NW
Washington, DC 20520

Department of Transportation
400 7th Street SW
Washington, DC 20590

Federal Procurement Data
Center
4040 N. Fairfax Drive, Suite
900
Arlington, VA 22203

Small Business Administration
1441 L Street NW
Washington, DC 20416

General Services
Administration
18th & F Streets NW
Washington, DC 20405

Government Printing Office
Main Bookstore
North Capitol & H Streets NW
Washington, DC 20402

RECOMMENDED PUBLICATIONS

The following is a partial list of publications I believe will be helpful additions to your proposal library. I stress both *partial* and *recommended* because a great deal depends on your special interests and needs, especially with regard to periodicals. In fact, few publications bear directly on the subject of proposal writing, but there are some that cover relevant subjects, such as marketing, writing, editing, and publications processes.

Books

Careful Writer, The, by Theodore Bernstein, Atheneum, New York, 1965.

Elements of Style, The, by William Strunk and E. B. White, Macmillan, New York, 1972.

How to Create a Winning Proposal, by Jill Ammon-Wexler and Catherine Carmel, Mercury Communications, 1976.

How to Make Money with Your Micro, by Herman Holtz, Wiley, New York, 1984.

How to Succeed as an Independent Consultant, by Herman Holtz, Wiley, New York, 1983.

Persuasive Writing, by Herman Holtz, McGraw-Hill, New York, 1983.

Thinking with a Pencil, by Henning Helms, Barnes & Noble, New York, 1964.

Words into Type (3rd ed.), by Henning Helms, Prentice Hall, Englewood Cliffs, N.J., 1974.

Word Processing for Business Publications, by Herman Holtz, McGraw-Hill, New York, Byte Books, 1985.

Writing for Results in Business, Government, the Sciences and the Professions, by David Ewing, Wiley, New York, 1979.

Periodicals

Government Sales Strategist, 10076 Boca Entrada Boulevard, Boca Raton, FL 33433.

Marketing Professional Services, 11800 NE 160 Street, Bothell, WA 98011.

Professional Marketing Report, POB 32387, Washington, DC 20007.

SUGGESTED STANDARD FORMATS

You can save a great deal of time by standardizing the formats of items you will use in all or nearly all your proposals. Some of the suggested items have been presented earlier in these pages, as have a few items designed to guide and help you in requirements analysis and development of approaches and strategies. A list of such items is offered here, and examples of additional items designed to help you follow. It would probably be useful to compile copies of these in a master file to be used in each proposal effort. If you are working with a computer, these can be entered as computer or word processor files, for even greater flexibility.

You may use these items in and for development of your proposals without change, choosing one from among several where alternatives were offered, or modifying and adapting them to your own needs, as you prefer.

Items That Have Appeared in Prior Pages

First steps in devising strategy	Figure 1
Proposal format	Figures 2 and 19
Exercise sheet: Consulting specialties	Figure 3
Bid/no bid analysis reporting form	Figure 4
RFP requirements checklists	Figures 5 and 6
Functional flowcharts	Figures 7 through 10
Value management (FAST) diagrams	Figures 13 through 16
Typical organization chart	Figure 21
Schedule, as table and as milestone chart	Figures 22 and 23
Resume format	Figure 24
Format for task/labor estimates	Figure 25
Format for and sample of response matrix	Figures 26 and 35
Pictorial diagram	Figure 27

Block diagram	Figure 28
Simple network	Figure 29
Standard drawing templates	Figure 31
Paste down and decal drawing aids	Figure 32
Logic tree	Figure 33
Sample title page	Figure 34

A FEW ADDITIONAL OFFERINGS

Modular Recent Project Presentation Format

For efficiency and flexibility in furnishing references and information on your current and past projects you can modularize your project descriptions so that they can be fitted into the format shown, while being reorganized (most relevant projects first) readily for each new proposal.

CURRENT AND RECENT PROJECTS	
PROJECT TITLE OR FUNCTIONAL NAME	**CLIENT ORGANIZATION**
Summary description, highlights, size (dollars, man hours, time, or other measure), record of performance with regard to schedule and budget, most impressive accomplishments	Contact: Name, address, telephone number of purchasing agent or other individual(s) responsible for monitoring project and able to furnish information
(Next project description)	

A modular format for describing other project experience.

Cost Summaries

Small projects are usually quoted by consultants with either a fixed price for the job or a consulting rate with, usually, an estimate of consulting time (hours, days, weeks, or other time unit) required. However, for a large project it is not unusual, especially in the case of government agencies, for the client to ask for details on how the cost estimate was established. Government agencies, especially those of the federal government, usually provide a standard for this. But even where clients do not provide such a form or prescribe the format, they ask for essentially the same inforation. In general, the following form serves the purpose quite well. This form is predicated on the assumption that there is no significant amount of materials required (businesses that are heavy in the materials area tend to have separate overhead rates for materials), that the accounting system does use a general & administrative (G&A) indirect expense pool to accommodate certain types of indirect costs, and that the overhead rate includes fringe benefits. Of course, if your own accounting system does not conform to this, does not include a G&A rate, and/or you list fringe benefits as an item separate from the overhead pool, you will modify this form to reflect that. And, if your fee is a flat figure and not a percentage, change that also.

G&A, by the way, is a rate that is applied to all costs that appear above it on this form. The same is true for the fee or profit rate.

This is to be used only when the client demands it and you are willing to reveal your various cost centers and burden rates to the client. In most cases the government will require it for any project running more than a few thousand dollars, perhaps $10,000, which is the current small purchase rate for non-military agencies. (Military agencies are currrently permitted small purchase authority to $25,000.) Commercial clients are less likely to demand this cost accounting, but those who do government work and subcontract to consultants tend to emulate government methods, and sometimes are even required by their government contracts to follow federal procurement methods in their subcontracting. But today even commercial organizations tend to impose this requirement for large contracts.

If you do not know precisely what your overhead rate is, and it is not uncommon for circumstances to create that uncertainty, especially for independent practitioners or practices in existence for only a year

Direct labor:

_____ _____ @ $ _____ = $ _____
(functional title)   (hours)   (rate)   (subtotal)

_____ _____ @ $ _____ = $ _____ $ _____
                                                          (dir. labor total)

Labor overhead:

$ _____ @ _____ % = $ _____
(direct labor)   (overhead rate)   (overhead total)

Other direct costs:

_____ $ _____
(itemize)

_____ $ _____ $ _____
                                                       (ODC total)

General & administrative cost: _____ % $ _____
                               (rate)

Fee or profit: _____ % $ _____

Grand total: $ _____

A general form for breaking down cost estimates.

or two, the usual practice is to estimate it as a "provisional" rate, subject to subsequent audit and adjustment. But that audit and adjustment is generally applicable only to contracts of at least $100,000, if then, in contracting with the federal government.

Experience and Qualifications (Resumes) Summary

For many projects the individual qualifications of the proposed staff are of primary concern to the client. The next illustration offers an efficient means for organizing that individual experience and qualifications record into a single, concentrated summary, a matrix in fact.

The cells of the matrix are developed according to the individual requirement. Each "item," for example, will be a given discipline, special skill, educational major, or specific experience, such as data processing, budget control, training, writing, or other. The set of items should, of course, represent all the qualifications required, and the candidate names will represent the professional and key staff offered for the project.

Sample Selling Headlines and Captions

The point was made earlier that in proposal writing every opportunity to drive home a sales message to make positive and persuasive arguments must be exploited, and that one of the most neglected areas for doing this is that of titles, headlines, and captions. Here, to illustrate this more clearly through a few "for instances," are some before and after examples.

However, even these are generalized and generic and can be further sharpened and made even more positive by expressing them in the specific terms of the requirement and relating them to your strategies, major promises, and proofs. For example, instead of "Proposed Ways to Cut Costs," a specific proposal to develop or revise a computer program might caption or title this, "A Tighter Program to Cut Operating Costs." Or, if the schedule is a tight one and there is some evident concern on the client's part about capability for meeting the deadline, the schedule item might be phrased, "How (your name) Will Deliver (the end item or service) by March 15." The idea is, of course, to concentrate on the client's worry items and in so doing make references to and reinforce those worry items, the benefits you promise to deliver, and the proofs that you can and will deliver on those promises. Those titles, headlines, and captions should be an unending series of reminders of the most important elements of your strategy and theme.

SOME FINAL WORDS: GUIDELINES TO CURE "BAD WRITING" AND MAXIMIZE CREDIBILITY

1. Avoid this common writing mistake: Don't start writing too soon. Too many proposals don't make it beyond the initial reading because they reveal that the writer began to write before he or she

PRO-POSED (Name)	EDUCATION (Degree/Univ.)	AREAS OF TRAINING/EXPERIENCE				
		(Item)	(Item)	(Item)	(Item)	(Item)

Format of qualifications and experience summary matrix.

BEFORE	AFTER
Costs	Cost Consciousness
Cost Considerations	Proposed Ways to Cut Costs
Schedule	Objectives That Will Be Met
Milestone Chart	Milestones Marking Success
Functional Flowchart	How the Problems Will Be Solved
Qualifications and Experience	Proof That _____ Can Do the Job
Qualifications Matrix	An Array of Capabilities
Understanding of the Requirement	The Essence of the Problem
Discussion	Specific Steps to Success
Proposed Program	Delivering on Our Promises
Our Facilities and Resources	Resources Placed in Your Service

Examples of selling titles, headlines, and captions.

fully understood the requirement, and never did bother to perfect his or her knowledge of what the client wanted.

Spend at least as much time in studying, analyzing, planning, researching, and otherwise *preparing* to write as in writing itself. It will be time well invested and will save you enough false starts and rewriting to more than compensate for the time it takes. Your ability to do all the other things listed here depends upon your first doing what is urged on you here.

2.   Don't allow yourself to wander aimlessly. (Many proposals are of the "river raft" type: They drift from one place to another, with no apparent destination. Draw up specific objectives—all the major points you must make in your proposal. Know in advance exactly where you wish to go. Otherwise, you are not likely to get to where you ought to be.

3.   Don't have vague ideas about how you will reach or achieve each objective. Draw up your subordinate objectives: Know in advance your itinerary—the route you plan to take to get there and the milestones (subordinate objectives) you must reach along the way.

4.   Don't try to work from plans in your head, or even from a generalized philosophy. Develop an outline in which all major points and objectives are specified, not an outline of what you will talk about in your proposal, but an outline of what you will say in your proposal.

5.   Don't expect to write a perfect first draft. Expert writers become expert writers because they know that first drafts are rarely as good as second and third drafts are. Expect to do some self-editing and rewriting.

Examine everything you have written, in your self-editing, and judge whether each sentence, paragraph, and other element achieves its objectives, and whether it not only can be understood, but cannot be misunderstood, that is, whether it is not only clear but unambiguous. (If it can be misunderstood, it will be. You may rely on that.)

6.   Don't be elegant, subtle, clever, or humorous in your writing style. All such characteristics are misplaced in proposals, which are read by busy people who probably do not enjoy reading at all, much less analyzing what they have read to see if they understand it correctly. (In fact, if what you have written brings from the reader a chuckle that is probably ominous.)

Focus only on meaning. Think about your reader and no one else, not even yourself.

7. Offer as much detail as possible in the areas you believe to be most important in influencing the client. Anyone can generalize and philosophize, and being able to do so suggests that you are glib but it does not prove that you are in complete command of the subject or possess the necessary capabilities. The ability to plan and describe in detail, to specify, on the other hand, indicates complete command of the subject and competence, both technical and managerial. It makes the proposal almost infinitely more credible than the one that is full of glib but general assurances.

8. Be sure that you do have a clear cut strategy rather than a vague idea or hope that the client will see you as superior to everyone else. Without such a clearly understood strategy underlying it, your proposal will probably not have a positive tone; it almost inevitably will come across as a defensive plaint. And without a clear strategy, properly implemented, you are not even partially in command of the situation.

9. Be sure that your proposal has a theme. The theme should be linked closely to the strategy, and should in effect reinforce the strategy on almost every page of your proposal. (If, for example, your strategy is based on low cost, your theme might well be along the lines of "efficiency and cost consciousness," and this could even be a running head or foot appearing on each page to remind the client of your promise.)

10. Finally, be sure that you have been absolutely explicit about what you promise to deliver, explicit both qualitatively and quantitatively, and stress the qualitative and quantitative terms as much as possible (but without hyperbole), so they come across distinctly as an offer and not as a plea.

INDEX

291